French Muslims

New Voices in Contemporary France

Sharif Gemie

UNIVERSITY OF WALES PRESS
CARDIFF
2010

British Library Cataloguing-in-Publication Data
A catalogue record for this book is available from the British Library.

ISBN   978-0-7083-2209-3 (hardback)
        978-0-7083-2320-5 (paperback)
e-ISBN 978-0-7083-2318-2

The right of Sharif Gemie to be identified as author of this work has
been asserted by him in accordance with sections 77, 78 and 79 of
the Copyright, Designs and Patents Act 1988.

Typeset by Mark Heslington Ltd, Scarborough, North Yorkshire
Printed by CPI Antony Rowe, Chippenham, Wiltshire

Contents

Series Editors' Preface

This series showcases the work of new and established scholars working within the fields of French and francophone studies. It publishes introductory texts aimed at a student readership, as well as research-orientated monographs at the cutting edge of their discipline area. The series aims to highlight shifting patterns of research in French and francophone studies, to re-evaluate traditional representations of French and francophone identities and to encourage the exchange of ideas and perspectives across a wide range of discipline areas. The emphasis throughout the series will be on the ways in which French and francophone communities across the world are evolving into the twenty-first century.

Hanna Diamond and Claire Gorrara

Acknowledgements

This is my fifth book. It would be nice to say that I find that they're getting easier; this has not been the case, and this work in particular has led me to analyse some new and difficult issues. However, I have truly enjoyed writing this book, and I hope that alongside the polemics and political passion that this book considers, this work will inspire readers to share my interest in these topics.

At various points I have called on friends and colleagues to help, advise, guide and even warn me about my many draft versions of this book. In no particular order, I'd like to thank, Paul Chambers, Ruth Kinna, Anthony Fiscella, Penny Richards, Brian Ireland, Laure Humbert, Gavin Edwards, Chris Meredith, Tom Cahill, Ali Wardak, Mona al-Honi and Louise Rees for assistance with particular awkward points; Sarah Lewis, the commissioning editor for University of Wales Press, for her encouragement and, in particular, for her invaluable assistance during a difficult moment in January 2008. And also Patricia Clark, for so much.

Glossary

CCMTF   Comité de coordination des musulmans turcs de France: Coordinating Committee of Turkish Muslims of France.

CFCM   Conseil français du Culte Musulman: French Council of the Muslim Faith. See chapter four.

CFDT   Confédération Française Démocratique du Travail: Democratic French Confederation of Labour. Created in 1964, it is now the largest trade union federation in France. Normally seen as moderate left.

CGT   Confédération générale du travail: General Confederation of Labour, created in 1895. The second largest trade union confederation in France, normally seen as left-wing.

CRCM   Conseil Regional du Culte Musulman: Regional Council of the Muslim Faith. There are twenty-five regional councils, all forming part of the CFCM.

EPT   Une école pour tou-te-s: A School for Everyone (with the French title specifying all girls and all boys). Organization formed to protest against the proposed law on religious symbols in schools in February 2004. See chapters four and six.

FNMF   Fédération Nationale des Musulmans de France: National Federation of Muslims of France, Moroccan linked Muslim organization, created in 1985 in opposition to the *grande mosquée*.

FSU   Fédération syndicale unitaire: United Syndical Federation. Founded in 1993, the FSU is the largest union of secondary school teachers.

LDH   Full title: Ligue française pour la défense des droits de l'homme et du citoyen, normally shortened to Ligue des Droits de l'homme: League of the Rights of Man. Founded in 1898, during the Dreyfus Affair, and dedicated to the defence of Human Rights. Often seen as a left-of-centre organization.

MIR   Mouvement des Indigènes de la République: Movement of the Natives of the Republic. Radical, anti-colonialist movement, created in 2004. See chapter six.

MRAP   Mouvement contre le racisme et pour l'amitié entre les peuples: Movement against Racism and for Friendship between Peoples, created in 1949. Left-wing anti-racist organization.

UOIF   Union des Organisation Islamiques de France: Union of Islamic Organizations of France, founded in 1983. See chapter four.

'We don't need people like you!'
'And do you think that I need you?'
'No, no, no. You and your veil, you can go back home!'
'But this is my home.'
'Your home? You'll never be at home here!'
'Is that so? What makes you more French than me?'
'The veil, it's not French! This is a Republic! Watch out! I've warned you!'

Street confrontation, Lille, c.2006–7[1]

Introduction
At the Funeral

We loved you so much.
Houria Bouteldja, 2005[1]

There were times when I could not stop myself from admiring Jacques Chirac. As president of the French Republic, he seemed to incarnate the dignity of statesmanship in a manner that left his contemporary, Tony Blair, looking amateurish. One of these moments occurred in September 2003. Readers may remember the extraordinary heatwave which swept across Europe during that summer, stifling dozens of old, frail people in many cities. In Paris, as elsewhere, there were tragic cases in which, days after their death, lonely anonymous corpses were found in cheap apartments, under bridges and in wastelands, the last remains of tramps, alcoholics and down-and-outs. Often no one came forward to claim them, despite the best efforts of the Parisian authorities to identify them and to locate relatives. Finally, in September 2003, a decision was taken to bury these wretched, lost victims, with the municipality arranging the procedures. At that moment, Chirac stepped in. He chose to attend these funerals, for even a dead tramp was a citizen of the Republic. Chirac's presence embodied a type of trans-political solidarity that transcended social, cultural and political divisions. This incident may have been the last occasion on which the values of French Republicanism were successfully presented as embodying ideals of social inclusion.

There were no cameras at the municipal funeral. Unlike Blair, Chirac understood the power of publicity without photographs: his gesture demonstrated a finely crafted political instinct, rooted in a perceptive evaluation of French people's sensibility, which eloquently asserted a principle without argument or conflict.

I was therefore amazed at some press reports early in December 2003. Chirac visited Tunis, and spoke to some school students. They raised the question of Muslim schoolgirls wearing veils. Chirac's response was astonishing. He explained to the Tunisian students that they had to understand that there was 'something aggressive' about the veil: wearing one to school raised a question of principle. Chirac referred to the Stasi Commission that was considering this question in the context of a larger study of the nature of *laïcité* (a term to be explored in the next chapter).[2] Chirac's comments on the veil were odd. There seemed to be something almost comic about the idea that the president of France was voicing his concern about aggressive schoolgirls. More seriously, there was also a stark contrast between these values and his previous pronouncements: if an anonymous tramp was recognized as a member of the Republic, shouldn't this quality also be extended to a veiled Muslim school-girl? And yet Chirac, the experienced statesman, chose to express this kind of exclusionary feeling in public, fully aware that his state-ments would be reported by the world's press.

Something was changing in France. Chirac's words presaged a small change in the regulations governing state schools (in effect, in March 2004 veil-wearing schoolgirls were banned) and illustrated a larger change in public attitudes to minorities. The new law provoked comment and debate in France and across the world. Many commentators were critical: people as varied as Jürgen Habermas, the respected German political philosopher, Rowan Williams, the archbishop of Canterbury, Christine Delphy, the French radical feminist philosopher, and Human Rights Watch all criticized the law's implications.[3] A range of anglophone academics also commented on the law. One interesting point to be gained from these rushed, critical responses was the wide range of disciplines represented: from women's studies (Caitlin Killian), anthropology (John Bowen), journalism (Emmanuel Terray and Jane Kramer – a rare supporter of the law), political science (Parvati Nair) to myself, previously principally a historian.[4]

As part of the preparation for my article, I gave a number of papers at conferences. An incident at once struck me. My paper had been placed next to a couple of papers on linked topics: the domin-ant tone of our panel was that we were puzzled by the new law, but certainly critical of it. Afterwards I spoke with a French academic. By mid-2004 I had learnt to be cautious when approaching French people about this topic. However, in this case, the lecturer was polite and welcoming. He'd enjoyed our papers, he said, and had realized that most British academics were critical of the law. Indeed, it did seem a bit ridiculous. Then, quite suddenly, his tone changed; he was staring into the middle distance and grew misty-eyed. 'But when I get to France' he said, his voice rising in passion, 'I remember the Republic and *laïcité*, I remember that I am French, and then …' Like Chirac at the tramps' funeral, he fell silent. Perhaps for him the argument was so obvious, that it did not need to be said.

In the months that followed, I made further trips to France, talking to Muslims and non-Muslims living there, and then discussing my impressions with colleagues and friends in Britain. I became sure that something was changing in France: there was a new tone emerging in academic and political circles. While the French lecturer that I'd met at the conference had fallen silent as he moved onto his vital point, others were prepared to state the argument explicitly. Several times I was told: 'You won't understand this, because you're not French.' This was a strange, unwelcome comment. When I'd been a postgraduate student in Lyon in the early 1980s, barely able to string together a grammatical sentence in French, and still confusing *tu* and *vous*, my research concerned the construction of the French schooling system and *laïcité*. No one had told me then that I wouldn't be able to understand my topic. Had I grown less intelligent during the years? Or had France changed?

Studying French Muslims

This work presents some reflections on these questions. It is not an analysis of the March 2004 law banning 'ostentatious' religious symbols from state schools, although it will include commentary on the debates that this measure provoked. What, then, is the main topic? This is a surprisingly difficult question to answer. In this section I will consider the issues raised by some previous studies, and then return to present this study's themes in the next section.

Today, France presents academics and other commentators with a valuable opportunity to study some unique cultural interactions, for it is – arguably – the first European country hosting a long-term, permanent presence of a substantial body of people who may be termed Muslims. In fact, their numbers have provoked one recent study to suggest that France can be counted as the world's fifteenth-largest Muslim country.[5] For these reasons alone, there have been many studies concerning Muslims in France.

Many works start with the presentation of a dichotomy, neatly illustrated by the title of Françoise Gaspard and Farhad Khosrokhavar's work, *Le Foulard et la République* (the headscarf and the Republic), or Oliver Roy's *La Laïcité face à l'Islam* (*laïcité* faces Islam).[6] These studies consider the context set by French legislation and the accumulated weight of French customs and practice, and then use sociological perspectives to explore the relationship between French cultures and the Muslim presence. Roy's work is particularly impressive in its analysis of *laïcité*, and how its nature is being changed by the new importance of Islam. Writers interested in social policy often adopt a similar perspective; the works by Laurence and Vaisse, and by Franck Frégosi, consider governmental policies and a variety of institutional responses towards French Muslims.[7] A rather more aggressive variant of the same format is represented by writers who could be considered *laïque* polemists, and whose writing can be linked to the revival of a nationalist Republicanism in France.[8] For writers such as Régis Debray and Michèle Vianès, Islam is at best a problem to be solved and at worst a threat to be defeated. Even the titles of their works suggest a threatening plot: Debray spoke of 'what the veil veils', and Vianès was concerned by a 'veil over the Republic'.[9] One potential counter-tendency to these polemical works is a book like Rachid Benzine's *Les Nouveaux Penseurs de l'Islam* (Islam's new thinkers), a work which outlines a history of reformist Muslim thinkers who could, perhaps, act as a bridge between the self-consciously liberal West and the apparently traditionalist East.[10] All these works concentrate on politics and policy: Islam features sometimes in a caricatured and simplified manner (as in the works by Debray and Vianès), sometimes more as a reactive force (as in Frégosi) and sometimes as an intellectual tradition (as in Benzine); only in the more perceptive works of Gaspard and Khosrokhavar, and Roy is there a fuller picture of Muslim dynamics, in interaction with the traditions of the West.

A second significant interpretative paradigm has been to start at the bottom, and to consider the lived reality of French Muslims. Anthropological writers have made some remarkable contributions in this form, and others have been inspired to adopt some quasi-anthropological methods in their depictions of Muslim life. One exceptional study which has not received the publicity it deserves is that by Dounia Bouzar and Saïda Kada.[11] Entitled 'One veiled, the other not', it presents a series of extended interviews with French Muslim women and comments on their experiences. The work reviews their many, varied forms of veil-wearing, from the authoritarian imposition of veil-wearing in some conservative Muslim households, to the more typical negotiations within families, to ideas of the veil as fashion accessory and symbol of identity or liberation. A second, more limited but perhaps better focused work is that edited by Ismahane Chouder, Malika Latrèche and Pierre Tevanian: they present a collection of interviews with veiled school students who were threatened with exclusion from their school in 2004. This provides an invaluable insight into the girls' experiences, but lacks any substantial analysis of its significance.[12] Sadek Hajji and Stéphanie Marteau's work draws on the older idea of travel-writing and provides some vivid descriptions of French Muslim *milieux*.[13] Farhad Khosrokhavar has edited a fascinating and chilling collection of interviews with prisoners accused of terrorist activity who publicly avow radical Islamist perspectives. Many are eloquent and thought-provoking, but the question of to what extent (if any!) these embittered young men can be cited as typical of any substantial section of French Muslims is left unanswered.[14] Two works by American academics – Trica D. Keaton and Paul A. Silverstein – are less satisfactory.[15] Their initial premise is to use anthropological perspectives to analyse particular communities in France. They base their studies on extended interviews. In practice, they encounter problems in transforming their data into coherent material for analysis. While individual interviewees produce valid or telling points concerning the lifestyles of modern Muslims, no collective voice emerges.

Finally, the third form of analysis has been sociological in nature, usually linked to specific groups or particular themes. Thomas Deltombe's work on 'imagined Islam' in the French media is an excellent work, informative and persuasive, and showing an intricate knowledge of his topic, but clearly is not designed as an analysis of the lives and aspirations of French Muslims.[16] Alec Hargreaves has studied the category of 'immigrants', and explores the serious difficulties which even second- and third-generation immigrant families experience in attempting to 'integrate': a term that, as

French Muslims

Hargreaves acknowledges, is exceptionally fraught with difficulty in
France. His work also shows the difficulty in making valid generalizations concerning this mass of very varied peoples.[17] The work
produced by the International Crisis Group (ICG) is something of a
curiosity: the ICG is better known for its excellent, informative
studies of crises in the Third World. The very publication of this
work about France suggests a type of post-colonial crisis, as the
distinctive mixture of impassioned and rebellious popular discontent, religion, and corrupt or unresponsive governmental structures
that has marked so many recent conflicts in the Third World now
appears to be replicated in France itself. Its work presents an exceptionally useful analysis of formal Muslim organizations, but leaves
open the question of the daily cultures of the mass of Muslims.[18]
Vincent Geisser and El Yamine Soum, two French sociologists, have
produced a well-argued and informative analysis of the internal
practices of French political practices in regard to minority ethnic
groups. They argue that while the new buzzword of 'diversity' has
changed the manner in which political parties treat such people, it
certainly has not produced any real or substantial integration of
minorities into political processes.[19] While their work is exceptionally informative about attitudes within mainstream political parties,
it says less about the situation of minorities outside of political
parties. In particular, Geisser and Soum seem to be deliberately
avoiding the use of the term 'Muslim'.

   This brief review of texts shows that the newly visible presence of
Muslims in contemporary France has stimulated a wide variety of
types of analysis, including religious studies, works on the sociology
of immigration, women's studies, the politics of the suburbs, social
policy and anthropology. From the simple issue of a few hundred
be-veiled schoolgirls, we move into a labyrinth of themes and
debates, which is almost impossible to structure into a neat example
of Cartesian dialectical logic. There is clearly no agreed framework
for debate on these topics, and certainly no canon of key works to
which all researchers refer. Furthermore, following the number of
exceptional, masterful studies already produced, one does need a
peculiar kind of temerity, of chutzpah, to dare to propose yet
another. This present work, however, does have a different starting
point from the studies listed above. I believe that a careful reading
of recent debates in France can provide an extremely valuable
lesson, even a universal lesson, about the dilemmas of nationhood

in today's world. While the French government and its loyal supporters constantly proclaim the universal nature of their Republican political culture, I find that the arguments with the strongest claim to universal significance are those developed by their marginalized opponents.

One problem which dogs the works listed above is the difficult choice of perspective: concentrating on the top – on institutions and philosophies – leads to a discussion concerning great abstract historical principles, with little reference to the real lives and cultures of modern French Muslims; while concentrating on the daily lives of French Muslims leads to patchy, piecemeal data flawed by real questions about its representative nature. In this work, I resolve this awkward dilemma by examining four thinkers who have put themselves forward, with some success, as speakers for their generation: Chahdortt Djavann, Fadela Amara, Tariq Ramadan and Houria Bouteldja. Each has featured extremely prominently in the French media, to the point where it would be no exaggeration to describe them as household names. Each might be categorized as a 'French Muslim', although each – in turn – suggests important qualifications to this term. I use these four as guides through the conceptual labyrinth. In part, this book will analyse in detail their thinking, but more often my aim is to contextualize and to explore, to re-construct the lifeworld from which their thinking emerges, to understand how they see French nationhood and the role of Muslims within it. None of these four, significantly, calls for a blunt rejection of French secular culture in the name of dogmatic religious values: this type of 'fundamentalism' (for want of a better term) is extremely rare in France, and has perhaps been best explored in the previously mentioned study by Khosrokhavar. Each calls for some form of debate with the Republic, even if the terms they set for such debates vary enormously. The four thinkers draw inspiration from different sources: they have links to different countries in the Muslim world (more specifically: Iran, Algeria and Egypt). Their political attitudes range from idealistic assimilation of French values, through a more cautious, pragmatic form of assimilation, an idealistic form of Islamic civic activism to a bitter, angry criticism of France as a political-cultural model. Through studying and contextualizing these four thinkers, we can gain a rich, composite picture of a set of cultures in transition, growing and developing distinctive strands, often outside the normal parameters of French political cultures. Arguably, the data which is uncovered through such an analysis is more representative of French Muslim experiences than either the philosophical-institutional or the anthropological approaches which have so far dominated studies.

These four thinkers represent a new generation, even a new form of Muslim politics: none of them (with the possible exception of Ramadan) could be described as professional intellectuals or as established religious authorities with a powerful institutional base. Significantly, none of them feature in Benzine's perceptive review of innovative, reformist Islamic thinking in the twentieth century. This concentration on this new generation of articulate, coherent, extra-institutional thinkers makes this work distinct from most previous studies on similar topics, which often have tended to assume that immigrants or minorities or Muslims are somehow fated to be the inarticulate victims of inexorable processes of prejudice or global-ization, pushed into social positions against their will, and that therefore they are incapable of responding except through the in-articulate violence of the city riot or through the escapist eloquence of religious mysticism. In this work, I wish to return a sense of agency to the subordinate voices, and to study how they have partici-pated in a wider national and international process.

This work will analyse the so-called 'debate' on Muslims and minorities that spluttered through the French media from 2002 to 2007. My concerns are largely bracketed between two presidential elections: the dramatic presidential elections of April–May 2002, which Jacques Chirac won, but in which Jean-Marie Le Pen, leader of the racist Front National, came second, to the elections of April–May 2007, when the dynamic rising star of the French Right, Nicholas Sarkozy, easily beat a type of sub-Blairite candidate from the Socialist Party, Ségolène Royal. Those principal actors – Chirac, Sarkozy and Royal – and their political struggles will feature in passing, but we will examine in more detail two of the lesser stars who contributed to their performance: Djavann and Amara, who will be analysed in chapters two and three. Both these writers won repeated plaudits, applause and publicity from the mainstream media. In the middle of this work we will pause to consider some of the institutions and organizations which play a limited part in the structuration of the presence of Muslims and minorities in main-stream French Republican culture (chapter four). Then, in the chapters five and six, we turn to two more challenging thinkers –

Ramadan and Bouteldja – whose ideas are caricatured and ridiculed by a complacent media that finds it difficult to accept that French Muslims may be producing original political ideas outside the established framework of Republican political culture.

Some extremely wide-ranging issues will be raised: we will cite examples from Turkey and Iran, from Algeria and Egypt, as well as reaching backwards over the past 250 years, considering the rival strands of historical memory which counterpose contrasting images of the same date or the same figure against each other, and so compare 8 May 1945 in Europe (VE Day) with 8 May 1945 in Algeria (the political violence in the port of Sétif, which provoked a massacre of thousands of Algerian Arabs), or distinguish the two legacies of Jules Ferry (1832–93), who was at once the grandfather of the modern French state school system and the pioneer of the French Empire.

Behind the scenes of the Republic

For much of this work, I have also been inspired by the older French concept of the *coulisses* of a topic: literally, the topic as seen from the wings, as in the wings of a theatre or, more idiomatically, from behind the scenes. From this position one can watch a production and see it not as a finished, believable representation of human life, but as a performance. While the audience suspends their disbelief, and is held by images that they are presented, those in the *coulisses* see both the artifices of the actors and the reactions of the audience. The term, I believe, was first used in a work published after the Boulangist adventure of 1886–9, when a dissident general raised what appeared to be a spontaneous coalition of the dispossessed, ranging from the urban proletariat, through the peasantry, the nationalist revanchists, angry with the powers of newly united Germany, to conservative, Catholic, monarchist aristocrats who had never accepted the Republic. *Les Coulisses de Boulangisme* aimed to unmask and demystify the movement; to reveal how what had seemed a spontaneous movement of the people had actually been created and manipulated by a skilful, powerful, conservative minority.[20] In order to write this kind of study, my most immediate models were not the academic and political studies listed above, but two rather unusual works. The first was François Maspero's *Les Passagers du Roissy-Express*, a type of anti-travel writing, which describes a three-week train journey from the north to the south of the Parisian conurbation in 1989.[21] The second was Azouz Begag's *Un Mouton dans le bagnoire* (a sheep in the bathroom), which tells of the lonely experience of a token Arab minister – the 'Arabe alibi' – in the Villepin government of 2005–7.[22] At first sight, these two works seem unrelated. They share, however, two concerns: both provide detailed commentary on the painful decline of a certain Republican faith, which upheld values of toleration and social solidarity. In a sense, whether knowingly or not, both of them are funeral elegies for the passing of this faith. And both provide an outsider perspective with which to interrogate and judge the world of the French insider.

The meaning of the term 'Muslim' is more complex than it may appear. It refers to a population who have a marginal presence in French society, and whose status is disputed to the point where some French republicans will even deny their existence as a discrete category of study. Alima Boumédienne-Thiery, a French Green euro-deputy, gave a speech to the European parliament in 2004 which included one of the most complete lists of the varied terms used to describe such people. She referred to a population that had been classified as 'natives, foreign workers, immigrants, descendants of immigration, *beurs* [French-Arab], North Africans and – today – Muslims and, according to some, potential terrorists'.[23] Given this terminological *embarras de richesses*, why privilege the religious term? First, and not very convincingly, because it is a term which circulates extremely frequently in the French media. But, secondly, because the term is applied in a way which makes it into a far broader category than readers may initially think. Obviously, Muslim can refer to someone who fulfils the ritual obligations of Islam: who recognises Allah as the unique god and Mohammed as his prophet, who prays five times a day, who respects Ramadan, who gives to charitable causes and who intends to go on pilgrimage to Mecca. But given the current state of Muslim observance in France, there are many who, while familiar with these rituals, respect them infrequently, or only in a perfunctory manner. Ramadan, for example, begins to function in a different manner, with the long nights, filled with music and conversation, assuming a greater importance than the austere days.[24] Some celebrate the end of

Ramadan by drinking a beer. Elsewhere this new generation has been identified by their food: they eat neither *choucroute* (almost a national dish in eastern France: pickled cabbage and pork) nor *couscous* (the best-known dish of North Africa, and approximately the French equivalent of curry in Britain), but McDonald's.[25] Taken as a whole, this is a group which is suffering not so much an identity crisis as a process of de-culturation. Tariq Ramadan refers to such people rather dismissively as 'Muslims without Islam', and calls for them to re-assert their true identity through a religious and spiritual revival.[26] Repeated surveys first give a global estimate for the number of Muslims in France, and then qualify the estimate with the proviso that only a certain number are 'practising': only 36 per cent according to an estimate in *Le Monde* in 2001, while another survey from 2003 suggested that only 5 per cent of those classified as Muslims regularly attended mosque.[27]

There is, however, a third use of the term 'Muslim': it also functions as an imposed identity in a society in which government and elites prefer to believe that social polarization and discrimination are a result of a willed effort by minorities to separate themselves from the majority culture, rather than a result of social policies pursued for decades, if not centuries, by the French state. Thus, during the urban riots of October and November 2005, some French commentators swiftly categorized the rioters as Muslims, labelled their rebellion an *intifada*, blamed the riots on fundamentalists and analysed the rioters' violence as a result of their failure to integrate.[28] (Police reports in following weeks revealed such analyses to be entirely baseless.[29]) In a similar manner, when Aïssa Dermouche was appointed as prefect for the Jura in January 2004, he was presented as France's first Muslim prefect. Why was this man's religious background highlighted? Why was the religious term used, in preference to – for example – terms such as 'from an immigrant family', 'Arab' or 'North African'? Previous appointments had not been announced as Jewish, Catholic or Protestant prefects. The answer seems to be that Sarkozy's Ministry of the Interior wished to demonstrate its commitment to 'diversity', and at that moment this religious category seemed the most appropriate marker of identity.[30] Such examples show that the term 'Muslim' can be not so much a concept which contributes to a sense of civic identity, but something more akin to a stigmatization.[31] The excellent study by Sadek Hajji and Stéphanie Marteau invents the

acronym FPMC – French Person(s) of Muslim Culture – to indicate
that their use of the word 'Muslim' refers as much to forms of political, social and cultural identity as to a practice or belief.[32] While this
term will not be used here, readers should remember that in this
work 'Muslim' can refer to at once a faith, a culture and a status,
and that it is in the last two categories that I am most interested.

Lastly, I am neither arguing that 'Muslim' is *the* correct term for
an analysis of this section of France's minorities, nor that it is an
incorrect term, merely that it is currently a widely circulating term.

Three minorities

In perhaps a rather over-schematic manner, it can be argued that
for the past three centuries French people have come into contact
with three distinct racialized sub-groups: Jews, black people and
Arabs. In each case, the results have been extremely mixed, yet for
two of three cases there is a strong tendency within French political
culture to celebrate these interactions as evidence of the Republic's
liberatory role.

Jews seemed to be the ultimate European minority in 1789. They
were largely ethnically, socially and religiously separate from the rest
of the population, and their lives were still structured in many parts
of Europe by the experience of living in ghettos: a practice which
was first enforced in Venice in 1516.[33] The French Revolution's
promise of a total civic and political emancipation was one which
the French-Jewish population found intoxicating, and the revolutionary reforms produced a deep-rooted, long-lasting form of
French-Jewish republican patriotism.[34] The Dreyfus Affair (1894–
1906) illustrates many facets of this evolving relationship: on the
one hand, the rapid conversion of an older religious anti-Semitism
into a right-wing, anti-republican creed, which would re-emerge in
the racial violence of the Vichy regime, resulting in the death of
some 75,000 French-Jews. On the other hand, many French-Jews
remained loyal patriots. Their political culture was exemplified in
the figure of Alfred Dreyfus himself, who remained so calm at his
trial and so stoical while imprisoned in Devil's Island because *he
knew* that the guilty verdict pronounced against him was wrong and
that, therefore, eventually French republican justice would recog-
nise his innocence. His attitude was very different from the noisy,
critical, libertarian protests that defended him and also – implicitly

– defended the cause of all minorities in the French Republic: as Péguy noted, the conservative, patriotic Dreyfus was precisely the sort of person who would never have been a Dreyfusard. Out of this proud, assimilationist creed, a unique approach to religious identity in the secular Republic evolved among French-Jews. They would be 'Jews indoors, French citizens outside'.[35] This was an attitude that was fully compatible with the ideal of *laïcité*. French-Jews accepted the idea that religion was properly a private matter, and that in all forms of public life it should be almost – if not entirely – invisible. In many cases, current French frustrations with the Muslim presence in France can be explained with reference to this Jewish assimilationist model: French critics are, in effect, often saying 'why can't Muslims be more like Jews?'.[36]

Initial contacts with black minorities came not through the assimilation of groups within France, but first through the slave trade, and then through colonial expansion, beginning in the seventeenth century. Once again, a narrative of republican liberation can be told, if one puts to one side the substantial French involvement in the slave trade. The Second Republic of 1848 ended slavery and introduced legal equality into the Caribbean. Allied to this, however, is a curious, often patronizing, affection for elements of black culture, exemplified in the now iconic (and politically unacceptable) advertisements from the 1920s and 1930s that showed grinning black Africans holding cups of Banania cocoa. French fascination with what was seen as the dark, primitive world of Africa also stimulated surrealism and guaranteed the showbusiness success of Josephine Baker: a singer who was stigmatized in her native USA, but who became in France the perfect embodiment of the amalgam of primitivism and hyper-modernism represented by jazz music.[37] To this day, black minorities in France meet less instinctive and automatic hostility to their presence than Arab or self-consciously Muslim groups: a point neatly illustrated by the repeated failure by French officials to recognize that one can be black *and* Muslim.[38]

In contrast, it is far more difficult to tell the history of the French contacts with Arabo-Muslim cultures as a story of liberation. French colonies in North Africa were extremely unequal societies, and showed little sign of growing more equal during the twentieth century. While French administrators could feel proud of some real technical advances – for example, the building of modern ports and railways, and the provision of some social services – the pervasive inequality of the colonial situation meant that Arab Muslims rarely received the benefit of these advances. Thus, in Algeria, the most important French colony, agricultural innovation went hand in hand with the legalized seizure of Arab land. Assimilation of the colonized into the colonizers' culture clearly did not take place and even French colonial policy shifted its goals, and often talked of a looser ideal of 'association' between the Republic and the colonized. The illusions drawn from colonial Algeria's image as an attractive, cheap holiday destination for French people were ended by the appalling violence of the last decade of French rule and left the French population with a gruesome impression of the failure of colonial rule. Worse still, the Algerian crisis threatened to spill over into metropolitan France as brutal police methods were used on Algerian workers in France, and hard-line colonialists terrorized the French Republic itself in 1958–62, raising the nightmare of a military coup.[39] Many French people came to feel doubts and even despair concerning the actions taken in the name of colonialism, but far fewer could identify with the struggle taken by Arab Algerian nationalists to liberate their country from colonialism.[40]

Turning this violent history into a positive story of Republican emancipation was a difficult challenge for even the most strident of the Republic's defenders. There was, however, one interpretative strategy: loyalists could re-cast French colonial powers as thwarted liberals, beaten by a chasm of misunderstanding that provoked first, the murderous, pseudo-Jacobin terrorism of the Front de Libération Nationale (FLN) and, secondly, political Islam. This alternative interpretative ploy became distinctively more viable during the 1990s, as an Islamic political party (the Front Islamique de Salut) was denied electoral victory in Algeria, and then split and decayed into a set of competing factions, some of them infiltrated, repressed and manipulated by outside forces, producing some of the most horrific examples of terrorist violence on a civilian population ever seen. In particular, one claim was consistently asserted: French colonialism had attempted to liberate Algerian women from the repression of Islam.[41] The 'proof' for this argument was produced by reference to the 'veil': a topic to be discussed in the next chapter.

The important point to stress here is that the history of Algerian colonialism left French people with a set of commonly circulating images by which to understand Muslim and/or Arab populations.[42]

(Indeed, one problem was precisely that the Algerian experience left many French people unable to distinguish between Arab and Muslim cultures.) The lessons drawn from 130 years of Algerian colonialism taught French people to see Islam as an enemy force, retrograde in its values and violent in its methods. This third colonial, racialized contact has also left a permanent suspicion about almost all forms of Muslim organization. A quip which is re-told by Muslim activists in France today states that: 'When a group of Bretons meet in the street, it's called regionalism; when it's a group of Portuguese, it's called folklore; and when it's a group of North Africans, it's called *communautarisme*.'[43] One point needs to be clarified here: France is probably the only country in the world in which a word linked to the term 'community' carries severely negative connotations. '*Communautarisme*' does not mean an innocent activity to build up a community: instead it means a challenge to the Republican ideal of a transparent, unified public sphere in which all citizens appear as approximate equals, as in the previously cited example of 'Jews indoors, French citizens outside'. Perhaps the best translation of the term is 'ghetto-ization', with the proviso that in this case it is understood as an example of the minority group 'ghetto-izing' itself.

This brief review of France's three contacts with racialized groups suggests how heavily the weight of centuries of history is acting to determine and to structure the apparently spontaneous, common-sense forms of political culture in France today.

Conclusion

This is a book about a group of people, Muslims, with the strong, clear qualification that this term is a provisional, constructed category, often an externally imposed category, which may be surpassed surprisingly quickly by events. While this work certainly makes frequent reference to a religion – Islam – its main purpose is not to study a faith. Instead, our principal topic is the difficult relationship between Muslims and the French Republic: a political form which, in the late nineteenth century, seemed to be the very embodiment of modernity; a form which was secular, democratic (if one is permitted to use this term to describe a regime in which women were denied the vote until 1944) and progressive; a form which seemed to unite diverse peoples in a common national culture. As the epigraph for this chapter suggests, these Republican ideals are at the centre of debates: the Republic was once a form which excited admiration and – in Bouteldja's words – even love from the non-French people who learnt about it. In studying the relationship between contemporary Muslims and the French Republic, we will note the decline of Republicanism as an effective political form. We will identify an unusual, probably unique, form of racism contained within the Republican form: a virtuous racism, in the words of Nacira Guénif-Souilamas, which could even be termed an anti-racist racism.[44]

This work will discuss how Republicanism has failed to adapt to the challenges of the twenty-first century. In the words of Yann Moulier Boutang, 'The Republic has become reactionary'.[45] Like President Chirac in September 2003, we are witnessing a silent state funeral.

Chapter One
The War of Symbols: a Chronicle of a Debate Foretold

The means by which French people were alerted to the issues raised in the previous chapter was through the presence of a few hundred veiled schoolgirls in French state schools. This chapter will first re-tell the story of the 'war of the veil', and then consider some key concepts and terms that this clash brought into prominence: *laïcité* (and the Republican tradition), the veil, integration and *beur*. My intention in examining these terms is to draw out some hidden political implications concerning how debate was structured: these assumptions form the context for the interventions by our four thinkers.

The war of the veil

It has become commonplace to suggest that the dispute surrounding the status of veiled schoolgirls in French state schools started, out of the blue, in September 1989.[1] In that month, three veiled schoolgirls were excluded from the Gabriel-Havez college in Creil, a small town north of Paris, on the grounds that their veils were not compatible with the *laïque* principles of the French state schooling system. Their veils were relatively light pieces of cloth covering their hair, but not their faces: nothing like the small tents that the Taliban imposed on the women of Kabul. (Indeed, 'headscarf' is probably a more accurate word, and was used more widely in the early 1990s. I will use 'veil' as it was the most commonly circulating word after 2000.) The Socialist Party was confused by the incident: a substantial minority in the party felt deep loyalty to the ideals of *laïcité* and therefore strongly supported criticisms of the girls' behaviour. Party lines were further muddled by the publication of a manifesto in the left-leaning *Nouvel*

Observateur weekly, signed by prominent intellectuals such as Elisabeth Badinter, Régis Debray and Alain Finkielkraut, which called for a stronger defence of *laïcité* against the threat represented by the schoolgirls. Christian Democrats, normally located in the centre or centre-right of the French political spectrum, were more tolerant of the veiled schoolgirls. A long, tortuous, legal-constitutional argument followed, and it was finally accepted in July 1995 that veil-wearing schoolgirls could be – reluctantly – tolerated in French state schools as long as they did not engage in active attempts to convert other pupils to Islam.[2] Disputes continued, and in the late 1990s about 150 cases each year went to a central arbitration body.[3]

In reality, it is clear that the episode in 1989 was a new chapter in a far longer story that could be dated back to 1830 (the French invasion of Algeria), if not still earlier.[4] The question returned to the political agenda in 2003, when the two daughters of a secular French-Jew converted to Islam. In October 2003, they returned to their school in Aubervilliers wearing headscarves. They were excluded from the school a few days later: it seems that some *laïque* militants in the school publicized their case, and therefore it was closely followed by the French media.

At first sight, these seem absurd episodes: how could the Republic be threatened by a few hundred (at most a thousand) schoolgirls choosing to wear veils on their heads? How could Chirac, in 2003, publicly associate himself with those who stated that they considered that wearing a veil to be an aggressive act? The contradictions in such arguments seem so obvious: does not Marianne, the buxom symbol of the French Republic, normally cover her hair? Are veil-wearing Catholic nuns also to be understood as aggressive?

At this point we have to consider at least three further dimensions to this issue. First, a general point: schooling occupies an intensely important position within French political culture, and it is no exaggeration to say that the school – understood principally as the *state* school – is the prime symbol of Republican values. French state schools have also performed reasonably effectively as a means of social promotion for some of the excluded and marginalized.[5] For some years, however, schoolteachers have been complaining of a decline in respect for their role, and – perhaps more seriously – of increased levels of aggression and violence in their schools. Such complaints received a powerful expression in a collection of essays and interviews edited by Emmanuel Brenner in 2004, with the

provocative, memorable title of *The Republic's Lost Territories.*[6] The
picture that emerges from this work is certainly alarming. Some 405
anti-Semitic acts were recorded in France between September 2000
and January 2002: many of these incidents were violent, and the
numbers recorded were undoubtedly increasing. Tags and graffiti
were becoming more common in many schools. Students were
growing more aggressive and ruder towards staff, and on occasion
would challenge teachers or simply refuse to follow lessons. While
Brenner was concerned about all forms of racism, he made it clear
that the rise in anti-Semitism was the most important issue facing
the Republic. He left his readers in no doubt about the cause of this
crisis: these acts were the result of a concerted move against
Republican values by some Muslims. 'To denounce the anti-Semitic,
anti-French and anti-Republican evolution of a section of the North
African community is not to stigmatize them,' he explained, 'but is
– on the contrary – to defend their right to integration in France.'[7]
More importantly, Brenner drew an impassioned moral lesson from
these events. He thundered to his readers: 'Let the Republic rise
again!'; they had grown too lax; they must fight to prevent 'the
decay' of the Republic's values. 'The whole of French society today
seems to be morally and intellectually disarmed when faced with the
assertion of religious and identity politics which is at work in the
Arabo-Muslim community.'[8] This book was also a passionate call to
revive a certain Republican activism.

Brenner also provided a clear, easy explanation for the increasing
numbers of Muslim women wearing headscarves in public. They
were, quite simply, part of an Islamist strategy to subvert the
Republic and evidence of a growing illiberalism among the Muslim
minority. (In reality, the dynamics and meanings of the veil are far
more complex than Brenner's hasty caricatures suggest: we will
return to this point in the next sections.)

Brenner's book was extremely influential, to the point where its
perspectives and analyses had some direct effect on the findings of
the Stasi Commission on *laïcité.*[9] Its analysis of the state of French
schooling can be questioned. One point which is particularly
worrying is the manner in which Brenner conflates all challenges to
the established school practices. Can it be argued that, for example,
a demand by pupils for special provision so that they can respect
Ramadan is the equivalent of a violent, anti-Semitic act? Can it be
argued that wearing a Palestinian *keffieh* is the equivalent of

spray-painting a tag on a school wall? These seemed to be the conclusions of the sensationalistic, undifferentiated – and often anecdotal – evidence cited by Brenner. Furthermore, as is nearly always the case in this type of conspiracy literature, the masterminds of the plot are never actually named. True, Brenner makes passing reference to the Union des Organisations Islamiques de France (UOIF: Union of Islamic Organizations of France – see chapter four), and also notes the activities of a tiny, largely Strasbourg-based party, the Parti des musulmans de France (PMF – Party of French Muslims).[10] But it is hard to believe that the UOIF, a group essentially concerned with the administration of mosques, or the tiny PMF have the power to control a plot which – supposedly – stretches across the whole of France's schools. Moving further from Brenner's emotionally charged perspectives, one notes how little he refers to social factors. Rather than blaming Muslims for a decline in courtesy and discipline in the schools, it seems more likely that these shifts are related to broader changes in the relationship between school, work and society, which have produced a context in which many young people have intuitively realized that working hard at school will not guarantee them a future in a fluctuating, uncertain and threatening work environment.[11] Finally, there is no sensitivity in Brenner's text to those who find the school to be 'an instrument of humiliation, of elimination, of yet more discrimination'.[12] Teachers, according to Brenner, are always benevolent, well-meaning liberals.

Alongside Brenner's Republican revivalism, there was also a political dimension in the renewal of interest in French Muslims in 2003–4. Since 1989, there had been a series of largely unsuccessful attempts to create some formal, institutional representation for French Muslims, similar to the organizations which exist for French Catholics, Protestants and Jews (see chapter four). This had been a relatively uncontroversial idea: during the presidential elections of 2002, none of the major candidates had made any prominent reference to this point and – indeed – even *laïcité* featured rarely in their programmes. Following the dramatic election, however, Chirac was in search of big political gestures which would allow him to appear as a truly national leader. He was also concerned by any successes by potential rivals on his right or left. In the course of 2003, the energetic Minister of the Interior, Sarkozy, seemed at last to be succeeding in building a representative structure for French

Muslims. In particular, he appeared to have a stable working relationship with the UOIF. Sarkozy even gave a speech to the organization at its prominent annual congress at Le Bourget, in April 2003. At one point he was noisily booed by the assembled listeners, but he did not come away with a desire to settle scores. It seems possible that this point initiated a political strategy by right-wing politicians loyal to Chirac. For some on the right, Sarkozy's approach to Islam was 'too politically correct'.[13] They were alarmed by the minister's growing popularity and sought to outmanoeuvre their rival. Their idea was to strengthen legislation on the presence of religious symbols at schools, specifically the veil, in order to force Sarkozy into a more confrontational position with the UOIF.[14]

Under these circumstances, veiled schoolgirls acquired a new importance in the national subconscious. They were no longer a few hundred eccentrically dressed youngsters, usually with impeccable school records and good classroom discipline: instead they were the visible representatives of a sinister conspiracy. An editorial in the left-of-centre daily *Libération* made this point clear: it spoke of 'a handful of veil-wearers who are exploited, whether voluntarily or not, by fundamentalist strategies'.[15] In many cases, discussions of schoolgirls with headscarves spiralled outwards in ever-increasing circles. Judith Kramer's article in the *New Yorker* is probably the finest example of this tendency to pile exaggeration on exaggeration: in a thirteen-page essay which begins by discussing the case of a veil-wearing teacher, the text moves on to cite Islamism in France, Islamism in the Arab world, Saudi funding for the Egyptian Muslim Brotherhood, the Algerian elections of 1991 (in which the Muslim FIS were denied their victory by military action), male violence, pornography, polygamy and female genital mutilation.[16] A dissident feminist publication discussing this type of writing accurately observed that 'veiled women became, in the French imagination, the sign of all the evils which threatened the Republic and its values'.[17]

These three dimensions – public concern with the condition of schooling, political machinations within the parliamentary right and the wild exaggeration of the importance of a few hundred headscarves – played a determining role in the deliberations of the Stasi Commission set up by Chirac, and the somewhat less important Debré Commission created by the National Assembly.

Early in 2003, Chirac chose Bernard Stasi to chair an enquiry into the application of *laïcité* in the Republic. The Commission opened on 3 July 2003, and presented its final report on 11 December 2003. It had twenty members, of whom six were women, and included nine academics, three officials from educational administration, three politicians, two lawyers, two activists from local associations and one representative from business. Politically, it represented a balance of left-wing and right-wing opinion.[18] It included three people with some personal experience of Muslim cultures: Mohammed Arkoun, a 75-year-old authority on Islamic thought, who appears to have remained surprisingly silent during debates; Hanifa Cherifi, the chief negotiator for the education ministry, who did not consider that there was a crisis in the schools, and Gaye Petek, the head of an association working to encourage the integration of Turks into France. The Commission conducted 104 public interviews and about forty private interviews (including contacts with five Masonic lodges).[19] It also received some two thousand letters. Questions have been raised about how people were selected for interview: Jean Baubérot, a Commission member, later wondered why all the teachers interviewed seemed to be so firmly anti-veil, when opinion polls indicated that the teaching body was divided on the question.[20] The dynamics operating in the Commission are still open to question: of its twenty members only one, the respected conservative historian René Rémond, dissented from its final conclusion. There was a surprising shift in attitudes by a number of Commission members who had previously refused to support legislation banning the veil from state schools. For example, the sociologist Alain Touraine had previously welcomed the 'modernism' of a new generation of veil-wearing schoolgirls.[21] Why did he change his mind?

It appears that the Stasi Commission initially decided not to interview any veiled schoolgirls. Its brief was to review *laïcité* in France: during their research, none of the Commission's members seem to have contacted any of France's numerous, well-informed and original analysts of Muslim culture. Stasi himself was a 70-year-old Christian Democrat who could remember French anti-Semitism during the Occupation. He was a man of impeccably liberal, anti-racist views, who could boast that each of his four grandparents came from a different nation: Tuscany, Corsica, Cuba and Spain.[22] 'I don't want to live in a country where there are only white people' he stated.[23] He later spoke out against the politicization of the question of immigration during the 2007 presidential election campaign. Stasi believed in France as a 'dynamic, living, exemplary' model of integration through *laïcité*.[24] His only direct contact with a Muslim culture, however, seemed to date from the late 1950s, when he had worked in Algeria in its last years as a French colony.[25] His Commission was confused by Muslim practices, and yet they chose to rely on their own resources. As one member later stated: 'The veil hid a forest, a dense forest, which was difficult to penetrate.'[26] The great bulk of the people they interviewed were not Muslims, and the evidence they heard tended to confirm the images previously established by Brenner: there were an increasing number of what might be termed 'border disputes' as Muslims began to make specific demands in schools, hospitals and prisons. There was even a broader social dimension: Commission members began to re-conceive the depressed and impoverished *banlieues* (suburbs) around Paris and other French cities as further examples of 'lost territories', 'in which Islamists run the show'.[27] The fact that accurate figures concerning the number of veiled schoolgirls were not available only worried the Commission still further. This was a further sign of laxity, of the frightening inability of Republican authorities to control the dense forest. Under these circumstances, the Commission members found it easiest to follow Brenner's analysis: there was an insidious plot to undermine the Republic.

Touraine seems to have been one of the few to retain some doubts. He belatedly insisted that the Commission hear from veil-wearing schoolgirls themselves, against Stasi's original proposal.[28] By this moment, most of the Commission members had made up their mind. One (or more?) of the handful of veiled schoolgirls they heard in private recounted 'the daily humiliation she felt when she was forced to wear the veil'.[29] (It seems likely that Chahdortt Djavann's interview also impressed some members.)[30] This was the last piece in the jigsaw: the Commission members now felt confident that in proposing that the veil should be banned from state schools, they were acting to emancipate a generation of Muslim schoolgirls. 'Thus, without any real debate,' records Jean Barbérot, 'it was suggested that one could not really believe in male-female equality and tolerate the headscarf in state schools.'[31] In the final report, Stasi declared that 'the Republic cannot stay deaf to the cries of distress from these young girls'.[32]

Having heard a litany of France's problems, the Commission was expected to act.[33] Some of its members still doubted whether banning veils from state schools would really solve these issues, but were then faced with the awkward dilemma of how to justify inactivity in the face of pressing problems. Brenner's book and Kramer's article show how issues appeared to the Commission members: not acting, not legislating, seemed to be accepting fundamentalism, the creation of ghettoes in France, the rise of intolerance and even female genital mutilation. The sense that they were expected to act weighed heavily on the Commission: Patrick Weill later recalled 'I must admit that I have never worked under this amount of public pressure coming from all sides.'[34] In this situation, it seemed better to do something. After all, the proposed law was 'the tracing of a border, a limit and not … an atavistic rejection of diversity'.[35] Stasi himself put great pressure on his Commission's members to maintain unity: one morning there was an informal show of hands among the Commission on the subject on banning 'ostensible' signs. Three members (including Touraine) voted against the proposal. Stasi spoke personally to all three, stressing how inactivity or neutrality would be perceived by the French public, and insisting on a second vote in the afternoon. Only one member persisted in voting against: Jean Baubérot.[36] Moreover, Stasi remained convinced that the purpose of his Commission was not so much to regulate the veil in schools, as to re-create *laïcité* for the twenty-first century. While excluding certain expressions of Muslim identity with one hand, the Commission devised twenty-six imaginative measures to integrate Muslims and other minorities with the other hand, including the official celebration of Muslim religious festivals in schools, the provision of halal food in school canteens, the provision of Muslim religious facilities in jails and – above all – creating a careful distinction between a legitimate (or 'discreet') religiosity and an unacceptable (or *ostensible*) religiosity in schools. (Unfortunately, while Jewish skull-caps and small crucifixes were deemed discreet, veils, headscarves or hijabs were not.) Commission members with doubts about their actions could therefore reassure themselves that their bulk of their proposals were not condemnatory and exclusionary: their ultimate purpose was to integrate.

Such subtle distinctions were of little concern to the press and to the mass of politicians. The one issue taken from the seventy-two-page report was the proposal to ban the *ostensible* veil in state schools. Stasi himself seems to have been genuinely surprised by this: 'What has disturbed me is how the debate has focused on the headscarf, while the mission [of the Commission] was far larger, far greater.'[37] Other Commission members shared his disappointment and bewilderment. Gaye Petek told *Le Monde* 'how many times did we say that the veil is not the main issue!'[38] In one television debate, Stasi proved surprisingly sensitive about criticisms of his work from a leading member of the UOIF. 'I won't let you say that I'm attacking the dignity of Muslims. It's not right to say that France is an anti-Muslim country. It's wrong, it's wrong, it's wrong! It's a lie!'[39] Yet the final effect of the Commission's report was a proposal to aid integration by excluding a few hundred schoolgirls.

Public reactions to this report and the wider 'debate' were predictable. In 2002, French people in general had been suspicious of the veil, but hardly saw it as an important issue. In the course of 2003–4, they were taught to be scared of it. There was a massive, sustained and extremely misleading coverage of questions concerning Muslims and minorities. Pierre Tevanian estimated that matters concerning the veil and/or *laïcité* were front-page headline news on at least 26 occasions in 2003 and that in the same year France's three leading daily papers – *Le Monde*, *Libération* and *Le Figaro* – contained 1,284 articles on these topics: more than one article per day per paper.[40] 'One gets the impression that this matter is the most serious and most urgent challenge facing our country' noted one sceptical journalist in *Le Monde*.[41] A record 150 deputies asked to speak in the relevant parliamentary debates early in February: in practice, only 120 actually spoke (about an eighth of their number in parliament) and of these, only 18 were women.[42] 'Everyone spoke of us, about us, but without us, and we had no way of replying' noted one veil-wearing Muslim activist.[43] The final result of this onslaught was summed up by the Catholic daily *La Croix*: the Stasi Commission had proved 'that there really exists a rampant islamisation among immigrant families'.[44]

Deputies were motivated by similar concerns to those which had shaped the Stasi report, and doubters were worried about appearing apathetic in the face of a pressing crisis. Voting for action, even inadequate and inappropriate action, seemed better than doing nothing. On 10 February 2004, 494 deputies voted for the law, 36 against, and 31 abstained. 90 per cent of the right-wing UMP deputies voted for, as did 94 per cent of the Socialist deputies. There was less certainty among the deputies of the centrist UDF (13 for, 12 abstentions and 4 against) and more opposition from the Communist deputies (7 for, 14 against). The Verts (Greens) were the only national party represented in the Chamber of Deputies who were openly critical of the law: two of their three deputies voted against, and the third abstained.[45]

Outside the National Assembly, the situation was somewhat more complex. Tevanian's research suggests that prior to this media campaign, there was little significant concern about veiled school-girls. In a study conducted in December 2003 among 125 students at Drancy (north of Paris), only one spontaneously raised the veil as an issue.[46] Certainly, when asked, French people showed themselves to be suspicious of the veil. A set of opinion polls from April 2003 suggested about 74 per cent of the French population were against the veil being worn in schools, but only 22 per cent wanted to exclude veil-wearing schoolgirls.[47] During the course of the media campaign, public opinion turned in favour of a law banning religious signs in state schools: from 49 per cent according to one opinion poll in April 2003 to 76 per cent in September 2004.[48] However, throughout this period, there was always one significant qualification: Muslims (however they were defined) were consistently recorded as being more sceptical about a law than the non-Muslim population.[49] Thus CSA opinion polls from December 2003 and January 2004 found 69 per cent of French public opinion in favour of the law, while only 42 per cent of French Muslims supported such a law.[50] There can be no doubt that the debate concerning this law played a part in encour-aging a clearer sense of difference among French Muslims from the bulk of the French population.

Some critical voices emerged in the media. There was a trenchant and hard-hitting editorial in *Le Monde* entitled 'The politics of fear', which accused Chirac of exploiting the public affection for *laïcité* and reducing the great principles it represented to an irrational fear of the veil.[51] The Council of Christian Churches – a representa-tive body which includes Catholics and Protestants – signalled its doubts about the drift from 'a calm *laïcité*' to 'fighting *laïcité*'.[52] Trade unions often seemed uncertain: thus the moderate-left CFDT welcomed the Stasi Report, but was worried by how it might be implemented.[53] The left-wing CGT re-affirmed its commitment to

another ways / to integrate

laïcité, but suggested that social and economic reform would be the best way to build a cohesive nation.[54] The FSU teachers' union also affirmed its loyalty to the principles of *laïcité*, but worried about how these were to be affirmed by a proposal to exclude pupils, and also raised the troubling question of how the law was to be interpreted.[55] At a local level, teachers themselves were often unsure. In the lycée Jean-Jaurès in Montreuil in November 2003, there were 12 veil-wearing pupils in a student body of 1,200. A strong minority of the teachers wanted their exclusion; the school management refused to act. Arguments among the teachers were bitter and divisive: seven general assemblies in two months did not create a united policy. Instead, there was an acrimonious debate on the nature of *laïcité*. 'I don't need a Muslim to tell me what *laïcité* is!' one angry teacher told *Libération*.[56] French human rights and anti-racist organizations were similarly divided. MRAP was consistently concerned with the manner in which the stigmatization of some Muslims as anti-French subversives easily led to a stigmatization of all Muslims.[57] The venerable Ligue des Droits de l'homme (LDH – League of the Rights of Man) preferred dialogue and social justice to a law that stigmatized part of the population.[58]

very relevant

The final result of this so-called 'debate' was to create a type of special status for French Muslims, putting their activities and proposals under particular scrutiny. John R. Bowen cites a good example: across France, many swimming pools had accepted requests from Jewish groups that there should be a few hours per week in which pools were reserved for women. However, when it was learnt in June 2003 that a group of Arab women made a similar request in Lille, this was immediately cited by hostile commentators as another example of Islamic *communautarisme* in practice.[59] *– what is this?*

There remained something unusual, even uncomfortable, about the debate. The volume of press articles and parliamentary speeches, the repeated variations on the same simple theme, all suggested more a nation trying to convince itself that it was right than a genuine consensus. More specifically, the debate cut across established political boundaries, often dividing long-term friends from each other.

Laïcité and the Republic

Observant readers may have noted that the term '*laïcité*' was used seventeen times in the last section – and yet no definition was given.

There is a simple reason for this: no commonly agreed definition is available.

The law which established the separation of church and state in France was passed in 1905: its text did not make use of the noun *laïcité* nor the adjective *laïque*. The first occasion that the term was cited in a constitutional document was in 1946, with the founding of the Fourth Republic; the term was then repeated in the constitution of the current Fifth Republic (1958).[60] For many Republicans, *laïcité* is a touchstone, not just a guarantee of French patriotism but also a type of indisputable proof of French identity.[61] The term also works to suggest a cultural contrast with other identities: according to the respected conservative historian Max Gallo, 'Islam opposes its concepts to ours, the first of which are *laïcité* and tolerance'.[62] Jacqueline Costa-Lascoux, a Stasi Commission member, writes in a similar manner that immigrants must be prepared to accept the values of *laïcité* in order to be integrated into France, noting that those who come from 'traditional or theocratic' societies will find it a difficult concept to understand.[63]

One or two commentators draw attention to some odd features of the concept. Nicolas Weill, a journalist from *Le Monde*, sent a French-language article on *laïcité* to a translator, and was amazed to learn that there was no English-language translation for the term.[64] The perceptive and articulate commentator Olivier Roy notes how despite its constitutional importance, no one has provided an accepted legal definition of what constitutes *laïcité*.[65] The so-called 'liberal mufti' of Marseilles, Soheib Bencheikh, finds it to be 'an imprecise concept' and notes that there is no official definition of what the term means.[66] But, as we will see, these are exceptional, atypical voices.

There are some odd features in the manner in which the concept has been used in the 'debate' of 2003–4. Consider the following interventions:

- Jacques Chirac: '[*Laïcité*] expresses our wish to live together in respect, dialogue and toleration.'[67]
- Christian Bourepaux: '[*Laïcité* is] the principle of a balance between the public sphere and the private sphere.'[68]
- Anne Vigerie and Anne Zelensky: '*Laïcité* is based on a neutral public sphere, one free of all religious belief.'[69]
- Jean Ayrault: '[*Laïcité*] is an emancipatory process which started

almost a hundred years ago ... It is a light to women imprisoned by obscurantism, it is hope for oppressed minorities.'[70]

- Une école pour tou-te-s: '*Laïcité*, as defined by the laws of 1881, 1882, 1886 and 1905, constitutes a guarantee for the liberty of conscience and the emancipation of men and women outside of religious dogma.'[71]
- François Fillon: 'This principle, the fruit of a long history, is based on the respect for the liberty of conscience and the affirmation of common values which create a national unity over and above particular loyalties.'[72]
- Jean-Pierre Raffarin: '*Laïcité*, our *laïcité*, is not the refusal of religion ... *laïcité* is ... a grammar which allows a calm, pacified dialogue between religions and the state within our country'.[73]
- Council of Christian Churches in France: 'In fact, *laïcité*'s aim is not to create spaces which are emptied of all religious presence, but to present a space where all, believer and non-believers, can debate ... what is acceptable and unacceptable, differences to be respected and errors to be avoided: and all this [in a context] of mutual understanding, without silencing the convictions and motivations of one another, but also without clashes and propaganda.'[74]

There are some surprising common features to these pronouncements. First, there can be no doubt concerning the importance with which each invest the principle of *laïcité*. Secondly, there is the curious assertive form which these pronouncements take: there is no reference whatsoever to exterior authorities, no footnote to the thirteen-volume tome by Professors J. Dullard and F. Raud (Dullsville University Press, 1994), nor even any reference to the actual practices of the French state – with the curious exception of Une école pour tou-te-s (a group to be considered in chapter four). And here, in this rare attempt to produce some contextualization, the Une école pour tou-te-s reference appears to be factually incorrect. Thirdly, during most of this debate, most commentators seemed to be blissfully unaware that contradictory claims were being made about the nature of *laïcité*. Occasionally, some left-wing critics argued that President Chirac presented too minimalist a concept of *laïcité*.[75] But apart from these rare dissonances, the 'debate' in 2003–4 seemed to take the form of a surrealistic ballet, in which each participant danced to a separate tune, while claiming

that the performance as a whole was an marvellous example of
coordinated national unity.

Looking at these varied interventions, some patterns emerge.
The concept is being exploited tactically, as a means of persuading
audiences of the speaker's mastery of words and ideals.[76] But in fact,
for all the references to universal values and rationalism, these
empty sound bites are the very opposite of rational debate and
analysis. *Laïcité* is perhaps the key concept which differentiates
contemporary French ideals about the state from British or
American ideals. Rather than seeing the state in its classical liberal
concept as a neutral arbiter between the competing claims of individuals, these emotionally charged references often refer back to
the rival, Rousseau-ian concept of the state as the embodiment of a
collective 'general will'. This concept can be linked to the origins of
modern political culture in France: the primary goal of the first
Republicans of the 1790s was not to create a political party, but to
re-configure France in such a form that its natural political unity
would be revealed and strengthened. A consequence of this stance
was the slow and uneven creation of modern political parties in
modern France: arguably, the first true national party was the
Radical Party, created in 1901.[77]

Since the collapse of the Soviet Union and the decline of
Marxism, there has been a re-creation of republicanism in France,
leading to a distinctive form of neo-republicanism which presents
republican ideals as a fully formed political philosophy, as intricate
and as demanding as Marxism.[78] To date, these initiatives have not
been successful in creating mass political movements, but they have
decisively changed the manner in which politics is debated in
France. The war of the veil was one episode in this development.

The political function of *laïcité* was illustrated in a comment by
Jean-Marc Ayrault, the leader of the Socialist Group in the Chamber
of Deputies: without a stronger assertion of *laïcité*, France would
become a land which was dominated by the principle of 'Each for
himself and God for all!'[79] *Laïcité* here is presented as a neo-
republican principle which binds isolated individuals together in
some collective endeavour. It carries a surprising social interven-
tionism: Régis Debray explicitly argues that *laïcité* has to be legislated,
it can never be produced spontaneously.[80] This is not a new feature.
Jean Baubérot, a Stasi Commission member, analysing the debates
that took place a century ago, notes a revealing contrast. Catholics

argued for 'freedom of teaching', meaning that churches and other groups should be allowed to create their own schools with minimal control from the state. Defenders of *laïcité* replied that what counted was 'the teaching of freedom': the Republican state had to intervene through the schooling system to ensure that the condition of freedom was created.[81] In a sense, the same debate is being replayed today: the chief aim for the state school is to equip its pupils with the necessary moral, political and cultural vocabulary to attain the neo-republican, quasi-Rousseau-ian state of freedom. The veil not only prevents the individual schoolgirl from attaining this condition, it also disrupts the teaching of freedom to the other pupils. Therefore, its ban is justified. Mohammed Abdi, a reluctant convert to the necessity of the law, explains his attitude by citing a quotation from abbé Grégoire, an important politician from the early years of the French Revolution: 'When comparing the weak and the strong, [it should be remembered] that it is liberty which oppresses the weak and it is the law which liberates them.'[82]

From this type of thinking also comes the stress by many left-leaning participants on the importance of 'dialogue' with veil-wearing girls rather than a simple process of immediate expulsion: for the self-image of the schooling system, one must attempt to win over even the lost sheep by an appeal to reason. As will be seen shortly, in practice the law worked differently.

There are many problems with such arguments. One is that it is clear that there are many incompatible, rival conceptions of this 'teaching of freedom'. For some, particularly those on the political left, *laïcité* expressed anti-clerical values and amounted to putting religion in its place: subordinate to the political sphere, faith was reduced to an individual practice within the private sphere, as in the example cited in the last chapter: 'Jews indoors, French citizens outside'. This interpretation was certainly the dominant idea a century ago. However, the practice of *laïcité* evolved over the decades: in the words of France's most senior religious representatives, it moved from 'fighting *laïcité*' to 'calm *laïcité*'.[83] The appearance of *laïcité* in the constitution of 1946 was an indication of a new spirit, as a revitalized France shook off the stains of collaboration and Occupation, and a new type of modern, liberal Catholicism accepted a form of moderate, consensual *laïcité*.[84] Thus, within the quotations cited above, Catholics and conservatives tend to refer to *laïcité* in more pragmatic terms, seeing it principally as a structure to enable the diverse elements of a society to negotiate competing claims peacefully. As the quotations from Chirac, Raffarin and Fillon demonstrate, such a stance can easily degenerate into an amorphous list of good causes which no one could contest. While the first concept of *laïcité* tends to be positively anti-clerical, the second is more genuinely neutral in spirit.

There are, however, some rather more fundamental problems. Given the diversity of opinions concerning *laïcité*, given its cloudy, semi-legal, semi-public nature, how does one ensure that one has understood and accepted these principles? The Muslim activist Dr Abdullah makes a telling point about such processes: 'often what is not said is more important than the principles to which people refer'.[85] For example, a Muslim woman is first informed that religious symbols are not permitted in her workplace, as they would break the code of *laïcité*. Later, she is told that, of course, a Christmas tree is not a religious symbol and so it is permitted. How is she to react?[86] To protest would merely reveal that she has not understood the principles of *laïcité*, which are immediately obvious to all true French citizens. *Laïcité*'s confused nature is thus politically useful: it permits inconsistencies and double standards where a clearer, more rational code would better enable minorities to situate themselves within French political culture.

Furthermore, while the values which are asserted in the name of *laïcité* may sound wholesome and uncontroversial – who could object to freedom and toleration? – the *assertion* of these values should not be confused with the real *embodiment* of them. Many pupils find their schooling to be an alienating, meaningless experience. Brenner describes a situation in which Muslim pupils bring prejudices into the school: he ignores another scenario, through which it is the teachers themselves who are prejudiced, and who abuse their position of power to bully and stigmatize pupils. The 'war of the veil' certainly provided many examples of ill-treatment, for it stimulated greater public hostility to Muslims in general and veiled women in particular. Examples of ill-treatment in schools are easy to find. First, there was the absurdity of the law, whereby non-Muslim girls were allowed to wear bandanas, but Muslims were often not allowed to do so, because their bandanas were defined by the school authorities as religious symbols. Thus Mona, at school in the Nord, was told that her bandana counted as 'ostensible' *because* she had been a veil-wearer.[87] Mariame experienced a ridiculous variant of the same theme: she was wrongly entered in the class register as 'Marianne', and therefore not suspected of being an Arab. Under these circumstances, she was allowed to wear a bandana.[88] As the law was enforced, more serious incidents took place. A 16-year-old girl, forced to remove her veil, recalls this as a moment of 'shame, guilt and a burning sense of injustice'. For her, the school becomes a place of 'hate, never-ending pain and bitterness'.[89] One veiled 15-year-old girl, temporarily excluded from classes in September 2004, reported that 'I was shut in a room with a window. I was forbidden to go out during the breaks. They treated me as if I was a monster! But I'm not a monster!'[90] Keltoum from Mantes-la-Jolie suffered a similar treatment: 'we were held in a separate room, as if we were wild beasts'.[91] Sonia was not allowed to go into the schoolyard during recreations, and was even kept out of sight.[92] Meetings between veil-wearers and teachers could take the form of tense confrontations as Mariame found out when a female teacher spoke to her.

> If you won't obey the law, you can always go back home.
> What do you mean by 'back home'?
> Well … back home!
> Yes, but for me, home is here. Where do you want me to go?
> You know exactly what I mean.[93]

Rather than 'liberating' these girls, the new law made their lives more difficult. Fadila comments 'I really think that people are more and more racist, as if the new law gives them a reason to dislike veiled girls. When I catch a bus, it's crazy. People make signs, jostle me, sneer, whisper as we pass, or shout out insults.'[94] Another veiled twelve-year-old had similar experiences. 'Last year, I was attacked by three men outside the school who spat in my face, hit me, and insulted me. At school, they tell us that we're weak-minded, and manipulated.' For these girls, the school is part of a continuum of racist practices in French society, not an oasis of liberty and toleration. As for the new law's promise of 'dialogue', the same veil-wearing girl found that in practice it meant 'obey or get out'.[95] Following the law, and her forced submission to its provisions, another schoolgirl's reaction was typical: 'I lost all my confidence: when a whole society and the entirety of the media show us as

submissive, fragile and deviant girls, you end up by believing it and
dropping out.'[96] Shifting our focus to universities, a revealing incident took place at a lecture in the Faculty of Pharmacy in Nantes
University on 20 January 2004. A few minutes into his presentation,
the lecturer suddenly stopped and stared at a veil-wearing student.
'What's that? What's that veil? Pick up your things and get out.'
There is no suggestion that the student in question had been
disruptive in any way. The lecturer later explained his actions to the
local paper. 'It's very upsetting for the lecturer. She was pissing me
about [elle vient se foutre devant moi en me narguant]… I saw it as
a provocation. I think of myself as a humanist, but I can't accept
someone trying to impose their vision of the world on me.'[97] The
blind hypocrisy implied by the lecturer's words is astonishing: there
is not a thought for the public humiliation suffered by the student
in question. The student's simple presence is interpreted as an
attack, while the lecturer's heavy-handed aggression is presented by
him as legitimate defence.

Veil-wearing women undoubtedly face forms of harassment and
hostility, running from a simple, unthinking fear of the unknown, to
more sinister forms of deliberately organized racism. Under these
circumstances, one might have expected that the representatives of
the Republic, those who pride themselves on their commitment to
fraternity and integration, would have chosen to demonstrate to the
people of France that these young women should also be accepted
as citizens of France. If Chirac could make this type of gesture for a
dead tramp, then why not for a veil-wearing schoolgirl? Instead, the
leaders of the French state chose to act in precisely the opposite
manner: they chose to add to the stigmatization and hostility which
these women face.

The call to defend *laïcité* echoes through these debates. In Tunis,
Chirac had described the veil as 'aggressive'. Brenner's calculated
use of military or colonial metaphors – 'the lost territories' – is a
second example of the same stance. To this was added a new presentation of *laïcité* as weak. Debray wrote of a vast theocratic
onslaught on vulnerable secular societies.[98] Chirac spoke of *laïcité*
as a 'subtle, precious and fragile balance'.[99] The conservative politician Debré wrote in his report that French inactivity in the face of
threats appeared as 'admitting weakness, a sign of impotence'.[100]

The veil constituted 'the start of an attack on republican *laïcité*', argued the *laïque* polemist Michèle Vianès.[101] Stasi spoke of teachers who felt that they were the 'victims' of a permanent guerrilla campaign against *laïcité*.[102]

These phrases are both dangerous and significant. They are dangerous because – as in the examples cited above – they encourage and justify aggressive actions against veil-wearing girls, on the grounds that this is a form of pre-emptive strike. But they are also significant, as they suggest an important shift in Republican political culture. Putting them together, one gets a picture of a Republic which is honest, slow to react to provocation, perhaps just a little too well-meaning and benevolent for its own good, which is being outmanoeuvred by a mysterious, malign and unnamed international conspiracy of highly organized militants … a near-perfect reproduction of the worldview of the anti-Semitic anti-Dreyfusards of the 1890s.[103] The far right is exploiting precisely this sort of discourse. Philippe de Villiers bemoans the fate of France, split between the France of 'globalized elites' and 'the France that is suffering'. 'The Republic has entrenched itself in a *laïc* citadel, on which the tsunami on Islamism is crashing down.'[104] The emotion which well-established politicians bring to the theme of *laïcité*, their unprincipled stigmatization of a minority group within French society as the base for a subversive conspiracy and their appeal to a sense of victimization among the mass of the French population produces a political culture which increasingly resembles that of the populist, anti-Semitic, proto-fascist new right of the late nineteenth century.[105]

The most curious point of all is the unity with which all major French political parties proclaim the need to defend *laïcité*, apparently under attack. But among France's main political traditions – the Front National, the Gaullists, Christian-Democrats and Socialists – one finds stout defences of *laïcité*. Among the more minor traditions – the Greens, Muslims, Communists and Trotskyists – one finds some debate and qualification about the nature of *laïcité*, but certainly nothing like a head-on attack. In fact, in the course of my research, I have only found one writer who criticized the basic principle of *laïcité*: a contribution to the anarchist weekly *Monde libertaire*, which was presented even in this publication as a minority opinion.[106] One can therefore question this basic premise that *laïcité* is faced with such a serious onslaught that radical measures are needed in order to defend it.

Attempting to reach a conclusion on such a multifaceted concept like *laïcité* is difficult. It has been of central importance in the formation of French society. It has worked as a means by which to construct a certain type of modernity, dependent on the evacuation of religious authorities from any integral status within the state and – rather confusingly – it has also created a political space for dialogue between peoples of faith and peoples without faith. More recently, in place of liberty, equality and fraternity, *laïcité* has become the concept that defines the nature of republicanism. For these reasons, it commands a deep, almost instinctive, sympathy from many French people. However, if one turns to consider how it functions today, the defence of *laïcité* appears not as the defence of a rational, constitutional principle, but as the construction of an intangible sense of French-ness, in a form which renders the accommodation of new cultures and identities singularly difficult.[107] In its current interpretations, it is a cultural ideal which is unsuitable for a world that is increasingly marked by the rapid and easy international transfer of goods, services, ideas and people.

The veil

There is a major problem in discussing this term: the veil does not exist. There is no single Arabic word for this garment, in the form that it is understood by French (and western) commentators.[108] And in truth, gentle reader, all my previous references should therefore have been to 'the veil' and not to the veil.

Let's begin our analysis of this term with a true story, from a school in eastern France. An elderly schoolteacher, liked and respected by her colleagues, is beginning her last year before retirement. To her colleagues' surprise, she appears on the first day of term wearing a Simone de Beauvoir-style bandana. Behind her back, they talk. Obviously, as the teacher in question is French, white and from a *laïque* family, covering her hair cannot be an indication of her Muslim faith. But why has she adopted it? Is it a fashion statement? Some, mischievously, suggest that she's been reading too much S de B. Others, more seriously, wonder whether she's beginning to go bald, and the bandana is to cover up her thinning, grey hair. Someone else points out that women who undergo chemical treatment for cancer often lose their hair: this point creates some sympathy for the teacher in question, but also inhibits her colleagues from directly asking her why she has taken to wearing a bandana. The teacher serves out her last year and leaves. Afterwards, the 'horrible' truth becomes known: this woman *was* a Muslim convert, and her bandana was an expression of her religious commitment.

One question that arises from this is: what is a veil? This is rather like the old philosophical conundrum: does a tree falling in a deserted forest make any noise? Does a piece of cloth that everyone recognizes as a bandana count as a veil? This point explains the difficulty in counting the number of veiled pupils in French schools: who is wearing a bandana, a large beret and an Islamic veil?

Let us now consider some representative statements by French commentators, all of whom participated in the 'debate' of 2003–4, concerning the veil and its meanings:

- Anne Vigerie and Anne Zelensky: '[The veil] symbolises the place of women in Islam as interpreted by Islamism. That place is in the shade: it's her relegation, her submission to men.'[109]
- Michèle Vianès: '[the veil is] ... a symbol of degradation ... it is a "marker" for discrimination, of sexual apartheid, preventing convergence, and preserving the tutelage of women.'[110]
- *Libération*: 'a symbol of oppression'.[111]
- Michel Gauchet: 'The veil is a religious symbol but, obviously, it's something else as well. It is fundamentally a sign of the subjection of women, and that's what causes the problem.'[112]
- François Bayrou: '[The veil means that] men and women have a relationship which is not one of equality.'[113]
- Union des familles laïques (The Union of Laïque Families): '[The veil is] symbolic of women's oppression.'[114]
- Raymonde Coudert and Thérèse Filippi: 'While the turban worn by Sikh boys and the kippa worn by practicing Jewish boys are not signs of sexual subjection, the headscarf is.'[115]
- Martine Billard: '[The veil] is, in all cases, either a sign of submission or a sign of alienation.'[116]

In these quotations, we can see some similarities with the manner in which *laïcité* is debated. There is the same tendency to make big, abstract, free-standing statements, with no attempt to provide evidence or contextualization, and no reference to the more serious, nuanced analyses of the topic. In this case, there is a surprising consensus among these varied commentators. However, it is important to identify the exact nature of this consensus. These commentators are not saying 'The rule of the Taliban in Kabul made women's lives a living hell, and their imposition of the *burqa* was the most visible sign of their authoritarian and tyrannical power.' These commentators are not saying 'The legal enforcement of veil-wearing on women in Saudi Arabia is an essential part of a law code which severely and unjustly oppresses women.' These commentators are not saying 'The regulations on veil-wearing in Iran are unjust, and produce a situation in which police authorities harass and humiliate women.' All these statements are empirically verifiable, politically sensitive and accurate. In the statements by the French commentators, there is a skidding between cause and effect: they sidestep issues of political and religious authority, they ignore context and they invest the veil *itself* with a particular and eternal meaning. The veil itself, however, is merely a piece of cloth: it has no more meaning than, for example, trousers. It is context which gives it meaning.

What is the origin of this idea that the veil itself is, intrinsically and irremediably, an instrument of women's oppression? It is not an explanation for its origins. The veil pre-dates Islam, and among the ancient societies that grew up around the Mediterranean it was 'a mark of exclusivity, status, privilege and privacy'.[117] It certainly cannot be found in the Koran. In fact, there is no direct reference to veiling in the Koran, although there is a specific instruction that women should not go topless, and there is a more general injunction that men and women should adopt modest dress. It is from this second reference that the connection between Islam and veiling starts: many Muslims have interpreted 'modest dress' to mean veiling. However, there is no implication that modest dress is a means to demonstrate female inferiority: on the contrary, it seems rather a way of affirming women's legitimate, public presence in society. In passing, we can note that veiling has certainly entered French culture in this way: for centuries, pious Catholic women have been expected to cover their hair in public and even Marianne herself was usually depicted by nineteenth-century illustrators with her hair covered.

Among the French veil-wearing Muslim women of our time, a variety of explanations are given for their choices. Hervé Flanquart conducted a series of in-depth interviews with twenty-five Muslims girls, of whom about half wore the veil. He found that all of them, veiled and unveiled, automatically refuted any element in Islam that seemed to contradict their belief in male–female equality.[118] For Sabrina, a 25-year-old law student, wearing a veil was a means to bring her closer to God.[119] For another girl, it was a means to surpass the Islam of her father and to find a pride in her Arab identity.[120] A third speaks of the veil as a form of vengeance for the suffering that her parents had experienced 'when they were forced to pray in garages'.[121] Commentators close to French Muslims produce a range of interpretations of the veil. Sophie Bessis, born in Tunis and working in France, makes the obvious – but necessary – points that the veil has no single meaning, and that the 'new veil ... is not a return to tradition'.[122] Hajji and Marteau, on their journey through Muslim France, present the interesting idea that the new veil carries a new significance: it is a way of asserting a double loyalty, to Islam and to France.[123] Gaspard and Khosrokhavar suggest a similar complexity: the new veil-wearers are French *and* Muslim, modern *and* veiled, autonomous *and* dressing in an Islamic manner.[124] Halima Zouhar, a Muslim activist, makes a similar comment about the dichotomy-bridging veil: 'these girls have adopted the emancipated lifestyle so praised by the West, while living according to the precepts of Islam.'[125] Caitlin Killian interviewed 100 Muslim women in France. She describes what could be termed 'the passport veil': the ability of the veil to act 'as a way to negotiate between the community of the parents and the French society in which they are immersed'.[126] Writing rather more eloquently, Lucette Valensi makes the same point, paraphrasing the typical young veil-wearer as saying 'father, mother, I am not betraying you. I share your values, and I am taking them to the public world'.[127]

Researchers working outside France who have interviewed or studied Muslim women have come to similar conclusions: they find a variety of explanations for veiling, but none report that Muslim women choose to veil in order to present themselves as inferior to men. Karin Ask and Marit Tjomsland, in a general review of women's lives and Islam, stress the heterogeneity of the religion, but also make the simple point that 'for the individual woman the veil materializes as a public statement of personal commitment'.[128] Jenny B. White, studying Islamist women in contemporary Turkey, identifies a 'new veil' which can be at once 'political symbol, marker of modesty and

… fashion'.[129] While she is aware of the contradictory nature of this symbolism, and of the manner in which the veil can contribute to frustrate women's aspirations to full political participation, she certainly does not consider that the veil is a symbol of inequality. Meena Dhanda, writing in the *Times Higher Education Supplement*, found that the veil worked as 'a means of seclusion from the rampant materialism of a hyper-commercial culture';[130] while Reina Lewis arrived at almost the opposite conclusion, noting how veil-wearing is developing its own fashion industry.[131] Karen Armstrong, a perceptive analyst of religions who was once a veil-wearing nun herself, considers that the new Muslim veil symbolizes 'resistance to oppression'.[132] Jen'nan Ghazal Read and John P. Bartkowski, interviewing Muslim women in Texas, found a sort of internationalism among them. The veil led to 'a feeling of connectedness with a broader religious community of other veiled Muslim women'.[133] The contrast between these analyses and the clichés that circulated among French politicians and in the media is obvious.

Muslim attitudes to the veil vary. One point to stress here is that non-Muslims often overestimate the unity of Muslim thought: in reality, Islam is a religion founded on debate and individual interpretations. A good example of this process is given by Bencheikh, who argues that the original purpose of veiling was to support women and ensure their status in the wider world. That role is now performed by the educational system: therefore Muslims should value the school over the veil.[134] Some Muslims refuse such arguments, some accept them. Certainly there are also some female French Muslims who have developed a deep resentment of the veil. *Libération* carried an interview with one such woman, who stated how she would like to tear the cloth from the heads of all veil-wearing girls: a comment that was used as a headline.[135] Abdelwahab Meddeb wrote strongly against veil-wearing, first because he found it a symbol of an ideological Islam, different from the pluralistic Sufi structures that he grew up with, and secondly because today it is a 'metaphor of sexual inequality'.[136] But if we focus our research on the voices of the veil-wearers, we find that while they certainly produce a variety of reasons for their choice of clothing (religion, identity, social status … and fashion?), none of them refer to a belief in female inferiority as a justification. As the veil-wearing Fatima, from Saint-Denis, notes: 'If my veil is a "symbol of oppression", am I then supposed to conclude that I'm oppressing myself?'[137]

The material surveyed in the paragraphs above therefore presents a sharp dichotomy: French veil-wearers produce a set of reasons for their choices, but these are not simply ignored by French political leaders, but even actively denied. Jean-Louis Debré considered that girls advancing modernist or emancipatory arguments in favour of the veil were demonstrating 'ignorance about the foundations of their own religion'.[138] Green deputy Martine Billard considered that 'whatever these individual interpretations that a minority of young Muslim girls give to the veil, it is in no way a symbol of emancipation'.[139] Stasi, to his credit, did note that the veil seemed to have different meanings, but then concluded that the paradigmatic case on which the Republic had to act was the veil as an instrument of oppression.[140] Veil-wearing schoolgirls who took seriously the law's promise of 'dialogue' met a similar wall of incomprehension and official arrogance: in September 2004 headteachers stood at the school gates and made snap judgements on their pupils' clothing, instructing them to push back their bandanas from their foreheads and ears. 'The law cannot be discussed' they told those who protested.[141] When the veil-wearing Zahra was isolated from her class in Décines (Rhône), she attempted to find out what she could wear to cover her hair that was not considered to be 'ostensible'. She received an official reply from her local educational authorities: 'it is for the school administration, and not for the young girl, to decide on the nature of a religious symbol'.[142] In Mantes-la-Ville, the school director was even more blunt: 'Law or no law, it's me who decides!'[143]

To return to our previous question, what are the origins of this infallible and exact knowledge of the meaning of the veil that French authorities possess: a knowledge that enables them to state with such ease and such certainty that the veil is and can only be a symbol of female inferiority? It has not been from studying Islam: to my knowledge, no official pronouncement by any Muslim group recommends wearing the veil in order to signal female inferiority. It has not been from reading the works of sociologists and other researchers. While French authorities do give a few references to the situation of women in Iran and Afghanistan, these hardly suggest any serious effort to engage with the complex social dynamics of these countries. Above all, the authorities' knowledge has not been gained from talking to the veil-wearing girls themselves: one recalls Stasi's original decision that the veil-wearers were inherently unsuitable for interview. This

leads to the inevitable conclusion that this rhetorical certainty is a
legacy of French colonialism, whose structures and administrations
were consistently based on the idea that French authorities possessed
an exact knowledge of the natives' cultures and lives.[144] For these
authorities, the idea that they were liberating the natives from the
oppression of their own culture was the most convincing justification
for their presence.[145]

One last point needs to be made here: the argument I have
presented is that while compulsory veiling is certainly an unacceptable infringement of women's rights, it is inaccurate to see the veil
itself as inherently oppressive. This does not imply that, therefore, I
consider the veil to be liberatory, merely that it carries many meanings. If required to define my position, I would describe myself as
neutral on this topic: as a general principle, people should be
allowed to wear what they wish. If veiling is to be criticized, then it
should be on the basis of knowledge, not prejudice. There is no
doubt that it is a practice that creates problems for its wearers: if the
primary injunction is to dress modestly, then wearing a veil in a
Western society seems, on the contrary, a means by which to draw
attention to oneself. If it is worn in order to achieve a certain public
recognition, then wearers themselves complain about the nature of
that recognition: 'they reduce me to my veil. And what a veil! A veil
like a yellow star, an accessory to rape!'[146] The simple banning of
veils from state schools, however, will not solve these problems.

Integration

To introduce an examination of this term, I wish to refer to an incident in Britain in October 2006. My reasons for briefly changing the
area of study are twofold: first, the incident provides an extremely
clear example of certain attitudes. But, secondly, it is also a
reminder that the problems which beset the French state are not
unique: if Britain has managed to avoid some of them, this is only a
difference of degree, not an absolute difference in quality.

As many readers will no doubt remember, Jack Straw, then leader
of the House of Commons, was visited in his MP's surgery by a
woman wearing a full veil – a *niqab* – which entirely covered her
face. She spoke English well, and had been educated in Lancaster.

Perhaps like Chirac considering a veiled schoolgirl, Straw later reported that he felt intimidated, and he asked her to remove her veil. More interesting, he then stated to the press that he considered her veil 'a barrier to social integration'.[147] This is a curious comment: this woman had learnt English, had succeeded in the British school system and had understood the British political system to the extent that she was able to make use of the appropriate administrative and political structures to raise a case with her MP: something which the great majority of the British population never do. In what sense was she 'not integrated'? At this point British culture comes to resemble French culture: she is described as 'not integrated' because she fails to conform to certain assumed norms. And what exactly are these norms? Here British culture grows as vague and cloudy as the speakers in the National Assemblies: those norms are the values of fair play, tolerance, moderation … Perhaps Straw meant that as this woman was wearing a *niqab*, she would find it difficult to institute the values of fair play by umpiring a cricket match? In truth, these oft-cited values are a remarkably poor summary of the values that govern most British people's lives, although they may have some relevance as ideals.

Migrants who attempt to accept these lessons concerning 'our values' are then trying to live their lives to a set of ideals which the 'native' population habitually ignores. Azouz Begag's political memoirs give countless examples of the moments when, having been characterized as a Muslim and as the child of an immigrant family, he was then required to live to a code of public morality which was *more strict* than that required for the other 'native' French ministers. This double-bind, Catch-22 logic has a demoralizing effect on the person caught in its contradictions. Begag speaks of an almost 'genetic' fear.

> I was terrified. From father to son, among us, we always have this fear of not being 'correct' [comme il faut] in the eyes of the French. We are afraid of hurting others. Afraid of shocking them, of betraying them, disappointing them, of being late. We are afraid of life, of death, of everything. My poor father left to me this genetic agony.[148]

The examples of Straw's visitor and Begag's experiences suggest that we need to rethink the concept of 'integration'.

A veil-wearing schoolgirl from Rennes observes: 'They tried to make people believe that we were deviants and that in order to "integrate" us we had to remove our veils. Yet we were extremely well integrated, and taking off our veil was humiliating.'[149] Her comments suggest that rather than thinking in terms of a monolithic 'integration' process, it would be better to imagine two processes: integration and assimilation. What Straw probably means by 'not integrated' is that this woman was 'not integrated in a form that he considered desirable'. Within this work, I will use 'integration' in an entirely value-free sense, to mean a comprehension of the manner in which a society works, or the acquisition of a competence to navigate one's way through a society, without any cloudy idealization of the values of fair play, toleration, motherhood and apple pie. This process is difficult, but young, ambitious migrants are often able to achieve it. Furthermore, there is the yet more difficult process of assimilation: this is where the question of values becomes important. Here, the migrant makes a choice to 'become like': to interiorize the values of the French (or British).

This is central to understanding the public significance of the veil: it is the clearest possible sign of someone who has decided to integrate *without* assimilating.[150]

Beurs

Our last key term is less controversial and, to some extent, I include it here simply in order to give information to the non-specialist.

There is a form of French slang known as *verlan*, based on the approximate inversion of the syllables of a word, which works best for two-syllable words. It is referred to in nineteenth-century novels, such as those of Balzac, and is probably older, for its logic makes most sense in an oral culture, and written examples will inevitably look forced or incomprehensible. Table 1.1 shows some common examples.

Table 1.1: Four French *verlan* terms

Orthodox French	Verlan
Mec (guy, bloke)	Keum
Pourri (rotten, corrupt)	Ripou
Juif (Jew)	Fij
Arabe	Beur

One point to stress here is that while these words are a very casual form of slang, they are not insulting. According to legend, *verlan* was devised by criminals or prisoners to prevent the police from being able to understand their conversations: its purpose was not to offend, but to conceal. In other words, 'beur' and 'fij' do not belong to that vast litany of hate words which all languages seem to accumulate. On the contrary, it is possible to present a positive reading of 'beur': it was a spontaneous creation, which marked the integration of Arab immigrant youth into the structures of French culture. A range of spin-offs evolved: *beurette* for a young, female Arab, and even *beur-geoisie* for that strata briefly known in English as Yummies: Young Upwardly Mobile Muslims.

The word *beur* acquired a political significance, for it is associated with two political movements. The first of these grew out of the *banlieues* of Lyon, in which a large, second-generation Arab immigrant population was concentrated, and in which there were constant problems of poverty, crime and police harassment.[151] An appeal was issued by a local militant, Toumi Djaïja, for a protest march across France, which was rapidly termed 'La marche des Beurs'. This movement acted as a forum through which the dispossessed *beurs* of the suburbs could meet middle-class *beur* professionals. It was through this movement that Fadela Amara first learnt of political organization.[152] Mainstream political parties grew interested in this movement, partly because they were genuinely moved by the spectacle of these usually secular, 'young, generous and apolitical' marchers,[153] whose first demand was entry into the structures of Republic. Robert Castel notes: 'They felt that they were French, and they knew that they would live in France.' Their movement marked the end of the old immigrant's illusion of a 'return', one day, to North Africa.[154] The parties were also in search of what became known as the 'Beur vote': they sought political mechanisms by which immigrant votes could be delivered as elections.[155]

In December 1984 a new organization was created, SOS-Racisme. This was linked to the Socialist Party and drew together *beur* militants, anti-racists and young socialists, with the avowed aim of stopping the rise of the anti-immigrant National Front. While this goal was worthy in itself, some aspects of SOS-Racisme's strategy were less praiseworthy. First, by concentrating solely on the National Front as *the* source of French racism, it turned attention away from the gentle, moderate, ambient racism that suffuses French society.

Secondly, SOS-Racisme's tactics were often quite patronizing: it is now best remembered for a briefly omnipresent badge, 'Touche pas à mon pote' (don't touch my mate), which was popular among a young, white, liberal audience. Lastly, the movement was firmly controlled by the Socialist Party, which enforced some crucial decisions concerning tactics and leaders.[156] There is a fairly well-founded suspicion that the Socialists were primarily interested in SOS-Racisme as a means to win the 'Beur vote'. Certainly, today, the organization is principally remembered among French Muslim activists as a model of how *not* to organize politically, and it is hard to point to a single real success it achieved.[157] The National Front vote continued to rise in the 1980s and 1990s, no North Africans were elected as deputies (in fact, none have been elected since 1962),[158] conditions in the *banlieues* got worse, and the Beur vote proved to be divided among lines of class and age – just like the rest of the French population.

Even the term 'beur' has fallen out of favour. When Michèle Lamont interviewed thirty North African workers in Paris in 1992–3, he found that none of them accepted the term.[159] Nasséra, a 19-year-old student interviewed by Bouzar and Kada, disliked the way it reduced a complex reality to a single word.[160] One rarely sees it being used by academics or researchers: Geisser and Soum's volume, published in 2008, is unusual in using it as a principal term of analysis. French Arabs I have talked to tend to shudder when they hear the word: once again, it is not pejorative, but it does sound outdated and even slightly patronizing. Instead, out of the disappointment with SOS-Racisme, a new generation began to look to Islam as a source of identity and values.

Conclusion: the little world of Marie L.

The 'debate' on the veil was decided in advance. Given the conceptual vocabulary used by leading politicians and the media there was never any doubt about the final decision of the Stasi Commission, or the ultimate consequences of its report. A revealing glimpse of the sub-culture which it created came to light in July 2004.[161] A young woman, whose full name was never revealed, reported that she had been attacked by four North Africans and two black people on a Parisian suburban train line: they told her that they would not allow Jews into their area, they cut off her hair and carved a swastika into her arm. The episode was reported extremely widely on French television and in the press: it was taken as another dreadful example of the innate violence of the immigrant population, whose actions revived the memories of the worst moments of French history. However, almost alone, the police investigating the case were suspicious: no evidence could be found to confirm Marie's experience. A few days later, she confessed: the whole episode was a fantasy. She had made it up, and was sentenced to four months in prison for making a false accusation. However, a society gets the insanity it deserves. Her sorry melodrama was an accurate reflection of the emotional charge within the case made by Brenner and Stasi: black people and Arabs were not to be trusted. More significantly, a double standard seemed to be operating. Anti-Semitic violence rightly aroused an immediate public revulsion among the media; other acts of racism somehow seemed less important, less central to the debate. Under these circumstances, why was it expected that immigrant families would accept Brenner and Stasi's protests that the Republic had instituted equality?

The contrast between the meanings ascribed to our two keywords is significant. All politicians loudly proclaim their loyalty to *laïcité*, but produce wildly divergent interpretations of what this term means. On the other hand, attitudes to the veil are consistent, if inaccurate. In other words, the positive principle, which is supposed to bind together the isolated citizens of the Republic into a united national community, is illusory, a mere politician's charade, while the negative principle, little more than an expression of educated prejudice, really does provide a type of cultural unity. The implications of this contradiction are extremely serious.

Chapter Two
Chahdortt Djavann:
Assimilation as Liberation

_____

I learnt my first words of French at the age of 25 … Today, I'm a writer: it's possible in France to pull yourself up, even if you haven't got a penny, even if you can't speak a word. So, I reject this sob-story language, and let's stop saying 'we live in difficult areas, we're poor …' [interruption from Houria Bouteldja] … Here, in France, I have not known racism.

Chahdortt Djavann, 2006[1]

Chahdortt Djavann and Houria Bouteldja were both guests on the ninety-minute-long television discussion programme *Culture et Dépendances* in January 2006. It was a strange occasion, with an odd selection of seven guests: among them, Vertan Berberian, a naturalized Armenian who proved to be more French than the French, Xavier Darcos, a sharp-suited and clean-shaven defender of the schools of Jules Ferry and a member of the government, the elephantine figure of Alain Finkielkraut, who seemed willing to talk for ninety-one minutes of the ninety-minute programme, and then the two women. Curiously, one could at least begin to describe them in similar terms. Both have mixed nationalities: Djavann is French-Iranian, Bouteldja French-Algerian. Both of them were brought up as Muslims, and both have raised questions about this faith. Both, in a sense, are rebels against established authorities: Djavann has been brave and forthright in her criticisms of the oppression of women by the Iranian Islamic Republic, while Bouteldja has criticized the racism of the French Republic. However, from the beginning of the programme, the differences between the two were obvious. It was even clear in their style of dress: Djavann had short, well-styled hair and wore an elegant, deep-red dress, an attractive example of that spontaneous, careless stylishness which French women spend hours achieving. Bouteldja dressed less fashionably, but was more willing to throw herself into debate. Djavann speaks with a slight but noticeable accent: she has no trouble expressing herself in French, but as the exchanges grew more heated it was noticeable that Bouteldja spoke louder and faster, while Djavann sounded angry, but more and more awkward, at one point even mistakenly addressing Bouteldja as 'Monsieur'. At crucial moments, Finkielkraut seemed to be speaking in her place. The exchanges between the two women were not simply bad tempered, not just one more example of the professionalized rhetorical exchanges into which French public figures regularly enter, but something deeper. The obvious, extreme tension generated by their disagreements represented an absolute clash of ideas, ideals and experiences with no possibility of compromise.

Why consider Chahdortt Djavann in a book on French Muslims? It could well be argued that she is neither French nor a Muslim. She is, however, a naturalized French citizen, and her frequent, prominent presence in the French media comes from her claim to speak about the Muslim condition. There can be no doubt that her books have played a significant role in structuring the dominant French attitudes to Muslims. For these reasons, she merits inclusion.

Djavann's France

The celebrated cultural critic Homi Bhabha has proposed the concept of a 'Third Space', suggesting a kind of parallel with the idea of the 'Third World': this would be a space between the developed and undeveloped world, in which 'unanticipated forms of historical agency' could emerge in forms which might transcend or confound the dominant paradigms.[2] In a similar manner, the cultural anthropologist Arjun Appadurai has argued that future cultural initiatives may well emerge from 'diasporic public spheres' which could contribute to a 'postnational political order'.[3] Both these writers put forward the hypothesis that the contemporary refugee communities may contain unique qualities that could produce radically different forms of political cultures, capable of superseding established political and cultural borders. Djavann's work can be understood as an extremely firm warning against such optimism, and against any easy idealization of the refugee condition. For Djavann, there is no question of constructing some form of comfortable synthesis between Iran and France, Islam and *laïcité*, East and West. Instead, one has to choose, and Djavann casts her vote for France.

Djavann is deliberately vague about her own biography. Looking at her works, one gathers that she was born in the late 1960s in Iran, and she lived through the Islamic revolution of 1978–9 and the disastrous, costly Iran–Iraq war of the 1980s. She was a student in Iran before leaving for France in 1991. She applied for French nationality, which was easily accorded to her, and she began a successful writing career (in French) in 2002. Since then, she has produced at least one book each year. Her first works were quite short, often less than a hundred pages, but each new work was slightly longer: her latest work weighs in at 422 pages. She normally writes in the first person.

Djavann came to public attention in the context of growing French disappointment with the Iranian Revolution. In 1978, this revolution was understood as a renewal of a revolutionary spirit in the Middle East: the first such assertion since Israel's 1967 victory over the combined forces of Egypt, Jordan and Syria, and the collapse of Nasser's Pan-Arabism.[4] There was an initial, ill-informed, French leftist celebration of the Iranian revolution, symbolized by a particularly maladroit text published by Michel Foucault. Then, slowly, the realization grew that the new rulers in Iran were certainly not secular republicans, nor even leftists making tactical use of Islamic vocabulary, but representatives of a genuinely new force: political Islam. The new regime's character was revealed, first, by the imposition of compulsory veiling for women in 1980, and then by the 'Rushdie Affair' of 1989.[5] French sympathy for the new regime declined, and was quickly replaced by some friendly interest in political refugees from this authoritarian regime. Djavann's first text, *I Come from Elsewhere*, was published in 2002 by Autrement, a publishing house normally specializing in 'alternative', left-of-centre works.[6] Her first major success was *Down with the Veils!*, a 47-page booklet, published by the more prestigious Gallimard publishing house in October 2003 during the second 'war of the veil': this provided a media context in which Djavann's work flourished.[7] She played a prominent place in subsequent debates. She was interviewed by the Stasi Commission, and immediately caused some comment with her proposal that veiling should be treated as a crime.[8] Stasi himself later publicly acknowledged how important her evidence had been for the Commission.[9] In general, she was treated extremely favourably in the press. Between September and December 2003, she was interviewed no less than fourteen times on

French television.[10] Magazine interviews followed: once again, Djavann's ideas on the veil were positively received; she was heralded as 'a ferocious defender of *laïcité*'.[11]

Her short pamphlet, *Down with the Veils!*, published in October 2003, was very well reviewed. *Le Monde* considered her pamphlet as the equivalent of Zola's famous open letter, 'J'accuse'.[12] *Le Figaro* found it to be clear, well argued and an appeal to common sense.[13] For the right-of-centre weekly *L'Express*, there was no better reply to the most recent betrayal of France by its intellectuals than her pamphlet.[14] In December 2003 the Communist daily *L'Humanité* invited her to address one of its regular public debates, there she met an enthusiastic reception from 'an audience which was won over to her cause'.[15] Even the anarchist weekly *Monde libertaire* cited her as a reputable authority on the veil.[16] In January 2004, following a small demonstration in favour of the right of schoolgirls to wear the veil, *Le Figaro* contrasted these demonstrators' clear lack of patriotism and confused ideas with clarity of the analysis offered by 'this brilliant pamphleteer from Iran'.[17] Her most recent work was favourably reviewed in *Le Monde* as 'an alarm call from an Iranian dissident'.[18]

Djavann's ideas are simple: she presents a clear contrast between Iran and France, and suggests that France is, in every sense, a better society. Let us begin by analysing her presentation of Iranian society.

Djavann normally writes in the first person, but it is hard to be certain exactly who is the 'I' in her narratives. Her name itself is odd. She claims to be the daughter of two Iranian communists, but is it likely that such parents would have named their child 'Shah's daughter'?[19] This problem with the author's identity is compounded by the style of writing she has chosen; of course, it is more than understandable that an exile who has been severely mistreated and abused by the Iranian police might wish to be secretive about her friends, relatives and past acquaintances, and might well prefer to elide certain episodes in her past life. Djavann herself speaks of 'reconstructing her life in French'.[20] But, given these constraints, why stick so rigidly to the first-person narrative? Why not write in a more abstract, more indirect style? The answer is that the conceptual basis for Djavann's work is precisely that it is a direct, transparent record of her life: she is not simply a commentator, but actually a witness with direct access to experiences that 'French intellectuals do not understand'.[21]

For Djavann, the Iranian Revolution of 1978–9 destroyed the promising developments of the Shah's 'White Revolution'. While the previous regime was authoritarian and non-democratic, it implemented great advances: the country was industrialized, contraception and abortion rights were introduced, educational facilities were expanded, a real intelligentsia developed and Iran became 'a *laïque* country'.[22] As the country grew more divided in the late 1970s, the Shah introduced new reforms, but 'the crowds were no longer listening'.[23] Djavann claims that her admiration for the previous regime is typical of contemporary Iranian opinion: 'the great majority of the population … miss the Shah's era'.[24]

Djavann remembers 1978 as a brief moment of 'a vague and immense hope' which quickly passed.[25] Soon Khomeini arrived, and conditions very rapidly got worse. Gun-wielding militants from Hezbollah (not to be confused with the Lebanese party of the same name) beat back Communists and other secular groups. Censorship was introduced in Djavann's school, and was enforced through a system of spies.[26] A new system of education was introduced: Djavann speaks with force and eloquence about the manner in which female pupils were treated. She was made to feel ashamed of her femininity and her periods, while wearing the veil made her suffer 'guilt about her shameful body'.[27] During the 1980s, the war with Iraq dominated everything: Iran became a country in which 'death counted for more than life'.[28] 'I learnt to be silent. To not resist. To not see, to not understand, to not feel. I learnt to be what I was not.'[29] Yet she could not help seeing some horrific sights, the worst being that of a 13-year-old girl, raped by her uncle, who gave birth in hospital. On the order of armed men from the local revolutionary committee, her experience was never recorded on the hospital register.[30] As the years passed, the new regime showed no sign of moderation or reform. Djavann's brief account of life in Islamic Iran ends with a horrific episode in which a Revolutionary Guard kills a little girl who had been caught playing in the street.[31] Djavann is left feeling 'an implacable hatred' for the regime and its religion.[32]

In contrast to bloody, guilt-ridden Islamic Iran, *laïque* France is a land of liberty. Even while in Iran, Paris was the city of which Djavann dreamed: it was a 'city of enlightenment'.[33] For Djavann

France is, above all, a country formed by its literary traditions: she cites Hugo, Molière, Balzac, Voltaire, Zola and Sartre.[34] It is through learning from this tradition, Djavann argues, that she becomes French.[35] Her novel which includes the description of her arrival in France and her acquisition of French nationality also includes an element of fantasy: she composes letters to Montesquieu, a writer who holds a particular importance for Djavann because of his *Persian Letters*. Within this work, one concept leads to another: as Djavann learns French, she learns of Montesquieu and his Enlightenment values; as she learns to write French, she writes to Montesquieu and gains more confidence in her new identity; lastly, in turn her letters then become the basis for her fifth published work in French.

Djavann's admiration for France seems limitless. She recounts how sometimes the simplest gestures fill her with pleasure. When she walked into an office to apply for her naturalization, the female official who was processing her claim immediately said 'Please sit down': according to Djavann such simple courtesy is unknown in Iran.[36] Throughout all her years of living in Paris, she has never once been hassled by a man on the city's streets.[37] Racism is defined as a crime in France, and therefore it does not exist.[38] Does Djavann make no criticisms of French society? Searching through her work, one can find one, ambiguous, critical reference to Western foreign policy and the Iran–Iraq war, in which Djavann berates all the Western nations not only for their failure to act to stop this conflict, but also for the profits they took from arms sales to both sides. Even here, however, Djavann's final point seems to be that the West should have prevented this conflict by intervening earlier to prevent the development of 'green fascism' in Iran.[39] Such pronouncements make one wonder if Djavann has really understood Montesquieu. After all, the purpose of the *Persian Letters* was not primarily to criticize eastern despotism – which appears to be what Djavann thinks – but to exploit a stereotypical image of the Orient as a means by which to introduce implicit criticisms of the French polity which could get past the relatively strict censorship of the early eighteenth century. This type of repetitive, boundless admiration for all things French is very far from the subtle, witty, self-critical prose of Montesquieu.

Djavann, the veil and global Islam

Given this stark contrast between Iranian oppression and French freedom, Djavann was therefore horrified to learn that there are French people who will not only support the right of French school-girls to wear the veil, but who will even defend the veil. Reluctantly, despite the emotions which the topic aroused in her, she turned to write about the veil.[40] She makes clear the nature of her topic: 'The veil. Not the veil in school, but the veil in itself.'[41] Her most memorable passage on this theme is her description of a return trip to Tehran in 1998 by plane. As the aircraft reaches Iranian airspace, Iranian laws apply and all the women in the plane are required to veil themselves:

> *An elegant voice announces 'We are beginning our descent to Tehran. Please attach your safety-belt and raise your seat' ...*
>
> *I pull my veil out of my bag, and twist it back and forth through my fingers: I want to tear it up but, like the other women, I pull it over my head and tie it under my neck. 'How stupid of me to go back to Iran!' I say to myself. My face tightens. It is as if our simultaneous act shows that we all accept that our bodies are just sexual objects, objects whose fate is controlled by others: I see this as the humiliation of being a woman. I swallow my rage, but I can feel the veil gripping round my face, controlling my life.*
>
> *In fact, all the other women are transformed: and even the men have now become Iranians. You can see a trace of smile on their lips, they turn round and look at their newly veiled neighbours.*
>
> *I want to tear this veil from my head: it proclaims a guilty sexuality. I had almost forgotten that feeling. I try to think about something else: about my family, who I will soon be seeing again. But I feel stifled each time my heart beats. My body has been transformed against my will, as if it was a diseased object, which must be locked up, a bad object which men desire. I feel dizzy. Suddenly, I lift my hand up from the arm of the chair, and I shrink down into my seat. My neighbour seems very comfortable: he stretches his legs, and pushes his shoulders back, then falls back into the chair with a sigh. His territory has grown. I try again to think about how happy I will be to see my family. We are getting nearer the ground: the plane will land any minute now. I am not sure what nostalgia really means, but I think I am feeling it extremely powerfully. Perhaps it is an illusion about an imaginary past. Whatever it is, it helps me last through the last moments.[42]*

This is Djavann's writing at its strongest: angry, detailed and convincing. The passage cleverly mixes something with which all readers will be familiar – a descent in a plane – with an experience with which few will be familiar, and provides the reader with enough details to identify with Djavann's feelings. As one reads the passage, it is impossible not to feel sympathy with her, and to understand the humiliation imposed by compulsory veiling.

However, problems remain with her writing. First, in the passage cited above – and in all her writing – Djavann is explicit. Her quarrel is not with *compulsory* veiling, but with *all* Islamic veiling practices. 'There has never been an innocent veil', she writes, 'the veil is an insult to all women.'[43] It is a way of marking out a young girl's body, similar to genital mutilation.[44] Perhaps there are a tiny minority of Muslim women who genuinely choose to wear a veil but then, remarks Djavann, they say that there are also some prostitutes who actually want to sell their bodies.[45] (This type of remark is regrettably typical of Djavann's writing, and illustrates some of her limitations. Obviously, any veil-wearing woman would find it extremely offensive, as would many Muslims, veiled or unveiled, male or female. But this is not the point: Djavann is not really writing to Muslims; she is not trying to persuade them of her case. Her real audience is white, Western, non-Muslim readers, who are open to quite different perspectives on Islam.) These types of arguments suggested that the debate over the veil was not about *laïcité*, nor about the rights to express one's religion, but actually concerned the most basic of human rights, the right to exist. Djavann was forceful – even offensive – in her argument that *all* forms of veiling were intrinsically wrong.

While putting herself forward as an authentic voice speaking on behalf of all oppressed Muslim women, it is clear that others have different perspectives. One could consider, for example, the intelligent and original Iranian feminist photographer Shadafarin Ghadirian. Her work has often portrayed Iranian women wearing headscarves, and one interviewer asked her whether she deliberately aimed to 'emphasize the headdress more than the woman'. Ghadiarian just dismissed the question: 'This really isn't our most pressing issue, and it's so interesting to me that all the foreigners seem to think it is.'[46] One can also contrast Djavann's analysis with that adopted by her compatriot Shirin Ebadi, the Iranian Nobel Prize-winning civil rights lawyer, whose work we will examine later.

Looking over the border into Iraq, one could cite the quite contrasting comments by the pseudonymous blogger 'Riverbend', who puts forward anti-fundamentalist, democratic ideas, often critical of the American military invasion. Her commentary on the veil begins by quoting a statement by Stanley Kurtz, an anthropologist at the Hoover Institution that 'a key purpose of veiling is to prevent outsiders from competing with a woman's cousins for marriage'. 'Riverbend' replies:

> *Thank you, Stanley Kurtz ...*
>
> *He took hundreds of years of wearing the veil for religious reasons and relegated it all to the oppression of female by their male cousins. Wow – human nature is that simple.*
>
> *I can see the image now – my cousins roaming the opening of our cave, holding clubs and keeping a wary eye on the female members of their clan ... and us cowed, frightened females all gathered in groups, murmuring behind their veils ...*
>
> *Muslim females do not wear a hijab or veil because their male cousins 'make' them wear it. They wear it for religious reasons. I personally don't wear a hijab or headscarf, but I know many females who do – in Baghdad, in Mosul, in Najaf, in Kerbela, in Falloojeh ... in Jordan, in Syria, in Lebanon, in Saudi Arabia ... and none of these females wear a headscarf because their 'cousins' make them wear it. They wear the headscarf out of a conviction that it is the correct thing to do and out of the comfort and security it gives them. Cousins have nothing to do with it and Dr. Kurtz's very simplistic explanation is an insult.*[47]

Looking still further afield, one can question the extent to which Djavann has understood the sexual politics of veiling. By presenting the veil only as oppression, she ignores the potential for the veil to stimulate a specifically Muslim debate concerning the commercialization of the female body. Consider, for example, the more challenging observations by Heba Ezzat, a leftist and libertarian Egyptian feminist.

> *When we say 'humility', and that the body should not be the domain for a competition between the small percentage of glamorously beautiful women in the world and the rest, this is because when you do not make the body the main focal-point of expression, people begin to look for more profound manifestations and expressions, including, conceivably, a political way forward.*[48]

Unlike Djavann, such dissidents refuse to accept Western free-market liberalism as the only model of freedom, and instead attempt the far more challenging task of attempting to learn from a variety of different and even contradictory cultures.

The contrast between 'Riverbend', Ezzat and Djavann is instructive, for it reveals the degree to which Djavann's work is unrepresentative of Muslim opinion. Djavann is not even a good guide to the policies adopted by Muslim states: they have shown far greater variety in their attitudes to male–female equality – including some real capacity for substantial reform – than she allows.[49] The frequent citations of her work in the French media as an unproblematic, authentic representation of Muslim and/or Iranian opinion is based on a misunderstanding. Djavann's writing is actually quite exceptional.

Djavann's attitude to Islam merits comment. Unlike her compatriot Shirin Ebadi, she finds no redeeming features in this religion. She refuses to differentiate between a violent, extremist version of Islam and a more benign mainstream, for 'the origin of Islamism is Islam'.[50] She even repeats the old, medieval, Christian underestimation of Islam: it contains nothing original, it contributes nothing which was not previously presented by Judaism and Christianity.[51] The one qualification that Djavann does allow is to note the difference between some variants of Islamic belief – principally the enlightened Sufis – and the practices embodied in Islamic institutions.[52] Outside of these powerless exceptions, Islam is a 'complete and closed system', 'political and conquering', clearly incompatible with democracy.[53] In no other country does pornography circulate as widely as in Islamic countries.[54] When Islam seizes power, it creates totalitarianism, as happened in Iran.[55] Implicit in such arguments is another assumption: for Djavann, Khomeini's Iran does not represent a distinctive and rather unusual interpretation, but it is *typical* of Islam. Perhaps at this point it should be remembered that forty-eight out of forty-nine Islamic states refused to accept Khomeini's fatwah against Salman Rushdie: a point which clearly illustrates the exceptional, atypical nature of the Islamic Republic.[56]

We must note that Djavann is not alone in expressing such opinions. In recent years there has been a flood of wildly exaggerated, nightmare visions of Islam: indeed, one researcher writes of an unquenchable American appetite for such works.[57] On occasion, one can feel sympathy for the authors. Ayaan Hirsi Ali's reliability as a witness has been brought into question, but one can understand the anger she feels. Her account of systematic misogynist violence in Somalia, unstopped by Islamic authorities, is a harrowing and eloquent record. She, too, voices extremely condemnatory opinions concerning Islam: 'Fanaticism in Islam is a reality, and its following is growing steadily.'[58] Less excusable are the silly excesses of Oriana Fallaci who – writing in 2006 – warns of the treacherous revival of Islam's centuries-old expansionism, its seizure of Marseille 'which is no longer a French city' and its advances into Europe which 'is by now a province or rather a colony of Islam'.[59] Like many French neo-republicans, Fallaci chooses the language of revivalism: 'Wake up, folks, wake up! ... A reverse Crusade is on march.'[60] Again, like them, she writes with a certainty and an absolute confidence in the accuracy of her analysis, dismissing any qualification or demand for evidence. 'About Islamic Fundamentalists, on the contrary, we Europeans know everything.'[61] Certainly, there is anger in this work, but there is something else as well, a despicable celebration of hatred: 'I spit in their faces.'[62] Another example of this growing hostility can be found in Israel, where the previously critical, radical historian Benny Morris has re-interpreted his own work as a justification both of Zionist expansionism and of armed confrontation with the Palestinians: 'The Arab world as it is today is barbarian'; Israel can only survive 'by force alone'.[63]

Similar sentiments have been expressed in France: one could cite Elisabeth Badinter, Philippe de Villiers and – most recently – the sad case of Robert Redeker, a philosophy teacher from Toulouse, who felt moved to write an anti-Islamic polemic when he heard that girls wearing thongs would be banned from sunbathing along the Seine in 2006. (In passing, one notes that is a curious issue on which to base a political case. Previously political activists fought for liberty, solidarity and emancipation. Redeker fights for the right to ogle girls' bottoms.) Redeker considered that this move by the Parisian municipality was an example of the creeping influence of Islam in French public life – of 'the islamization of minds' – and provided readers with a concise analysis of Islam. The Koran was a work of 'unheard-of violence', while 'Jesus was the master of love, Mohamed was the master of hate', and the works and practices of Islam 'exalt violence and hatred'.[64] The case took a tragic turn: following the publication of his article, Redeker received death threats which the police judged to be serious, and he had to be protected. Many

French intellectuals rallied to his defence in order to uphold the principle of freedom of speech; but others felt misgivings, and wanted to present a more nuanced case: while condemning the death threats, they also wished to signal that they could not accept Redeker's silly, hateful caricature of Islam.[65]

There is, therefore, a wider context for Djavann's writing: to see her as a single writer 'who fights political Islam with the only weapons she possesses: her words' is to misrepresent her status.[66] She contributes to a wider continuum of anti-Islamic polemics which seem to be growing in their frequency and virulence, and – perhaps indirectly – her words also serve to justify Western foreign policy decisions. Djavann rarely refers to this external framework: her first-person narratives concentrate on presenting her personal experiences and are therefore poor vehicles for making connections and citing other similar authors, although at one point she does acknowledge the influence of Samuel Huntington.[67] His *Clash of Civilizations*, first published in 1997, laid out the intellectual basis for the new anti-Islamism. Like Djavann, Huntington puts forward the hypothesis that societies are first and foremost defined by their religions, not by their economies, their forms of popular culture or their political systems.[68] Thus Huntington cites the example of Islamic terrorists who wear Western-style jeans, drink Coke and listen to rap: while accepting elements of Western culture, their religion marks them out as permanently separate, different and *therefore* opposed to the West.[69] Like Djavann, Huntington explicitly refuses to distinguish between a moderate mainstream Islam and an extremist minority: 'the underlying problem for the West is not Islamic fundamentalism. It is Islam, a different civilization whose people are convinced of the superiority of their culture and are obsessed with the inferiority of their power.'[70] This radical, arrogant refusal of dialogue is obviously in danger of becoming a self-fulfilling prophecy: as authorities and governments increasingly identify their enemies as Muslims, as they treat these peoples with greater suspicion and hostility, it is inevitable that both global and national conflicts grow in frequency and virulence.

Djavann pursues arguments like those presented by Huntington to their logical end. In her writing, there is very little affection for any aspect of Iran. Its people form weak, fickle crowds, incapable of understanding the reformist intentions of the Shah, and worthy of analysis by the pioneering nineteenth-century crowd psychologist,

Gustave Le Bon.[71] The Iranian people are unable to think for themselves.[72] The Iranian middle classes are decadent, self-obsessed
people, happy with their parties at which illegal whisky is drunk and
where fashionably dressed, high-heeled women try to imitate the
latest American screen idols. Widespread corruption allows such
privileged people to survive within the regime.[73] Intelligent, brave,
critical voices like Shirin Ebadi are dismissed by Djavann as 'soft'.[74]
Searching through her works for some positive reference to Iranian
culture, one finds that Djavann feels some fondness for medieval
Persian poetry.[75] There is also a word of praise for the Persian poet
and mathematician Omar Khayyam, but with the qualification that
he cannot be seen as an Islamic poet.[76] Islamic Iran is a totalitarian
regime, a mixture of Nazism and Stalinism.[77] The veil is like the
swastika, like the yellow star forced on the Jews.[78] At this point, one
begins to realize some of the weaknesses of Djavann's writing. How
can the veil be *both* like the swastika and the yellow star? This
suggests not simply a mixing of metaphors, but a real intellectual
clumsiness, an inability to think in coherent political terms. What
can one say about a political commentator who uncritically relies on
Le Petit Robert for her definition of totalitarianism?[79] Even the swift
comparison of Islamic political culture in Iran and fascism is not as
logical as Djavann suggests. Certainly, there are many important
objections which could be raised about the Islamic Republic,
relating to gender equality, democracy, human rights and social
equality. But do these objections mean that it is a 'fascist' regime?
Stefan Durand makes some obvious rejoinders to such sloppy
comparisons: the new Islamists are trans-nationalists rather than
nationalists, they lack the distinctive economic corporatism of
fascism, they do not create mass parties, and they make little – if any
– reference to social eugenicism.[80] 'Islamo-fascism' is a clumsy and
inaccurate term.

   Djavann's willingness to sidestep numerous awkward issues is also
obvious. She gained French nationality at a time when this process
is being made more difficult for most applicants, but she reduces
her narration of this event to 'a miracle', with no thought of those
who failed the test, or for the implications of the changes in policy.[81]
She recommends the provision of cheap air flights home as a means
to solve the social problems raised by the development of an underclass in France.[82] Even her writing on the veil is open to question.
'Imagine veiled Muslim men!' she writes, as if this was logically

impossible.[83] But almost any work on the topic will inform readers that male Muslim veiling does exist, specifically among the Tuareg tribes of north-west Africa.[84] Above all, her whole work relies on a type of conceptual telescoping: the violence and repression in Iran in the 1980s is typical of the entire record of the Islamic Republic; Islamic Iran is typical of the Muslim world; and it is these same Islamic norms which are typical of the opinions of French Muslims in twenty-first-century France.

Djavann herself is sensitive to criticisms of her limitations, and at one point even insists that she is presenting an analysis, not an eye-witness account.[85] But this claim denies the ontological basis of her writing: 'I know what I am talking about.'[86] For every problem, she refers first to her direct personal experience or, worse still, to a representation of her memory of that experience. Thus racism does not exist in France, because she has not experienced it. Islam is a totalitarian, fascist, Stalinist, Nazi system, because this is the form of Islam she has experienced. The veil is humiliating, oppressive and an instrument of a guilty and hypocritical sexualization, because this is how she has experienced it. No alternative, no other interpret-ation is possible within Djavann's world-view: above all, no coherent political perspective emerges from this simple, polemical writing.

Above all, Djavann is not an example for others. What practical policy can she suggest for reform in Iran? One possible implication of her latest work is that Western forces should invade Iran, just as they invaded Iraq. According to Djavann, 'for more than a quarter of a century the Iranian people have been waiting for the Americans to arrive'.[87] There is good reason to doubt this judgement: one of the few genuinely popular moves in Iran by conservative religious authorities has been to call for national unity against a foreign invader. Furthermore, what would happen if Iran's 11 million female students read her work, and then decided that they too would emigrate to France? Would the French state welcome these 'barbarian' Muslims with open arms? Beyond telling her Iranian readers 'become French!' and re-assuring her French readers that all Iranians admire France, Djavann has nothing to say. Her work is a passionate plea for an educated elite to reject all elements of their culture and religion, and to enter a dead-end street, a backward-looking, romanticized vision of a past French literary culture, circumscribed and policed by the demands of French politics. This is far from a meaningful liberation: like her comrade-in-arms, Hirsi Ali,

Djavann implies that Muslims should accept directions from the West. 'We need the help of the liberal West', writes Hirsi Ali, 'intellectuals and authorities must assist us in our pursuit of reason.'[88] Rather than proposing the emancipation of women, these angry anti-Islamic polemicists are offering them a new form of subordination which is compatible with the recent international policies adopted by the USA and other Western powers.

France's Djavann

Yet, as Djavann reminds us, France is the country that has produced such intellectual giants as Hugo, Molière, Balzac, Voltaire, Zola and Sartre. Why does this country take Djavann's simple polemics so seriously? If French people want to understand Muslim cultures, why don't they look to the Muslim countries with which they have the most connections: to Algeria, Morocco and Tunisia? The answer must be that Djavann has gained such respect because she plays her part so well. She tells nationalist-minded neo-republicans exactly what they want to hear. She tells them that France is right, and that it is morally and politically better than other countries. By virtue of her status as an Iranian, her words provide the evidence that French policies on the veil cannot be racist.[89] She tells Republicans that they are right to be suspicious of dissident voices who question the ever-changing interpretations of *laïcité*. She tells them, above all, to be suspicious of Muslims: these are people who cannot adapt to the democracy and moral values of the French Republic, and therefore should be watched, controlled, disciplined and re-educated. There is no need for further research, no awkward questions to re-think: the only mistake that the French have made is that they have not been faithful enough to their own traditions – 'may your acts follow your words!'[90] – and that they have been too soft, too indulgent, too slow with their enemies. Once again, one can note how perfectly this mimics the anti-Semitic, anti-Dreyfusard rhetoric of the 1890s, which presented a similar picture of the decent, ordinary, average French patriot, outwitted by sinister foreigners.

An alternative Iran

Much of Djavann's status relies on the idea that she is a representative voice of an oppressed Iranian majority. Certainly, Iran is an oppressive country, and many Iranians have protested in different ways against their government, but it seems unlikely that Djavann represents any substantial number of them. Her analysis of the country's development lacks subtlety. One important point that she ignores is the massive expansion of female education under the Islamic Republic, to the point where in June 2006 some 11 million of Iran's 22 million students were women. This large number of well-educated women have formed the basis of a stubborn, clear-thinking women's movement, often organized around NGOs, which has had some success in reforming elements of Iran's repressive law codes.[91] Despite repeated – and sometimes violent – police crackdowns, this movement has not been defeated. Its most prominent representative is Shirin Ebadi, who in September 2003 was awarded a Nobel Prize for her contribution to international peace.

The contrast between Ebadi's work and Djavann's perspectives could not be more obvious. Like most Iranian dissidents, Ebadi writes of the last years of the Shah with a certain caution; she remembers wearing mini-skirts, and participating in angry anti-Shah demonstrations. While Djavann is unable to explain *why* the Islamic mullahs became so popular so quickly, Ebadi notes their cleverness in identifying the corruption of the Shah's court, in publicizing the poisonous effects of American influences in Iran and – above all – in creating a critical language with which they could speak to the people.[92] Ebadi writes with an honesty and a self-critical quality absent in Djavann's work. She notes how, in participating in the demonstrations against the Shah, she also brought about her own downfall: she lost her position as one of Iran's top judges. In February 1979, as the Shah left, she felt proud:

That day, a feeling of pride washed over me that in hindsight makes me laugh. I felt that I too had won, alongside this victorious revolution. It took scarcely a month for me to realize that, in fact, I had willingly and enthusiastically participated in my own demise. I was a woman, and this revolution's victory demanded my defeat.[93]

She criticizes the imposition of the veil on women in 1980, but is far more exact and clear than Djavann about its significance for Iran's women: it was 'a symbol of their broader lack of rights'.[94] There is no polemic here about the inherent, sexualized evil of the garment, no confused rhetoric about a totalitarian, fascist, Stalinist, Nazi regime, but a sober, critical assessment based on a coherent political philosophy that sets a clear political aim: the development of human rights in Iran.

While Djavann achieves a sort of fame for her renunciation of Islam, Ebadi has a quite different approach to the religion. When arrested and imprisoned in 2000, she found comfort in Islam, and prayed five times a day.[95] She is certainly sensitive to the ways in which this religion can be abused, but realizes also how it can promote progress, leading to 'female equality in an Islamic framework'.[96] She highlights the idea of *ijtihād* – the right to interpret the Koran. '*Ijtihād* is central to Islamic law, because sharia is more a set of principles than a codified set of rules.'[97] Unlike Djavann, Ebadi is sensitive to the varieties and contexts of Islam, and carefully avoids simplistic generalizations from the Iranian experience.

Above all, throughout her work Ebadi remains sceptical of the Western interest in Iran, seeing it as, at best, counter-productive and, at worst, exploitative, corrupting and destructive. Unlike Djavann, she remains a patriot, someone who believes in her country and its ability to reform itself.[98] A comparison between the two writers demonstrates how shallow Djavann's claim is to speak for Iranian women, let alone for all Muslim women.

Conclusion

In place of Bhabha's and Appadurai's beautiful dreams of a liberatory, transnational 'third space', Djavann shows us another vision of globalization, predicated on fear and a desperate quest to belong. Her world vision seems closer to that of which Zygmunt Bauman warns: a world 'sliced into poorly coordinated fragments'.[99] Rather than constructing bridges between France and Iran, she creates new walls. We can easily imagine her standing next to Chirac at the funeral.

Yet Djavann is right. A woman like her, hostile to the rituals of Islam, terrorized by Iran's rulers, in love with French literary culture and – above all – ambitious, could never feel at home in the Islamic Republic. Her migration to France, and her success in winning a certain literary reputation, have undoubtedly allowed her a freer, more fulfilling lifestyle than she could ever have lived in Iran. But is this really a liberation? Her position is dependent on her constant, repeated, implacable renunciation of everything she learnt in her first twenty-three years. She must be the only woman in France who has become famous for *not* being a Muslim, and it is this essentially negative position that defines and limits her work. Instead of creating her own autonomous voice, she offers conservative French people an ersatz vision of their own idealized identity, replete with the necessary homage to dead literary giants. No doubt her accent, her exoticism and the strained simplicity of her prose all add to the appeal of her contribution and the welcome she has received. But if ever the West lost its fear of Islam, and if French society came to terms with its position as the world's fifteenth-largest Muslim power, Djavann would no longer have any role to play.

Chapter Three
Fadela Amara: Assimilation as Social Reform

---

*My France ... is the France of the Enlightenment, the France of the Republic,
the France of Marianne, the Dreyfusards, the Communards, the Resistance.
In brief, the France of Liberty, Equality and Fraternity.*

                                                            Fadela Amara, 2003[1]

Of our four thinkers, Fadela Amara is the only one who can be
described as 'French Muslim' without any qualification. She was
born in 1964 in the city of Clermont-Ferrand: both her parents are
Muslims, both born in Kabyle region of Algeria, and she remains a
practising Muslim. There are some similarities between Amara and
Djavann: Amara also stresses the value of her experience, and at
times will stress her personal knowledge of a topic, often stating 'I
know this' during debates, or speaking of her familiarity with the
'grass-roots' (*terrain*), when discussing themes beyond the experience of her interviewer.[2] But Amara's claim to knowledge and
accuracy is less absolute than that presented by Djavann, and she
has been willing to acknowledge her own mistakes. And while
Djavann's favoured literary form is the first-person narrative, Amara
seems more reluctant to write down her thoughts, and her three
published works all take the form of long, extended interviews,
sometimes in the form of dialogues with a co-author. Unlike
Djavann, Amara is a combative, confident speaker, fully capable of
dealing with hostile crowds, and not afraid to confront her audience's expectations and assumptions. Her speeches could never be
described as lyrical, and in fact – when written down – often seem
shallow and unstructured, shifting from one topic to another
without a clear line of logic. But if she lacks eloquence, her spoken
performances have a tough, gritty quality, often close to anger,
which can make her an extremely persuasive speaker.

Une fille des banlieues

Amara belongs to a new generation. Her father emigrated to France in 1955, following a severe economic crisis in the Kabyle region of Algeria. He did not speak French when he arrived, and has never learnt to speak it well. He remains illiterate. He began working in Algeria when he was eleven. When he first arrived in France, he had nowhere to sleep, and so slept in the building site where he was employed.[3] He returned to Algeria briefly in 1960, when a marriage was arranged with Amara's mother, fifteen years his junior, who speaks French well, and is literate. Her father retained his connections with Algeria, and would regularly threaten his wife that if she did not run the household well, he would go back to Algeria and find another wife.

Amara was one of ten children. She grew up in a tiny flat in a slum area outside Clermont-Ferrand, and lived for fifteen years in an estate designed to provide cheap housing, an area in which, she recalls, 99 per cent of the population were Arab.[4] Her mother was a strong influence on her: she was a model of feminine domesticity, working hard to ensure that all her children were clean, healthy and properly dressed. Her father refused to let her go out to work: a prohibition which many Arab immigrant families followed.[5] It was her mother who introduced Amara to Islam.[6] Amara says little about her faith, but – unlike Djavann – in her brief references, she speaks of it with respect, praising the poetic beauty of the Koran.[7] Her mother had a deep fear of all French authorities, and Amara recalls her nervousness before every school medical: her mother was terrified that she would be blamed for any physical defect detected in her children.[8] Amara's first contact with the French state was through the school. She remembers it as very distant from her home life, and she found it hard to concentrate on the lessons.[9] It was through her teacher that she learnt that her foreign origins and her religion made her different from the majority of people in France.[10] Her father treated his sons and daughters very differently. While the boys were allowed some freedom, for the girls there was to be no access to any outside space: they were to return home immediately after school.[11] In one sense, however, these were the good years: the French economy was still expanding in the 1960s and early 1970s. There was always work for her father, and a reasonable expectation that at least the boys of the family would also be able to find jobs.

Much changed for Amara in the late 1970s. One stimulus was the school which, for all its distance from her family, still provided a model of a different lifestyle. At least in the school, she saw women who had careers outside the home.[12] 'Apart from the education my parents gave me', she notes, 'what made me what I am was the republican school.'[13] In her later works, she also stresses its politicizing and liberatory role. 'It was at the republican school that I learnt to love what is most noble about France: the Republic.'[14] But outside school, conditions were getting worse. The immigrants' housing estates deteriorated. Mass unemployment ended many immigrant families' hopes for a better future. Drug-taking, spreading to all areas of France, created an illegal, parallel economy in their housing estates.[15] Amara's elder brother was arrested and imprisoned, thus breaking the chain of male hierarchy in her family.[16] Amara took his role, leading her father to bestow on her the ambiguous compliment that she was worth ten men ('why not ten women?' she would later tease him).[17] Amara participated in the Marche des Beurs of 1983, and then joined SOS-Racisme: this movement, for her, was something extraordinary.[18] Despite her parents' opposition, she attended meetings regularly, and began to be chosen for official positions. In 2000 she was elected as the head of its Fédération National des Maisons des Potes (FNMP, which could be very approximately translated as 'National Federation of Friends' Houses').[19]

Within this organization, there was a specific concern about women's lives in the housing estates: this led to the publication of a manifesto in 2002 entitled 'Ni Putes ni Soumises' – a difficult phrase to translate. This point is more revealing than it might appear: at a number of key moments in her public life, Amara has become notorious for her use of informal, colourful, slang terms in formal contexts. In a sense, she has brought the language of the housing estates into a parliamentary and political arena. 'Pute' is one such term: it is a regrettably common French slang term for prostitute. 'Soumises' is also an ambiguous term; literally 'submissive women', it has been pointed out that the origins of the terms 'Islam' and 'Muslim' are in an Arabic word for submission: a Muslim is one who submits to God. It is therefore possible to read 'soumises' as referring to female Muslims. The entire phrase could be translated as meaning something along the lines of 'Neither slags nor doormats'. The manifesto was favourably received by some, and eventually an organization with the same name was created in April 2003.

We will return to this organization below. However, in order to understand more clearly Amara's status in French political life, we need to consider where she came from. We will then turn to consider her political record.

The crisis of the *banlieues*

While it would be easy to translate *banlieues* as suburbs, the French term actually signifies something quite different. The term's shifting resonances suggest a summary of almost two centuries of social experimentation. Its origins lie in nineteenth-century reformists' concern with working-class housing and lifestyle. The obvious answer seemed to be planned, designed areas, guaranteeing the inhabitants space, light, cleanliness and decency. Innovative architects such as Le Corbusier produced plans for 'la cité radieuse' (the light-filled city) in the early twentieth century, but it was not until the post-1945 era that such plans were finally put into practice, and there was a concerted move to eradicate the ill-equipped slums and shanty towns in which many workers still lived. In 1955, it was estimated that 11 million French people still lived in substandard housing.[20] These social projects were part of a more profound shift in French capitalism, away from the liberal, laissez-faire model of the nineteenth century, and towards the more technocratic, self-consciously modern, state-orientated capitalism of the 'thirty glorious years', the three decades of near uninterrupted expansion from 1945 to 1976.[21] This was, indeed, a different France: the population was increasing, the demographic weight of the working class was growing and the economy always needed more workers. Immigrants, principally from North Africa, Spain and Portugal, poured into France: approximately 1.7 million lived in France in 1954, 4.1 million by 1975.[22] In order to accommodate them, 195 zones à urbaniser en priorité (ZUPs – priority zones for urbanization) were created: these often took the form of vast new housing estates far from the old city centres, in areas where it was expected that new industries would develop.[23] Originally, these were fairly tightly directed by local municipalities, usually with left-wing majorities, who would engage in their own miniature socio-political experiments, ensuring that the first tenants in these new, clean, modern blocks were skilled workers and council employees.[24] A few critics warned of the loneliness within the estates; others raised concerns about their geographic isolation and poor transport links.[25] Such dissidents were, however, exceptional.

The immigrants of the 1950s, such as the fathers of Begag and Amara, often lived in shanty towns, in cheap hotels and in slums. They were concentrated in the unskilled sectors of the economy. Initially, most immigrants were single men, but particularly in the 1960s the French state favoured a policy of regrouping families. At this point, the immigrants were caught between two myths.[26] On the one hand, there was the myth of return: the dream that eventually they would 'return' to a country which, frankly, had become foreign to them. On the other hand, there was the ambiguous promise of naturalization and integration into France. Surprisingly, perhaps, many of them continued to be Muslims. Relying on their own resources, cellars and garages were converted into prayer rooms, and a generation of worker-imams ensured their faith's survival in France. It was estimated that in 1970 there were about a hundred such places in the region around Paris.[27] They were rarely noticed by outside observers, except on special occasion such as the ceremonies to mark Nasser's death in September 1970.

In the 1970s and 1980s conditions in the estates deteriorated. Municipalities' budgets were cut, and the physical conditions of the buildings worsened. The richer inhabitants moved out, often seeking detached houses as a new symbol of their status. Immigrant families now moved in to the worn-out, ill-kept estates. As early as 1977 official reports warned of their worsening social conditions. In 1981 two estates near Lyon acquired a fearsome reputation for car stealing, violence, theft, drug dealing and riots.[28] Reports began to slip over different concepts: 'everyone knew that' all the estates were violent, all were full of immigrants and all the immigrants were Muslims. Journalists were sent out to uncover increasingly macabre and blood-thirsty stories. They knew little about these now distant areas, and they frequently addressed the people they met in the patronizing and familiar 'tu' form: therefore they were met with resentment.[29] This was the lost world that François Maspero traversed in 1989, just before the bicentenary of the French Revolution: he knew of the stories that used needles from heroin injections could be found in every housing estate stairwell, and he certainly noted apathy, poverty, exhaustion and hopelessness among people he met. But Maspero also noted other aspects of people's lives: the quiet pleasure of walks and fishing along canals, the lively cafes, the exuberance of the girls, proud of their clothes and hairstyles, and the decent, retired petit-bourgeois living in their detached houses and cottages. He noted a paradoxical, perhaps unwelcome, success of the housing schemes: 'it's hard to leave: [the estates] are turned in on themselves, they offer a territory, a type of security.'[30] Passing a cheap hotel offering rooms to migrant African workers, he wondered 'refuge, ghetto, oasis [or] citadel'?[31] Above all, he was conscious of the great political irony of the contrast between this curiously empty, dejected landscape, and the sorry attempts of ill-equipped municipal councils to recreate a loyal Republican patriotism, worthy of the bicentenary of 1789.

Maspero's intuitions were both perceptive and prescient. The worst parts of these areas are not 'ghettoes' in any real sense of the word, but they have now been re-classified as zones urbaines sensibles (ZUS – difficult urban zones), within which 4.46 million of France's population live.[32] Despite the difficulty of obtaining accurate statistics relating to ethnicity in France, one point is clear: the majority of their population are *not* from immigrant families, but a mixture of the poor, the rejected, the underemployed and the foreign.[33] One persistent problem that their inhabitants face is the suspicion that their initiatives and their cultures meet from authorities. Olivier Masclet retells a sad little story which can be taken to illustrate the general problem of political culture in the *banlieues* and, more specifically, of the left and immigrants.[34] His research concerns Gennevilliers, to the north-west of Paris, which has been run by the Communist Party (PCF) since the Second World War. Historically, the PCF has worked extremely well as a vehicle for the acculturation and education of the poor. To its credit, in Gennevilliers the PCF refused to reduce the social problems of the housing estates to a simple security issue which could be solved by tough policing. However, even the PCF was influenced by colonial fears concerning Muslims, and was reluctant to recruit or to promote activists from the new wave of immigrants into its organizations. Suspicions concerning the second and third generation of immigrant families grew more pronounced in the 1990s, and the local council became apprehensive about a youth club in the Luth district, a tiny building of 50 square metres, and one of the few local facilities available to young people from Algerian or Moroccan families. The council worried that it was being used by fundamentalists as a place of recruitment. In reality, observes Masclet, there were few Islamists in Luth, and they were poorly organized and not really fundamentalists. As part of the policy to combat fundamentalism, the council insisted that the youth club implement a strict sexual equality policy. This caused problems: there were a few women in the youth club, present both as organizers and as ordinary members. But they were clearly in a minority. Most of the district's girls did not want to attend the youth club, most of the young men appreciated its largely masculine culture, and most local families would have disapproved of a place in which young people of both sexes could meet without parental supervision. It therefore proved to be impossible to meet the councils' new demands; the municipal subsidy was withdrawn, and the club was closed in 1996. The young men who had previously met there, under the direction of both male and female organizers, were now left to hang around the streets. An apparently liberal policy, seemingly designed to promote equality and integration, had actually produced almost exactly the opposite effect.

This type of self-fulfilling prophecy has been repeated many times over. Particularly after the rise of the anti-immigrant National Front, left-wing councils grew reluctant to encourage immigrants or immigrants' children to stand for local elections, for fear that they would be criticized for being 'soft' on immigration: this led to a gradual disengagement of immigrants' children from politics.[35] In place of policies to promote and integrate such people, security-orientated policies became the norm, even in the Socialist Party, in the early 1990s.[36] If integration had not taken place, then this was now seen as the fault of the immigrants themselves for 'too many immigrants cannot imagine that they can be the equals of the native French population', as one Stasi Commission member commented.[37] The effects of the new concentration on security are illustrated by anti-terrorist 'Vigipirate' operation, mounted in 2000, which resulted in three million identity checks being enforced: the majority of these concerned people travelling to and from the *banlieues*, and so had the effect of further isolating the estates from town centres. One joke which circulated was that in order *not* to be stopped by the police, all one had to do was to display that quintessential symbol of bourgeois propriety: a briefcase.[38] Police checks were often experienced as another humiliation: frequently the police would be laughing as they stopped yet another Arab, and would use the familiar *tu* when talking to them.[39] 'The police are not fascists', notes Yann Boutang, 'they are just too white.'[40]

Since Maspero's eloquent description, another expert observer has stepped forward to describe the *banlieues*: a teenage girl from one of these estates. Faïza Guène's first novel, *Kiffe Kiffe Demain*, is a well-written, observant and even funny account of life in the *banlieues*, sprinkled with dictionary-busting *verlan* terms. (The title is an untranslatable French-Arabic phrase; the English-language version has the title *Just Like Tomorrow*.) A vivid and convincing picture is presented of a family whose members are split between France and Morocco, but whose culture is clearly more French than Arab. The main character lives in a world in which people observe Ramadan without making any reference to its religious significance, and where 100 per cent halal speedburgers are an ordinary part of their diet.[41] The possibility of any 'return' to Morocco is swiftly dismissed by the teenage narrator: 'There, if you've two little bumps for breasts, if you know how to shut up when you're told to and how to bake bread, then you're ready to be married.'[42] The teachers and social workers who surround the estates are not bad people, not racist, but perhaps patronizing, distant and not very effective. Her mother's employer calls all his female Arab workers Fatima, all his female black workers Mamadou, and all the Chinese Ping-Pong.[43] He can leave every weekend in his little blue van for a pretty village in old France for Sunday Mass, wholemeal bread, traditional Roquefort cheese and dried sausage.[44] While the people living in the estates certainly know of this world, they have no access to it. Certainly there is poverty, but – perhaps worse still – there is a realization that there is no way out of this situation, and that others around them have better lives, but are separated by barriers as emphatic as the Maginot Line or the Berlin Wall.[45] To this new generation, the dominant French culture is not so much incomprehensible as meaningless. At one point the narrator wonders why a nearby school is named after Louis Blanc, and looks up his name in a dictionary. She learns that Blanc was a journalist, a socialist and a reformist. She comments, accurately: 'In France, if you've got three words that end in -ist, that's enough for them to name a school, a street, a library or an underground station after you.'[46] The narrator's friends are stuck in the estate's filthy towers, where the lifts stink of piss and dog-ends. Nothing in their world seems whole, proper or authentic: even the Barbie dolls she plays with are not real Barbies, but 'dolls for the poor', bought in the local cut-price store.[47] It is like living in a film by an incompetent writer.[48]

It was these kinds of frustrations that sparked off the riots which erupted across France in October and November 2005. The police wanted to check the IDs of three teenage boys: they ran off, tried to hide in an electricity power station, and were electrocuted. Riots followed: by 7 November a state of emergency had been declared which covered one quarter of French territory. After two weeks of riots, 8,400 cars had been burnt in over 100 different towns, and one person had died. Sarkozy, then Minster of the Interior, uttered his now-notorious comment about how he would use high-pressure hoses to clean away the scum: a comment which provoked the rioters to greater violence.[49] Some three and a half thousand were arrested; of these, some five hundred were eventually found guilty of offences.[50] Questions were immediately asked concerning who had organized these riots. *Le Figaro* reported that Islamist sites were calling the riots 'a new jihad',[51] but a reporter from *Le Monde* who followed one group of rioters was surprised to find that there was 'no strategy ... no organization ... neither the [criminal] gangs nor the Islamists seemed to be in charge'.[52] It seems unlikely that the majority of the rioters could either be described as Arab or Muslims: many of France's Muslims had tried their hardest to calm the rioters. The UOIF issued a fatwa condemning the violence. In Rosny, near Paris, a UOIF section mounted a patrol at night to try to persuade the rioters to go home. The patrol attempted to talk to the rioters: they would start by saying 'Salam Aleykum', and normally the young men would reply 'bon soir'.[53] Other aspects of the riots are also worth stressing: nearly all the rioters were young men. The women of the *banlieues* rarely participated, but tended not to condemn the rioters. The older men disapproved.[54] Moreover, the overwhelming majority of people in the *banlieues* did not participate – even if they did feel some sympathy for the rioters.[55]

Some critics drew some apocalyptic lessons from these events. Stasi considered that they would provoke a rough, difficult awakening among the French people.[56] For Yann Boutang 'the French model of integration was burnt by the riots'.[57] Tariq Ramadan argued that the events showed that 'the unity of the Republic, a quality which is idealised to the point of madness by political discourse, is – in terms of French society – a myth and a lie'.[58] This was 'a crisis of meaning, of values of identity for the whole nation', considered Azouz Begag – who also noted that he was the only member of the government who had lived on the estates, but nobody wanted to talk to him about the riots.[59] Michel Pialoux considered that after the riots, it was as if the idea of progress had disappeared.[60] Fadela Amara drew a different lesson: she stressed the point that the girls of the *banlieues* had not rioted.[61]

Ni Putes ni Soumises, 2003–6

Since 1975 there had been a vague awareness that living conditions were deteriorating in the estates, and that those living in them were unable to access the ordinary resources of French society. The disturbances of 1981 and the Marche des Beurs of 1983 were both attempts to draw greater attention to this problem and to demand action. SOS-Racisme was one attempt to respond to this demand, but was largely unsuccessful. Ni Putes ni Soumises was, in a sense, a more sophisticated attempt to respond to the same agenda.

Amara had grown up in the type of area from which the riots were organized. Her political values were formed in those estates, and the organization she joined constantly made reference back to that situation. Amara worked from 2000 to 2003 to identify common problems faced by women in the *banlieues*. One effective means of doing this was through publicizing some instances of horrific sexual violence in the *banlieues*, such as the ghastly death of Sohane, a young woman who was burnt alive in a dustbin by a spurned lover, or the dreadful experience of Samira Bellil, who survived three incidences of gang rape. Amara led protests and demonstrations to publicize these crimes, and then added two other themes. She protested against what she termed 'the green fascism' of self-proclaimed imams, and she raised the issue of the daily harassment that some women faced in the estates.[62]

In February and March 2003 the new organization – Ni Putes ni Soumises – was launched by a month's march through twenty-three towns: a tactic which recalled the 'Marche des Beurs' of 1983.[63] The march ended on 8 March 2003, International Women's Day, in Paris, where between 10,000 and 30,000 young women marched behind the banner of Ni Putes ni Soumises. In a powerful symbolic gesture, the organization produced an exhibition of fourteen young women from the *banlieues* in the pose of Marianne, the female symbol of the French Republic, 'who represents the values of a liberating and protecting Republic, to whom the women of the estates want to give homage, and of whom the deputies are the guarantors'.[64] As had been the case with SOS-Racisme, the media reaction was generally favourable. *Le Monde* celebrated these 'beaming, proud young women with blusher on their cheeks, marching shoulder to shoulder, accompanied by ululations'.[65] Amara, in particular, attracted positive attention: the right-of-centre *L'Express* weekly applauded 'this energetic little woman who has become the speaker for the girls of the *banlieues*'.[66] In general, the media welcomed the appearance of the *beurette*, the young French-Arab woman, as an acceptable alternative to the more threatening figures of the rioting youth and the veiled woman.[67] The movement grew rapidly. In October 2003, there were twenty-three Ni Putes ni Soumises committees and five linked associations.[68] In February 2004, it claimed 1,750 members and some 30 local committees, by 2006 there were 60 committees.[69] This was 'France's noisiest feminist movement' noted an enthusiastic report in the *Guardian*.[70] Soon links were made with politicians: by October 2005, Amara was in regular contact with Laurent Fabius, then general secretary of the Socialist Party, and referred to him as 'a mate'.[71] Sarkozy had also requested to meet her.[72]

Unfortunately, all was not as simple or as successful as the press suggested. Created early in 2003, Ni Putes ni Soumises was promptly called to serve in 'the war of the veil'. Amara's first pronouncements on this matter were cautious and sensible. She noted how the focus on the veil diverted attention away from more pressing social problems. Banning the veil in schools could also make young people from the *banlieues* feel, once more, stigmatized and rejected by French society. All Muslims would feel threatened. The veil was not a religious question, however: it was 'an instrument of oppression, alienation, discrimination, a form of men's power over women'.[73] Amara herself, a practising Muslim, had never felt the need to wear one. Her conclusion? Amara certainly implied that she was against legislation on the matter, but ended with a typical piece of obfuscation: she would prefer girls to wear a Phrygian bonnet, like Marianne, rather than a veil. Events moved quickly. In December 2003, Amara added her signature to a petition organised by *Elle* calling on Chirac to support a law banning the veil in school.[74] Following the publication of the Stasi report, Amara voiced her approval of its conclusions.[75] By 8 March 2004, the annual International Women's Day march in Paris faced a real problem: would it accept women wearing veils? Should they be excluded? Ni *marginalised by association*

Putes ni Soumises supported a call to ban veil-wearing women from
the march. By all accounts, this became quite a tense issue: veiled
women reported being jeered and spat at by other contingents.[76]
The next year, the 2,500 women of the Ni Putes ni Soumises contingent joined a separate, *laïque* demonstration, after the official
demonstration refused to ban veiled women from participating in
the march.[77] This was not simply a point of demonstration etiquette:
a policy decision had been made that henceforth '*laïcité* is an essential value in our struggle'.[78] Veiled women had joined the first
march by Ni Putes ni Soumises in 2003;[79] by 2005 it was clear that
they were no longer welcome. (This position has led Ni Putes ni
Soumises into some contradictory poses: its publicity photos show a
variety of cheerful, confident-looking young Frenchwomen – and a
few men – all of them emphatically unveiled. However, the organization has developed some links abroad, including Morocco. The
publicity photos to illustrate this show cheerful, confident-looking
young Moroccan women – with about half of them wearing veils.
Are readers supposed to assume that wearing a veil in France is a
symbol of adhesion to the values of green fascism, but in Morocco it
means a love of democratic *laïcité*?)[80]

In the months that followed, something like a political position
evolved, structured around Amara's own writing and the organization's increasing visibility. Ni Putes ni Soumises spoke eloquently
about the growing daily degradation of women in the *banlieues*.[81]
Amara was clear on this point: their lives were getting worse. This
point was illustrated by more terrifying incidents: the horrific knife
attack on Khadidja by her husband in 2004, and by a series of gang
rapes. As unemployment got worse, fathers lost their authority as
bread-winners, family structures broke down and unemployed,
young men began to rule the streets. Some of them harassed girls
who they saw as betraying their communities by growing too
friendly with the French; at times these same young men seemed to
want to impose a puritanical code: it was reported that they attacked
girls wearing sexually provocative clothing. 'Their only form of
power is their rule over girls.'[82] There were fewer and fewer places
where boys and girls could meet as equals.[83] The only form of sexual
education in the *banlieues* was that gained from pornographic
videos.[84] Under these circumstances, wearing make-up became a
form of resistance.[85] Ni Putes ni Soumises even co-organized a
competition with *Elle*, whose prizes allowed the winners to work in

the fashion industry.[86] The plight of these young women had been largely ignored by French feminists and political parties: the issues which concerned mainstream French feminists were simply light years away from the concerns of the young women of the *banlieues*.[87] In a memorable phrase, Amara said that talking to *banlieue* girls about equal opportunities was like talking to them about the sales at Hermès (an extremely exclusive fashion store in Paris): it was something so distant as to be irrelevant.[88] For some young women living under this form of domination, there was only one way out: through the Republican school.[89] Outside of the estates, they could find everything that had been denied to them: boyfriends, films, fashion and freedom.[90] The organization itself was like a bridge which could aid the girls' escape from the *banlieues*.[91]

Amara repeatedly stressed the threat represented by Islamism or 'green fascism'. Imam were emerging from the cellars and garages (where they organized improvised prayer rooms), and were being accepted by local authorities as legitimate representatives of the estates.[92] Many of these new religious authorities were illegal immigrants from the Middle East and Pakistan, benefitting from foreign funding. They preached to the boys, and next the boys began to adopt hostile attitudes to their sisters.[93] The imams' presence was a clear challenge to the laws of the Republic.[94] (We will return to this issue in the next chapter.)

This clearly constitutes a grim picture of life in the *banlieues*. However, it is open to question whether it is coherent. Like Brenner, Amara tends to line up a list of undesirable practices, and then point to Islamism as the culprit. There are problems with each point of her argument. First, these Islamist groups remain extremely vague: aside from claiming that the UOIF makes tactical use of the accusation of Islamophobia,[95] we are given very little hard information concerning the specific activities of specific groups in specific places.

Secondly, there is a further contradiction in suggesting that Islamists are somehow responsible for the horrific – but, thankfully, relatively rare – cases of sexual violence. When interviewed, Belill explicitly denied that religion had any relevance to her dreadful experiences.[96] At this point, it is worth remembering that one reason why the first generation of long-term immigrants to France worked so hard to preserve Islam in their communities was precisely to safeguard a sense of morality within the difficult and corrupting conditions in which they lived in France.[97] Furthermore, however 'fundamentalism' is defined, it is a rigorous creed which demands extremely high moral standards from its followers. Converts in particular experience their discovery of hard-line Islam as a moralization of their lives: they give up drugs, petty theft and improper sexual experimentation.[98] Many of them, of course, may have curious and objectionable views concerning sexuality, but to push together horrific examples of sexual violence and Islamism is – like Brenner – to skid from one concept to another. While there is some evidence to suggest that women in the *banlieues* face street harassment, it seems that this is more likely to come from a sub-elite of petty criminals attempting to exert control over neighbourhoods than from any religious group.[99]

Thirdly, within a lot of Amara's writing there is the unproven assumption that sexual violence in the *banlieues* is particularly horrific. The sad truth is that male violence against women can be found in all sectors of French society: Amara is actually honest enough to acknowledge that she was shocked to realize this.[100] Amara's critics have often concentrated on this theme, arguing that the repeated and powerful publicity which her organization gives to acts of sexual violence in the *banlieues* contributes to a more general stigmatization of Arabs as savage, rapacious and uncivilized.[101] According to Fatima Ouassak, Ni Putes ni Soumises reduce the general problem of sexism to the particular problem of male Arabs' sexism: 'Above all, whites are implicitly presented as "better" on the question of male/female equality.'[102] Thomas Deltombe describes the evolution of the organization's propaganda thus: 'the complete abandon of social and economic analyses ... Out went problems of segregation and a flexible work force, [and] the leaders of the Ni Putes ni Soumises now based [their analysis] on a security- and culture-orientated analysis: individuals and cultures were responsible' for all that was wrong in the *banlieues*.[103]

Amara's strident loyalty to the Republic and its schools also represents a difficult political choice. The people of the *banlieues* can draw on other inspirations; for many, the defining moment in the construction of their political identity was the Algerian struggle for national liberation: an example of a struggle *against* France. More distantly, they can also admire the Palestinian *intifada*. Amara's unreserved praise for French institutions is often rejected by such radicals. Significantly, Amara simply denies the possibility of a Muslim feminism: for her, women's emancipation must be *laïque*.[104]

The final contradiction, however, relates to the tone of much of Amara's writing. She presents herself – and is often accepted – as a representative of the women of the *banlieues*, who can campaign on their behalf. But much of her writing actually seems very critical of those who live in the *banlieues*. She lectures them, often in a hectoring manner. They have to work harder at school, they have to respect the Republic more, they have to adopt reasonable and acceptable forms of Islam, they must reject the veil. When addressed in Arabic, she replies quite curtly: 'Speak in French.'[105] There is a rather grim, Samuel Smiles-esque ethic here. One could argue that this is making the best of a bad situation: given the French state's unwillingness to invest in a programme to renovate the *banlieues*, all its inhabitants have left are their own resources. The final goal, according to Ni Putes ni Soumises, is to get out. Here, Amara's analysis runs into the same contradiction as that represented by Djavann's analysis: is this really feasible? Is this really desirable? No doubt a talented and imaginative writer like Guène might have benefitted from a better school and greater encouragement for her talents. No doubt the lucky winner of the *Elle*-Ni Putes ni Soumises competition did earn more money and work in a more dignified and more pleasant place than her sisters who stayed behind. But there are about 4.5 million people living in the ZUS: how practical is it to tell them 'get out'? And particularly when, as in the case of Djavann, moving out also means giving up certain forms of religious practice, and – more seriously – cutting oneself off from family support networks, often the only viable form of self-help network that many people of the *banlieues* possess.

Ni Putes ni Soumises, 2006–8

2006 may well have represented the year in which Ni Putes ni Soumises achieved its greatest success. In this year it sponsored a brave and imaginative lecture tour: Ni Putes ni Soumises remains one of the few groups which will openly and publicly raise questions about sexual morality in the *banlieues*, and this has included discussions on the taboo topic of the 'gay *banlieue*'. It established a permanent meeting-place and social centre in Paris, which offered facilities to receive and advise women who had suffered violence. This was opened on the symbolic date of 8 March 2006, and Chirac and Bertrand Delanoë (the Socialist mayor of Paris) attended its opening ceremony.[106] Furthermore, a new, hi-tech website was created, which included numerous video clips. All these initiatives proved their worth. Meetings organized by Ni Putes ni Soumises regularly attracted a respectable one or two hundred people across France.[107] The Parisian centre for abused women dealt with 1,700 cases in 2005, and 1,750 in 2006. Of the cases in 2006, 19 per cent concerned forced marriages, 24 per cent domestic violence and 9 per cent rapes.[108] The website attracted an average of about 600 visitors per day.[109] The 116-page report issued at the end of 2006 presents a convincing account of a reasonably successful organization: its claim that Ni Putes ni Soumises had won 'its place in the political and social landscape' seems justified.[110]

Questions and doubts about the organization's ultimate aim, however, remain and grew more pertinent when the organization was gripped by a political and administrative crisis in 2007. One point relates simply to numbers. The annual demonstration of 8 March in Paris was presented as central to its activities: it allowed 'the daughters of immigrants to show publicly their wish to be an integral part of French society'.[111] Yet the available figures suggest that Ni Putes ni Soumises was, year by year, actually mobilizing fewer people to attend this event (see table 3.1).

This gives the odd impression of an organization which is actually losing support from its designated audience while it gains financial support from exterior bodies. A chance remark by a critical commentator on the 8 March 2003 demonstration also reflects some of these concerns: it was noted that the Ni Putes ni Soumises contingent came equipped with an ear-splitting sound system and a prominent helium-filled balloon – 'all the massive resources of a

Table 3.1: Numbers marching in the Ni Putes ni Soumises contingent at the International Women's Day demonstration, Paris[112]

Year	Numbers present
2003	30,000
2004	10,000
2005	2,600

major political party, all the media support that goes with such a status … but no more ability to mobilize than a little local group.'[113] Deltombe notes how quickly the organization became 'a televisual machine', reliant – like the earlier SOS-Racisme – on badges, T-shirts and simplistic slogans.[114] In 2005 Tariq Ramadan described the organization as 'a handful of people'.[115] In 2006 Ni Putes ni Soumises was claiming sixty local committees: how many people did this actually represent? When the organization declares its aim to 'mobilize today's youth', does it have the resources to do this?[116]

In May 2007 Sarkozy was elected president of France. At first sight, this looked like an ominous sign for Ni Putes ni Soumises. Sarkozy was famous for his declaration to sweep the scum off the streets, and headed an emphatically right-wing political organization. While Ni Putes ni Soumises had never explicitly 'cast its vote', its proximity to the Socialist Party was obvious to all: Amara had been a Socialist councillor in Clermont-Ferrand, her advisors came from the Socialist Party, and her switch of attitude about the law on the veil was widely assumed to be a result of pressure from the Socialists. On the other hand, Amara seemed reluctant to condemn Sarkozy publicly, and even seemed to be prepared to forgive his reference to 'the scum'. In 2006, her main criticism of him was that he was too close to the UOIF.[117] In June 2007, to the amazement of many, she accepted the post of Secretary of State responsible for urban policy in his cabinet. (In France, there is a long tradition of offering cabinet posts to people who are not elected politicians.) According to *Le Monde*, the current president of SOS-Racisme burst into laughter when he heard the news: he could not believe that Amara, staunch defender of *laïcité*, was going to accept a post subordinate to the Catholic Christine Boutin (then Minister of Urban Development), who had waved a bible during her speech criticizing a bill that permitted the civic union of homosexual couples.[118] To some extent, a move like this was hinted at in one of her earlier books, when she states that *banlieues* did not need the announcement of another great law or another fine speech: what was needed was a return to the grassroots, a more modest effort, to be pursued relentlessly, day after day.[119] This kind of perspective de-politicizes issues, and one can see that Amara might be just the right kind of person to perform this sort of labour. As for the contradiction of a

Muslim entering a right-wing cabinet which included people who had spoken against the presence of immigrants in France, Begag had already answered the question: in the twenty-five years since the Marche des Beurs, the left had not appointed a single cabinet minister from an immigrant background. Amara remained a member of Ni Putes ni Soumises, but she resigned her post as president, handing the position over to Sihem Habchi.

Members of Ni Putes ni Soumises were horrified by her move. An internal document asked: 'is there life after Amara?'[120] Some members spoke to the press about their discontent with the organization, and twenty-six local committees resigned.[121] This incident also sheds some light on the manner in which Ni Putes ni Soumises had been functioning. First, many members could not accept Amara's adhesion to a right-wing government. The principal complaints about this were that she was serving under a Catholic minister who did not seem to accept the ideal of *laïcité*, and that the government as whole took a security-orientated approach to the problems of the *banlieues*. A more general worry was whether the organization could still claim to be politically independent if it was so publicly linked to the government. But other complaints about the organization itself also emerged: it has not been functioning in a democratic manner. Questions concerning Amara's move were simply ignored. Committees which complained were dismissed by Mohamed Abdi, her advisor. Even the committees which remained loyal accepted that 'the way in which the organization functions lacks transparency and democracy'.[122] Faced with the prospect of twenty-six committees leaving, the loyalists comforted themselves with the thought that half of the protesting committees were already dead, and the other half had never been really active: a revealing comment on the manner in which Ni Putes ni Soumises had been functioning.

The protestors formed a new organization, 'Les insoumis-es'. The continuity with the previous organization was clear: it proclaimed the values of *laïcité*, it defended the universal values of republican feminism, and it would fight against both fundamentalism and racism.[123] The contest between the two seems to have grown tense, with at least one accusation by the Insoumis-es that they had been violently attacked by persons connected with their former organization.[124]

The original organization continues, but it does appear to be significantly reduced in strength. The Lorient committee, which has a particularly well-documented website, reported that it had seventy members in July 2007, and that numbers declined afterwards.[125] In August 2008, twenty-two local committees remained. Of these, only four offered facilities to help women who had suffered abuse: a good test of the real strength of a particular committee. One could use the figures of the Lorient committee to provide an approximate estimation of the organization's current strength: if we assume that post-Amara, each of the 22 committees has 60 members (which may well be a generous estimate), then the total strength of the movement is about 1,320. Obviously, it does have a wider 'resonance', and more people may well participate in the events it organizes. But this seems a slim base for a movement which was once seen as representing 'the girls from the *banlieues*'.

The political goals of Ni Putes ni Soumises seem to be growing less clear. It still makes every effort to demonstrate its commitment to *laïcité*. A good example of its attitudes was presented in July 2008. There was a rather mysterious case of a Moroccan woman, resident in France, married to a Frenchman and the mother of three children born in France. She applied for French nationality, which was refused to her. The woman in question followed a strict interpretation of Islam, and wore a burqa which covered her face. Many suspected that she had been refused French nationality simply because of her burqa; others claimed that it was because of what the burqa represented; and there were still others who argued that in fact the Conseil d'État – the relevant decision-making body – had ignored her clothing.[126] Surprisingly, Ni Putes ni Soumises put out a press statement almost immediately, applauding the decision of the grounds that it constituted a reaffirmation of *laïcité*.[127] One has to note that this is a movement that seems to have moved very fast: in 2006 Amara was still working to aid women in irregular situations gain French nationality;[128] by 2008 the organization that she had created was celebrating the refusal of French nationality to a woman in a complex and unclear case. The desire to proclaim *laïcité* seemed to be taking priority over all other goals.

What is the role of this organization? If helping women who have suffered sexual violence is its priority, then how is it different from the other French organizations that carry out this valuable role? If it is a type of 'sister organization' to the Socialist Party, then how can it continue with its most celebrated member working in a right-wing government? If it is to defend *laïcité*, how is it different from the countless other organizations that have set themselves the same goal? Above all, if its role is to represent the opinions of the 'girls from the *banlieues*', how can it do this while adopting such a hostile and patronizing attitude to their lifestyles and cultures? More and more, Ni Putes ni Soumises seems to resemble a transmission belt for orders and directives from above, rather than a democratic organization that represents opinion from below. After eight years, Ni Putes ni Soumises still seems to be an organization in search of a cause. At the time of writing, it is too soon to make any judgement on Amara's performance as a government minister. Like Begag, it does appear that she is finding it difficult to be accepted as an equal partner, and – as yet – there is little sign of her urban policy achieving concrete results.

lack of identity

Conclusion

The people living in the *banlieues* suffer multiple discriminations. There is a dreadful overlapping of exclusions, whether social, economic, ethnic or religious in nature. One issue which repeatedly arises is their status in French society: as Zygmunt Bauman notes, a distinctive sign of a modern underclass is their collective absence of identity.[129] The solution proposed by Fadela Amara and Ni Putes ni Soumises is a traditional one: it reduces debate to a simple binary division between the friends of liberty (defined through the legacy of 1789) and the enemies, identified as Islamist. For the people of the *banlieues* to acquire a status as citizens in this context, they must be *like*; they must stand with the president of the Republic.[130] However, as distinct from the stance taken by Djavann, this allegiance is not unconditional. Amara wants to negotiate: she wants to choose which elements of French republican traditions she will validate (as indicated by the epigraph to this chapter), and she notes some of the failures of French social policies.

how they can integrate

Ni Putes ni Soumises may well serve as a 'safety net' for some who suffer a particular abuse; it is to be applauded for raising the questions of sexual morality and the double standard in the context of the *banlieues*. Its policies and activities certainly can produce tangible benefits for talented individuals within its organization, but it cannot be proposed as an effective, collective solution to a shared problem.

Chapter Four
Organizations and Institutions

Marianne, don't be afraid!
Demonstrator's slogan, February 2004

It makes an immigrant laugh to hear the fears of the nationalist, scared of
infection, penetration, miscegenation, when this is small fry, peanuts,
compared to what the immigrant fears – dissolution, disappearance.

Zadie Smith[1]

When immigrants to France considered that their stay would be
temporary, they did not expect any substantial institutional support
for their cultural or religious needs. The first mosques to be
constructed in France, such as the *grande mosquée* of Paris, were
understood as exceptional: the Parisian mosque was a tribute to
honour the 24,000 Algerian Arabs who died fighting for France
during the First World War.[2] This context changed in the late twentieth century: it was the decision to stay that initiated a deep-rooted
identity crisis. In a curious and unexpected manner, migrants, and
more particularly migrants' children and grandchildren, often grew
more determined to define themselves as Muslims.

Such developments are not unique to France: in the first years
of the twenty-first century, more Muslims are making Europe
their home. It has been estimated that there are between 11 and
12 million Muslims in the EU, amounting to about 4 per cent of
the total population. Of these, about 3.7 million come from
North Africa and other Arab regions, 3.1 million from Turkey and
0.8 million from the Indian sub-continent. Within the EU, France
has the highest proportion (about 7 per cent of its population),
followed by countries such as the Netherlands with 4.6 per cent,
Germany with 3 per cent and the UK with 2.7 per cent.[3]

This is a radically new situation. While Islam has had a long-term –
and largely beneficial – influence on European society, in the past
this has usually been produced by long-distance, indirect, temporary

contacts and, on occasion, through military conflict.[4] Today, Muslims are permanent residents. This is an innovation which has the potential to change both Islam and Europe profoundly.[5] The simple point that Muslims constitute a minority within a majority Christian-secular culture demands new thinking by Muslims concerning the status of Islam, which has normally flourished within sympathetic states. This situation has pushed Muslims, almost against their will, into new types of deterritorialized, diasporic belief, in which the internet is as important as the minaret, quite different from the previous forms that have dominated in the Middle East and Asia.[6]

In this chapter we will consider some institutions and organizations which have attempted to assist the integration of Muslims into French society. (As stated in chapter one, I will be using the term 'integration' in a morally neutral manner, meaning a competence to navigate one's way through a new society.) We will first consider some obstacles to this integration, and discuss the largely unsuccessful attempts by Muslims and others to create political organizations to oppose the March 2004 law on religious symbols. We will then consider the Conseil Français du Culte Musulman (CFCM – French Council of the Muslim Faith), an official representative body formed with the aim of creating a structure of dialogue between the French state and French Muslims, and the Union des Organisations Islamiques de France (UOIF – Union of Islamic Organizations of France), probably the largest Muslim organization in France. Lastly, this chapter will examine the vexed question of Muslim fundamentalism in France.

Placing Muslims in France

The first problem which this developing Muslim presence faced was simple: a lack of resources. In 1989 there was only one Islamic cemetery in France (at Bobigny). French Muslims lacked cemeteries, schools, mosques, meeting rooms, halal butchers and appropriate canteens in hospitals, schools and barracks.[7] Of course, some French people were concerned by these problems, and were sympathetic to proposals to aid the integration of Muslims into French society. One could cite the public appeal by the archbishop of Paris for Catholics to 'meet Muslims without fear',[8] or the recognition by Alain Boyer, a sub-prefect in Reims with much experience in this area, that the French state had a duty to provide Muslims with decent conditions for them to practice their religion.[9] Whether motivated by an ecumenical wish to welcome believers from a different faith, or a desire to provide hospitality to newcomers, or just a belief that the state's provisions should be interpreted fairly for the benefit of all French citizens, there have been French people who have worked to accommodate the new Muslim presence. Unfortunately, however, they have been in a minority.

Majority opinion was clearly revealed during the 'war of the veil'. One journalist even spoke of a 'veil test' to be applied to Muslim organizations and institutions, from which one could judge whether they were fit to be integrated into French society.[10] This is a revealing comment: it was certainly a test for which Muslims were ill-prepared and which they usually failed. The Stasi Commission's report and the resulting law placed French Muslims under great strain. Fear, hostility and suspicions concerning Muslims were voiced by many prominent public figures from Chirac downwards, usually with little effort to check evidence. The image of a mysterious conspiracy, developed and repeated by Brenner and Stasi, was an easy means by which to represent a little-known community to a wider public. Worse still, many politicians seem to have decided that voicing hostility to Muslims was an effective means by which to gain support. Sarkozy illustrates this turn towards open hostility. In 2002–3 he had led a bold endeavour to build bridges with Muslim organizations, developing a type of rapprochement with the UOIF. By 2007, however, as he presented himself as a presidential candidate, Sarkozy seemed to throw himself into voicing some of the most sensationalistic criticisms of Muslim beliefs and lifestyles.[11] In a television interview he told viewers

I wish to stress very firmly: no one has to live in France. And if you love France, then you must respect it … You must respect its rules, which means that you can only have one wife, that you do not allow the mutilation of your daughters, that you don't kill sheep in your flat and that you respect the laws of the Republic.[12]

The fact these practices had very little relevance whatsoever to the real lives of third-generation migrants was ignored: Sarkozy's aim was not to analyse Muslim cultures but to create a negative integration, a unity of French people against a mythical enemy. The result of such speeches was – obviously – increased hostility to Muslims.

Unfortunately, Sarkozy's speech was not exceptional. Similar sentiments were repeated constantly in the media. A series of 'bad news' stories constructed a radically negative image of all Muslims. These included:

- Philippe de Villiers' declaration in April 2006 that the UOIF was using its influence among Muslim workers at the Charles de Gaulle airport to impose sharia law on the site.
- the absurd, repellent court case in June 2008 when a marriage between two Muslims was annulled after the husband discovered that his bride was not a virgin.
- a court case in February 2007, brought by the CFCM and the UOIF against the satirical weekly, *Charlie-Hebdo*, which republished the now-notorious Danish caricatures of Mohammed, plus a series of new cartoons on the same theme.

The importance of these incidents lies in the manner in which they were interpreted by the media. First, they were presented as representative and typical of the opinions and morality of all French Muslims. The lesson to be learnt was that France harboured hundreds of thousands of unrepentant and dangerous opponents. Islam 'must renounce the most flagrant archaisms of its dogma', thundered *L'Express*, it must learn the lessons of 1789, 1806 (Napoleon's creation of the Consistoire for French Jews) and 1905 (the separation of the church and state).[13] The trial of *Charlie-Hebdo* was 'a trial from another age ... an obscurantist quarrel' according to *Le Monde*.[14] De Villiers called for the CFCM to be disbanded in order to facilitate a better adaptation of Islam to the French Republic and French lifestyles.[15] Regrettably, an essential act for all the Muslim organizations was, constantly, to issue denials and rebuttals of these pernicious rumours.[16]

Yet it was possible to see these incidents in a different light. For example, considering the case involving *Charlie-Hebdo*, if the CFCM chose to appeal to French laws to serve its interests, was it not making use of the facilities available to all French citizens? Was this not proof of the CFCM's *integration* into French legal and political structures? This illustrates – once again – the problems with the manner in which 'integration' is interpreted: it should not be interpreted as blind, uncritical loyalty to a series of absolute moral or political principles, but rather a willingness to accept a common framework within which to debate sometimes conflicting interests. Thus, for example, there are many points of Catholic dogma which potentially conflict with the Republican state's requirements, but few argue today that therefore the Catholic church should not or cannot be integrated into a *laïque* structure. French laws are quite clear on this point: the *laïque* state cannot intervene in matters of dogma, even if such dogma affirms points which contradict the laws.[17] The reception to the CFCM's court action suggested that a different standard was being applied to Islam. Hostile critics were demanding that French Islam be domesticated, adapted and reformed in a manner that has never been applied to the Catholic church.

The ultimate importance of these nasty newspaper stories, however, lies elsewhere. It has to be remembered that the mass of French Muslims did not think of these stories as the dilemmas which were splitting their community: indeed, there is little evidence for their strong interest in any of them. Instead, they are further examples of outside commentators seizing isolated incidents and telling the wider public: *this* is Islam.

The hostility directed towards Muslims did not only take the form of intangible rumours or verbal insults, it also had a practical effect on social policies. When Alain Morvan, the official in charge of educational facilities in the region around Lyon, refused to allow a Muslim group to open a school, he explained his decision: 'We are facing a plot against the Republic and its laws ... I do not want to see France sold off, bit by bit.'[18] In 2007, municipal councillors of the anti-immigrant MNR party used delaying tactics to obstruct the construction of a mosque in Montreuil (Seine-Saint-Denis).[19] In March 2004 two prayer-rooms near Annecy (Haute-Savoie) were burnt down.[20] In April 2008 148 Muslim graves in a military cemetery in the Pas-de-Calais were desecrated.[21] According to one estimate, between October 2003 and October 2004, twenty-eight mosques and prayer-rooms suffered attacks, and Muslim graves in eleven cemeteries were vandalized.[22] Alongside this, discrimination in work and housing, and a nasty, petty harassment is a daily experience for most Arabs and Muslims living in France: a point which was noted by the Stasi report in a single paragraph, but which must be constantly borne in mind when considering French Muslims' political and religious initiatives.[23]

Organizing for 'the war of the veil'

We must start by recognizing a basic conceptual problem: in general, Muslims really did not understand why the French population were so concerned about a few hundred veiled schoolgirls. In 1989, as the first battle in the war of the veil was fought out at Creil, neither the UOIF nor the Moroccan-linked FNMF intervened: in fact, no Muslim organization was publicly involved.[24] Fourteen years later, they were still puzzled. A typical reaction was that of the Etudiants musulmans de France (EMF – Muslim Students of France, an organization that is part of the UOIF). They asked: how can a bit of cloth bring down a 200-year-old Republic?[25] At first sight, this might seem like a piece of clever rhetoric: I would suggest that readers should take the statement at face value, an honest expression of bewilderment.

As was seen in chapter one, there was no unified Muslim attitude to the veil. However, most studies found that a small majority of Muslims were against the proposed law. One opinion poll in January 2004 found that 53 per cent of them opposed it, and 42 per cent supported the law. (The same poll also found that 95 per cent of Muslims believed in equality between the sexes, and 71 per cent thought that they had heard too much about the veil and schools.)[26] French Muslims' divergent attitudes made it difficult for their organizations to express a clear, united attitude to an awkward problem.

Some Muslims strongly criticized the proposed law. Why is *laïcité* receptive to other religions, but coercive towards Muslims? Why didn't the Stasi Commission hear from veiled girls until the last moment? asked one Muslim.[27] The biggest and best-established Muslim organizations, however, did not encourage their members to oppose the law. The CFCM was pointedly restrained in its pronouncements on the matter. It had never been intended as a fighting organization, and its divergent members did not share a common position. Its president, Dalil Boubakeur, issued a statement actually approving the bulk of the Stasi report – whose principal subject, after all, was meant to be *laïcité* – but raising some questions about the proposal to ban *ostensible* religious signs from schools.[28]

During the war of the veil, Sarkozy bypassed the CFCM. He flew to Cairo to request a judgement from the venerable Islamic authorities in the Al-Azhar University.[29] If even Sarkozy considered that this foreign institution was the ultimate authority on such matters, then what was the point of the CFCM?

Organized opposition to the proposed law came from a range of divergent sources outside the CFCM. The tiny and ultra-militant Parti des Musulmans Français (PMF – French Muslims' Party), created in 1997, organized a demonstration in Strasbourg on 21 December 2003: about 650 people attended.[30] On the same date there was a rather different demonstration, largely organized from a website – *www.ma-liberte.com* – run by three female students, whose appeal was then also publicized by an established independent Muslim website, *www.oumma.com*, not linked to any of the bigger religious organizations. This demonstration attracted about a thousand demonstrators, most of them young and female.[31] While small in size, the protest caused both astonishment and concern in the media. Was this the beginning of a larger Muslim backlash? The French press were suspicious about this event: the manner in which it was organized was 'a story which is too good to be true', commented one journalist,[32] while another considered that there was 'a dreadful lack of transparency' concerning its organization.[33] The demonstrators had arranged for a group of male Muslims to provide a security service: given the tense climate, it was understandable that the female protestors were concerned for their safety. For the French press, however, there was only one way to interpret this: it was an example of fundamentalism in practice. Many observers simply refused to accept that women could freely demonstrate for the right to wear the veil: it was repeatedly claimed that they must be acting under instructions, or even that they had been intimidated. One article concerning a later, similar demonstration considered that 'Islamist bigots' must have been behind these women: 'They can stone them, veil them, mutilate them, and they make them demonstrate.'[34] 'The veil is a pretext, and the veiled girls are ... the Trojan horse for Islamism in the Republic.'[35] This was the work of radical imams, avoiding the light of publicity, who worked to develop 'a militant *communautarisme*'.[36] At least two daily papers and one weekly circulated rumours suggesting a type of connection between these demonstrations and the far-right National Front, usually only in the indirect form that the National Front was the sole political group which would benefit from the protests, but it was also hinted that 'a conjunction of subversive interests' existed.[37]

The fact that the CFCM refused to lead opposition, that the UOIF did not participate in the demonstrations, and that the controversial Tariq Ramadan held a seminar in Evry rather than lead Muslims to protest, were all points which – paradoxically – also aroused suspicion. Journalists expected and even wanted to see militant fundamentalist fanatics in the street, and seemed disappointed to hear Ramadan telling his mixed audience of men and women, Muslims and non-Muslims, to use legal means to oppose the proposed law.[38]

A second set of demonstrations and protests to oppose the proposed law began in mid-January 2004. More than 10,000 marched in Paris, and there may have been another 4,000 in Lille and 1,800 in Marseille. While the UOIF did not participate in the biggest demonstration in Paris, some of its provincial branches joined the smaller protests.[39] To the fury of some French patriots, the demonstrators sang the *Marseillaise*, waved tricolour flags, held up voting cards and chanted a variety of provocative slogans: 'It wasn't because of my big brother, my father or my husband ... it was *I* who chose to wear the veil!'[40] 'Marianne, don't be afraid!'[41] 'Veiled women, unveiled women: solidarity!'[42] On 5 February, a group of largely secular organizations lobbied the National Assembly: about 1,000 people were present in Paris, and another 400 in Strasbourg.[43] This cycle of protests and demonstrations ended on 8 March 2004 when a contingent of 5,000 people, all protestors against the law, mainly women, some veiled, joined the annual International Women's Day march in Paris.[44] They faced some ferocious opposition from *laïcistes* within the main demonstration: they were jeered, jostled and spat on.

These protests were either ignored or condemned by the most prominent Muslim authorities. Dalil Boubakeur, speaking as president of the CFCM, explicitly advised Muslims not to attend one demonstration. He also noted that the demonstrations on 17 January 2004 represented less than 0.6 per cent of the Muslims of France.[45] The presence of the tiny PMF may also have discouraged some from participating. Many commentators remained suspicious of the UOIF because of its *lack* of participation in these protests: for some, this suggested that it favoured the law in order to encourage Muslim private schools.[46] Others considered that it was attempting to appear 'moderate' because of its involvement with the CFCM, but it still retained a fundamentalist base.[47] The truth seems to be that these new Muslim associations, often created for a religious, administrative or charitable role, were genuinely uncertain about how to react in these difficult circumstances. Indecisive or ambiguous pronouncements were an expression of a lack of political confidence, rather than an expression of some subtle and mysterious strategy.

One of the most interesting developments from this political clash was an indirect result of an initiative by Tariq Ramadan, which led to the formation of a radically new organization, Une école pour tou-te-s (EPT – a school for everyone – the French title specifies that this means all boys and all girls). This brought together libertarian-minded activists from left-wing groups and feminist organizations with more politically orientated strands among Muslims. It did not include the UOIF directly, although the UOIF's student and youth organizations were involved. The Trotskyist Ligue Communiste Révolutionnaire (LCR – Communist Revolutionary League) refused to participate, but its youth wing, the Jeunesse Communiste Révolutionnaire (JCR – Communist Revolutionary Youth), joined. There were contacts with the older civil liberties organization LDH, and the anti-racist MRAP, but neither joined.[48] EPT's first appeal was issued on 23 January 2004, and signed by the prominent French feminist Christine Delphy, the Green Euro-deputy Alima Boumédienne-Thiery, and the leading Green activist, Noël Mamère. Its members were aware that the force of public opinion was now clearly against them: one internal document spoke of the need to 'deconstruct the negative image' created by a 'systematic stigmatization'.[49] While proclaiming their loyalty to the principles of *laïcité*, they insisted that this admirable principle should not be interpreted to stigmatize and penalize young women.[50] An EPT leaflet circulating in Rennes proclaimed: 'Yes to *laïcité*! No to laws which exclude!'[51] Throughout the spring and summer it was often assumed that the EPT was preparing for a wave of protests in September 2004, when the law would be applied for the first time in the schools. In practice, Une école pour tou-te-s did succeed in organizing some events – a film-show here, a protest meeting there – but did not lead a substantial movement.[52] External events later stifled most protests, as will be shown.

In August 2004 the UOIF finally organized some protest activities: it formed a '15 March Committee', named after the date when the law was adopted. It offered support to veiled schoolgirls in conflict with their schools. It was clear that this was a scrupulously legalistic body which sought to exploit the inherent ambiguity within the law – after all, what exactly constitutes an *ostensible* sign? One of its first statements read: 'The committee strongly stresses its apolitical nature, its absence of any ambition other than that of working for the pupils, and its refusal to transform itself into a pressure group.'[53] Once again, this hardly sounds like the fanatical fundamentalism that the press so desperately wanted to find behind the protests.

The context changed dramatically when two French journalists were taken hostage in Iraq by a mysterious Islamist group, which threatened to kill them if veiled schoolgirls were banned from attending school in September 2004. The response among French Muslims was clear: they were horrified by this development. Fatima Ajbli, a leading member of the UOIF, made an eloquent statement. 'I am terrified that my headscarf will be associated with people like that. I refuse to allow my headscarf to be stained with blood.'[54] For perhaps the first time, politicians and the media looked to CFCM to act: it did not disappoint them. The CFCM firmly and unequivocally condemned the hostage taking, and even sent a delegation out to Iraq to attempt to negotiate with the group. Lhaj Thami Brèze, the president of UOIF, accurately observed that French 'Muslims have shown a massive, spontaneous support for France. They have shown that they need no foreign guidance.'[55] The Minister of the Interior, Dominique Villepin, even appeared at the *grande mosquée* of Paris to thank Muslims publicly for their support. The small groups – the PMF, EPT and the 15 March Committee – which had prepared to contest the law, in whatever manner, now felt intimidated, and were far more reluctant to act.

Under these circumstances, the return to school in September 2004 was a subdued affair. The UOIF still protested that the bandana was not outlawed, and Luc Ferry, the Minister for Education, once more demonstrated his extraordinarily detailed and perceptive understanding of Islamic practices by stating that there were ordinary bandanas and Islamic bandanas.[56] The situation in French schools remains confused: veil-wearing and *ostensible* signs are certainly prohibited, but not even the Minister of Education has been able to define exactly what this means.

The conflicts and protests which unfolded in 2003–4 have some wider significance. These constitute – arguably – the first occasion on which the majority French population were informed of the lifestyles and cultures of ordinary French Muslims. The lessons they learnt were clearly misleading. This point also clarifies the context in which Muslims tried to organize their lives and their faith. As a general rule, they faced opposition from ignorant and prejudiced people.

In search of French Islam: towards the CFCM

The question of how to represent French Muslims to the French state has been a long-running debate, leading to a series of questions concerning the nature of Islam in France. Here, we will first briefly review the manner in which Islam is understood by Western commentators and scholars, and then turn to consider the French policies which led to the creation of the CFCM.

One common misconception about Islam concerns its structures and hierarchies. There is an assumption, particularly among critics, that Islam is a cruel religion, therefore a tyrannical religion, and therefore a strictly structured and hierarchical religion. This short book is not intended to reveal 'the truth' about Islam: suffice it to say that while there is much to criticize in Islamic traditions, criticisms should be based on accurate information. In reality, Muslim structures are not centralized and strict, but loose, informal and often provisional in nature, for Islam stresses the direct relationship between the believer and God. As Karen Armstrong notes: 'Each Muslim had a unique responsibility to obey God's commands, and no religious authority, no institution … and no specialized group of "clergy" could come between God and the individual Muslim.'[57] Islam's structures are therefore 'amorphous' rather than tyrannical.[58] It is even possible to argue that while Islam is a faith, it is not a church.[59] It has neither a baptism ritual nor a procedure for the registration of births: in order to consider oneself a Muslim, it is enough to believe it, notes Soheib Bencheikh.[60] Since the ninth century, scholars – or *ulama* – have acted as a co-ordinating force through which to preserve unity and common identity across Islam, but even they have been divided into diverse strands, opposed by other social forces, and their work has never taken the form of a single vision imposed on all believers.[61]

Religious faith proved surprisingly resilient among the first generation of Muslim immigrants in France. Neil MacMaster notes how it formed 'a crucial psychological defence, a means of preserving a sense of identity and personal cohesion ... an anchor, a means of resisting depersonalization' in the difficult context within which the immigrants lived and worked.[62] A process of 're-Islamization' is now taking place among second- and third-generation immigrant families. This can be seen as a form of rational choice for those who find that they no longer fit into the old or new countries. Their new Islam is not the Islam of their parents or grandparents. Bencheikh probably speaks for a whole generation when he describes his parents' religion as a 'series of strict duties and a never-ending list of proscriptions, given without any intelligent or convincing explanations'.[63] Instead, re-Islamization encourages a new form of faith, compatible with the status of a migrant. One interviewee explained to Yamina Benguigi that she felt caught between two cultures: 'I had to find a refuge, somewhere in the middle ... For me, this came from Islam. Thanks to the headscarf, I found a religious identity.'[64]

In recent decades the Muslim presence in France has expanded. French Muslims are concentrated in the main cities of France (Paris, Lyon and Marseilles), with a subsidiary presence out to the north-east in Lille and Strasbourg (see table 4.1).

Table 4.1: Estimates of the proportion of Muslims living in France, by region, 2001[65]

Region	Proportion of France's Muslims
Ile-de-France	35%
PACA (Provence, Alpes, Côte d'Azur)	20%
Rhône-Alpes	15%
Nord-Pas-de-Calais	10%

At first sight, one gains an impression of the rapid development of institutions and facilities in these areas. In 2001 there were 1,500 mosques and prayer rooms in France, by 2008, 2,000, with 16 new mosques being opened each year.[66] However, relatively speaking, facilities for Muslims in France remain scarce and underequipped. In a survey of 1,685 Muslim places of worship in 2005, it was found that only 20 could hold more than 1,000 people, and a further 54 could contain between 500 and 1,000 people. Two-thirds of them were actually just small rooms, with space for at most 50 people.[67] Compared to France's other religions, Muslims clearly have less access to places of worship (see table 4.2).

Table 4.2: Places of worship per believer in France, 2006[68]

Religion	Places of worship per believer
Judaism	1 per 234
Protestantism	1 per 671
Catholicism	1 per 1,033
Islam	1 per 2,967

The slowly growing urban visibility of Islam is not the equivalent of the construction of a united religious identity: many mosques are run by locally based associations. Even within particular towns, Muslims are divided among themselves. A proposal to build a giant 'cathedral mosque' in Marseilles, ended – in part – because the mayor was not able to negotiate with divergent and even rival Muslim groups. He was surprised by this: his initial expectation was that all Muslims would share common interests.[69] Differences between Muslims take various forms: sometimes they are ethnic in character, with the Islams of sub-Saharans, of Turks and of Asians taking a distinctly different form from those of North Africans.[70] There is a significant difference between those who consider that Islam is an individualist, even mystical religion and those who stress formal, collective worship. There are also differences in the interpretation of Islam, particularly between those – like Tariq Ramadan – who believe that Muslims should be active *as Muslims* in their respective societies, and those – like the Tabligh, to be discussed below – whose Islam leads to withdrawal from society.

An estimate from 2001 found that only 36 per cent of French Muslims could be considered as practicing Muslims: they were concentrated among the richest and poorest. About 20 per cent regularly attended mosques every Friday: 29 per cent of Muslim men, and 8 per cent of women.[71] One point needs to be stressed here: Islam is not necessarily as 'church-centred' a religion as Christianity. One can regard oneself as a sincere Muslim, one can practise the prescribed ritual of praying five times a day, *without* going to a mosque. There is also a general convention that collective praying is sexually segregated: in the smaller prayer-rooms this is obviously impractical and so – regrettably – female access to places for collective prayer is often severely restricted.

French Muslims are also politically divided. For those living in the depressed *banlieues*, apathy and alienation from the political process has become the norm, with a corresponding failure to register as voters.[72] Among the more active, there are some constants: a greater proportion of Muslims sympathise with left-wing parties than among the wider population. An enquiry in December 2003 found that 49 per cent of Muslims intended to vote for left-wing parties, while only 35 per cent of the French population had similar sympathies.[73] More detailed information can be seen in an opinion poll from April 2003 (see table 4.3).

Table 4.3: Political sympathies of French Muslims, April 2003[74]

Political tendency	Proportion of French-Muslim support
Far Left	7%
Communist Party	6%
Socialist Party	38%
Greens	14%
UDF	3%
UMP	13%
FN/MNR	1%
No Party	11%

In the 1990s there was an interesting point of contact between experienced *beur* activists and the Greens, who seemed less dogmatically attached to *laïque* doctrines than the Socialists or Communists.[75] The figures in table 4.3 show how the Greens continue to attract a relatively high level of support from French Muslims. However, following the mainstream parties' recent espousal of 'diversity' as means by which to combat discrimination, individual Muslims can be found across the political spectrum, including in the right-wing parties: Begag's entry to the Villepin government and Amara's adhesion to Sarkozy are merely the most prominent examples of this tendency. Even the National Front can boast Farid Smahi, a member since 1997, and elected as its representative on Regional Council for the Ile-de-France in 1998–2002.[76]

The first image of Muslims that circulates in the media suggests a disciplined, conspiratorial force, launching its schoolgirl soldiers into every school in France to subvert the Republic. The most basic research suggests a more complex reality: a varied mosaic of divergent, inexperienced and generally under-equipped associations and organizations, whose complexity cannot be understood through the clichéd categories of moderates and extremists. On the other hand, all these people do share something: they are members of France's fastest growing religion. Obviously, it could be argued that developing and structuring Islam in France is something which should be left to Muslims to organize. In practice, this type of policy would allow foreign powers to finance and therefore shape French Islam. One comment from 1995 noted the results of such policies: French Islam was 'administratively Algerian, financially Saudi Arabian, and theologically Egyptian'.[77] Another estimate in 2003 found that 90 per cent of French imams were foreigners, and half of them could not speak French.[78] Nearly all French politicians fear these foreign influences within French society, and so prefer the idea of creating – and therefore paying for – a *French* Islam.

There was an established solution to some of these issues, provided by the *grande mosquée* of Paris. This was an old, prestigious institution, with close links to both the French and Algerian governments. In 1995 the then Minister of the Interior, the conservative Charles Pasqua, returned to the older policy of treating it as a privileged interlocutor. He even negotiated a 'Charter for the Muslim Faith in France' with the mosque's director Dalil Boubakeur. This was signed by eighty-two prominent Muslim personalities.[79] The problem with this policy was that it was obvious that the *grande mosquée* had a weak claim to represent French Muslims: in particular, it had few links to the new local associations. In 2000 a later Minister of the Interior, the leftist and firmly republican Jean-Pierre Chevènement, chose to concentrate his efforts on the creation of a new representative structure through dialogue with the wider Muslim community.[80] The CFCM of 2003 was the final result.

Chevènement's initial discussions were inconclusive. After 2002, Sarkozy adopted a different approach: he made it almost his personal mission to unite the divergent organizations into a stable and coherent institution. A key term, frequently repeated by commentators, was the idea of finding 'a balance' between them.[81] Rather than privileging the *grande mosquée* of Paris, Sarkozy negotiated directly with other Muslim associations, to the surprise of many in his own party (the conservative UMP). In particular, he met the UOIF.[82] This decision to concentrate on the established organizations was significant: on the one hand, the three biggest Muslim associations represented about 60 per cent of all French Muslims in established organizations; on the other hand, they still only represented about one-tenth of all French Muslims.[83] By concentrating on the organizations, Sarkozy was in danger of ignoring the masses.

Sarkozy's record in this field is still difficult to judge. In May 2003 he clearly succeeded in establishing an institution which claimed to represent all French Muslims: something of which no previous minister had been capable. But in the long run, the CFCM has not performed well, and each year seems to have drawn it into ever more serious crises. According to Tariq Ramadan, it was broken when it was created, and it has remained out of order ever since,[84] while the general secretary of the UOIF, Fouad Alaoui, describes it as in 'permanent crisis'.[85]

A complex, indirect and quite heavily qualified voting procedure was introduced to elect both regional councils (CRCM) and a central CFCM council. There was an immediate problem concerning how to identify and authenticate the electorate. Given the tradition of 'neutral' censuses, the French state possessed no reliable data on who was a Muslim.[86] How were voting rights to be distributed? After much discussion, it was decided to use the criteria of the size of mosques and prayer rooms, measured in square metres. This rewarded success: those who had acquired funds and municipal authorization were now granted representation. Those who had not succeeded, or who did not go to a mosque, were denied direct access to the CFCM. Hajji and Marteau estimate that about 3 million French Muslims were disenfranchised in this way.[87] Significantly, an opinion poll from April 2003 found that 42 per cent of French Muslims had not heard of the CFCM.[88]

A substantial number of mosques and prayer rooms refused to participate. Experts' estimates on this point vary, but the substantial point cannot be denied. Thus Frank Peter considers that some 1,200 out of the 1,600 registered mosques and prayer rooms participated in the elections, raising the obvious question of why approximately a quarter did not.[89] From these participating institutions, 4,042 electors were chosen, who in turn elected a 41 (later 43) member council.[90] The results of the two elections in 2003 and 2005 are shown in table 4.4.

Table 4.4: Results of elections to the CFCM, 2003 and 2005[91]

	UOIF	FNMF	Grande mosquée	Independents	CCMTF
2003	13	16	6	4	2
2005	10	19	10	3	1

CCMTF = Comité de coordination des musulmans turcs de France (Coordinating Committee of Turkish Muslims of France)

Negotiations in 2002 had fixed limits to the electoral process. It was agreed that Boubakeur, the director of the *grande mosquée* of Paris since 1992, would serve as the president of the CFCM, however many votes his organization gained. The greatest interest concerned the rivalry between the UOIF and the Moroccan-linked FNMF. While the latter was a smaller and less well-structured organization, it benefitted from the strong support of the Moroccan embassy, whose efforts were successful in persuading Moroccans to vote for the FNMF.[92] While it was possible to see these elections as an approximate equivalent to a parliamentary process, the truth seems to be that they seemed irrelevant to most French Muslims. The elections thus inadvertently demonstrated the weakness of the top-down approach pioneered by Sarkozy.[93]

By July 2004, the CFCM still had no direct subsidy from the state, no public phone number or website, little media presence and clearly was not working as a force to unify (or merely coordinate) the more organized federations it claimed to represent. It possessed no legislative ability.[94] Its principal role was unclear: was it 'theological, bureaucratic or representative'?[95] It did not seem to represent a large proportion of young, third-generation Muslims whose principal point of contact with their faith was through more locally based associations.[96] (Tariq Ramadan, on occasion, could claim to speak for this sector.) In the CFCM, Boubakeur attempted to preserve the privileged status of the *grande mosquée*, while the FNMF and UOIF opposed this: the FNMF by exploiting its connections with the Moroccan government, the UOIF by attempting to develop a base in France.[97] One perpetual source of discord is the right to certificate halal meat: this is a useful source of revenue, one of the few available to these groups from within France.

One rule in the game quickly became established: organizations attempting to gain the government's support would label themselves as 'moderate' and stigmatize their opponents as 'fundamentalists' or 'extremists'. As the terms were never defined, either term could easily be applied to any of the involved groups. Thus when the UOIF called a meeting of CRCM leaders to protest about the delays in the CFCM elections, Boubakeur promptly denounced them as fundamentalists.[98]

Boubakeur made the mistake of thinking that, in the last analysis, the French government would always support him, and hence made a number of well-publicized threats to walk out of the CFCM. The first of these took place in September 2004; on this occasion a private meeting with Sarkozy persuaded him to remain, but in return the minister accepted that Boubakeur would remain president of the CFCM whoever won the 2005 elections to its council. In May 2005 the UOIF's Alaoui resigned from the CFCM. His resignation was rather a provisional gesture: he was waiting for the forthcoming elections. In an interview with *Libération* he still defended the institution, arguing that it 'was a major achievement for the insertion and normalization of Islam into a French context'.[99] In 2008 Boubakeur attempted the same tactic once again. This time, there was nobody in the government to support him – he was a pontiff without a church, comments Frégosi[100] – and the CFCM elections were then held without the participation of the *grande mosquée* of Paris.

A pernicious mixture of internal tensions within the federations themselves, external tensions from the demands of consulates and other foreign powers, and a significant gap between the organization and the mass of French Muslims has led to the CFCM performing extremely badly.[101]

The UOIF

UOIF was created in 1983 by a small group of French-Tunisians in the eastern department of the Meurthe-et-Moselle. In 1990 it made a small but significant change to its name, from the original Union des Organisations Islamiques *en* (in) France to Union des Organisations Islamiques *de* (of) France. This shift could be seen as encapsulating the whole history of the Muslim presence: no longer temporary residents *in* a land, they were now claiming to be part *of* that country.

At its origins, the UOIF was linked to the Muslim Brothers, often seen as the world's first fundamentalist group. This group was created in Egypt in 1926 and was responsible for several unsuccessful assassination attempts on Nasser, and for the killing of Sadat in 1981. It is still officially banned in Egypt, although it has built up a substantial semi-legal presence. This certainly sounds terrifying, but it has to be remembered that before Nasser came to power, the group was largely non-violent and throughout its history it has shown a real commitment to social reform. In contemporary Egypt, it has a prominent (if illegal) women's organization and has promoted the creation of schools and hospitals.[102] In other words, the simple equation 'UOIF = Muslim Brothers = fundamentalism = terrorists' distorts a more complex political and religious reality.[103] Moreover, one should allow for the possibility that a group can evolve: the large and increasingly experienced UOIF of 2008 is very different from the ill-equipped grouping of 1983. By December 2002 it directly controlled about 30 mosques, and had influence over between 150 and 200 others.[104] In the mosques it directs, the sermons are usually in French: another obvious sign of its willingness to adapt. In 2005 it had approximately 50,000 members, making it the largest Muslim organization in France.[105] It offers them an Islam stripped of national or ethnic traits, described by Alaoui as a 'true Islam: centrist, integrated, republican and open'.[106] During the course of its existence, its single most obvious trait has been its quest for power: it was more than willing to cooperate with Sarkozy, reluctant to fight on the issue of the veil, and keen to develop its position with the CFCM as a means to acquiring greater influence. Its leading members are 'bearded men in suits and ties, carrying briefcases': quite different from the media stereotype of the eccentrically or exotically dressed fundamentalist.[107]

The UOIF quickly developed a type of showcase event: its annual congress cum fair cum marketplace at Le Bourget, near Paris which has also been labelled 'France's leading Muslim matrimonial agency'.[108] Five thousand people attended this event in December 1989, 30,000 in 2000 and 60,000 in May 2001, making it the best-attended Muslim event in Europe.[109] Press reports marvelled at the range of Islamic products on sale at this event, from translations of the Koran, through hijabs and other Islamically correct forms of dress, Moroccan-style furniture, to a sweet fizzy beverage labelled 'Muslim Up', an Islamic alternative to Coca-Cola.[110] Over the past decades, a series of prominent politicians have attended. Sarkozy used the event as a platform to speak to the UOIF in April 2003. He was warmly welcomed: delegates saw him as a friend to the organization. Nonetheless, during his speech, he was loudly booed when he insisted that French identity cards must carry pictures of unveiled women.[111] In April 2007, as the campaign for the presidential election grew fiercer, only one elected politician attended the congress: François Grosdidier, the UMP's national secretary. Presidential candidates from the major parties had been invited, but clearly had considered that it was not in their interest to attend.[112]

The UOIF has faced serious internal problems. In 2002, issues came to a head in the UOIF's youth wing, JMF. Many of its leading members resigned. Farid Abdelkrim, ex-president of the JMF, explained that 'among the members of the administration council, I was the only one who was born in France'. This tension has been sometimes described as a conflict between *blédards*, meaning those from the rural areas of North Africa, and *chebab*, opinionated urban youth who have grown up in France.[113] In general, the *blédards* tend to be conservative and seek social mobility upwards in France, while the *chebab* are more likely to be leftist and work within associations. The *blédards* have the advantage of being able to speak Arabic fluently, permitting links with the Gulf states and thus with their financial resources. This financial support has been important; but it is clear that the UOIF is working as hard as it can to achieve its autonomy. Alaoui claimed, in 2004, that the Gulf states' contribution to the UOIF's budget was down to 10 per cent.[114] An article in *Le Monde* estimated that in 2006 about a fifth of the UOIF's budget came from abroad.[115] This point is important to the UOIF itself, which tries hard to present itself as a genuinely French movement, quite different from the *grande mosquée* of Paris and the FNMF, with their respective Algerian and Moroccan links.[116]

In general, the UOIF is reluctant to support public demonstrations: it never participated in any of the Parisian demonstrations to protest against the law on the veil, although some of its provincial groups did join regional demonstrations. Its decision in November 2004 to back a demonstration which protested against anti-Semitism and islamophobia was genuinely exceptional.[117] In November 2005, apparently against the advice of other members of the CFCM, the UOIF issued a statement voicing despair concerning the urban riots which raged in the *banlieues*, and calling for a return to calm. It later even issued a fatwa, condemning participation in the riots.[118] Significantly, therefore, one of its most important public political acts in recent years was to recommend an *end* to action. This point tells us something about the nature of the organization: it is not a grouping of political militants. Most of its members join because they admire the UOIF's commitment to efficient administration, because they see it as a means to integrate Islam into French society, or because they have a religious commitment to Islam, not because they are motivated by a political project.

In June 2004 the UOIF issued a position statement on the issue of the veil. It was painstakingly legalistic, pointing out that the new law did not ban all head-coverings, warning against 'exaggerated reactions' and recommending that pupils should not renounce their studies. It offered 'moral support' to all pupils who found themselves in conflict with their schools, but recommended that they contact their CRCM to discuss it.[119] Frustratingly, this was reported in *Le Monde* as 'the UOIF invites Muslims to ignore the law': in reality, it was asking its members to respect the letter of the law, but to use whatever opportunities they could find within the law to save their headscarves.[120]

The elections of 2005 and 2008 suggested that the UOIF was losing influence within the CFCM. It has failed to translate its position as France's biggest Muslim organization into real power; it seems to frustrate both the upwardly mobile (by not advancing their integration into political structures) and the underclass (by failing to achieve the development of resources for the disinherited).

Fundamentalism in France

Once again, we must start by noting the media myth, according to which: 'Islam is growing ideological due to the activities of exiled militant islamists who indoctrinate young Muslims in the *banlieues* who are searching for an identity.'[121] Such reports have an obvious problem: they never define exactly what they mean by 'fundamentalism', *intégrisme* or 'islamism', and thus they allow readers to imagine that any eccentrically dressed Muslim in the *banlieues* is a member of a dedicated conspiratorial group. When reading such reports, one can readily sympathize with Bencheikh's weary comment: French journalists 'have only one word to describe anything that moves: *intégrisme*.'[122]

The main problem with the term 'fundamentalism' is that it is drawn from a tendency within Christianity to purify faith by a return to the apparent primitive simplicity of the Bible. Islam, however, had always been a far more book-centred religion than Christianity. Indeed, for centuries, the first task of many Muslim schools was to teach their pupils to memorize the entire Koran. Thus, the Christian model of 'fundamentalism' is difficult to apply to any particular Muslim tendency. Backward-looking tendencies exist within Islam, and some stress this type of inspiration as the defining characteristic of Islamic fundamentalism. Thus Aziz Al-Azmeh writes: 'I define fundamentalism as that moment in all religions which gives primitivism and primevalism precedence over history, which seeks to eliminate history and regard it as, at best, an illegitimate accretion onto the pristine beginning.'[123] It is open to question whether this type of definition is coherent or genuinely perceptive. The Turkish sociologist of religion, Ayşe Saktander, produces a more subtle, contextualized characterization: 'A discourse of moral transformation which has helped to tend the wounds of the long-lasting political powerlessness of Muslims before the hegemonic power of the West.'[124] In this analysis, Saktander suggests a dialectic of power defining the relationship between Western authorities and Islamic communities, and sees fundamentalism as an element within this contest. Of all the various analyses, however, that produced by Olivier Roy is probably the most convincing. He distinguishes between an original fundamentalism which attempted to create a morally pure society through action by a state: post-1979 Iran might be the best example of this. Such attempts clearly failed. Contemporary fundamentalist movements are therefore, for Roy, actually *neo*-fundamentalisms, which substitute individual actions and social movements for the failed project of state action. Neo-fundamentalism is 'the demand by the believer to live out their faith fully, to shape all aspects of their life, including political and social aspects, to a religious norm'.[125] Roy's definition concentrates our attention on the actions of the individual believer, and is probably most useful in a discussion concerning French Muslims.

The issue of fundamentalism (or *intégrisme*) has certainly worried the French state, particularly after a number of terrorist attacks in France linked to the mysterious Algerian group, the GIA.[126] This issue has provided a focus for the French police as they monitor activities of groups that they consider may try to emulate the GIA's terrorism. Their research, however, often runs into the familiar problem of confusing cause and effect, and is frequently structured along the lines of Brenner's muddled conceptualization.

A police report from July 2004 stated that of 630 'difficult areas', over 300 were experiencing a *repli communautaire*, a turning in on themselves, even a 'self-ghettoization'. (This would amount to about 1.8 million people.) It was significant how the police researchers defined a *repli communataire*. Its signs included the opening of ethnic shops, the development of Islam and the presence of non-French speakers. North African women in these areas who followed European lifestyles could be insulted in the streets. The report highlighted the growth of Salafist and Tabligh groups.[127] Police researchers also noted how the face of some urban quarters seemed to be changing. A report concerning Seine-Saint-Denis, the department to the north of Paris, described an area defined by halal butchers, Islamic bookshops, kebab fast-food stores, travel agents offering trips to Mecca, phone facilities to call back home and North African hairdressers. On Fridays, the mosques are full, and young men listen, patiently, to an hour-long sermon in Arabic (which they do not understand) followed by a five-minute French-language summary. At first sight, this could all be seen as evidence of a concerted urban take-over by Muslim forces. However, local activists pointed out that no particular group was directing Muslim initiatives. Salafist groups seemed to be gaining new recruits, the Tabligh seemed to be losing members. But no one was 'in charge' of this urban transformation. And the older tendencies were still present: those who could get out, left. One local Muslim activist predicted that in a few years, the only organisations left in such *banlieues* would be Muslim associations, a few football teams and the National Front.[128]

A police report from July 2005 drew on interviews with 1,610 people identified as 'radical Muslims'. In general, they were young men, with an average age of thirty-two. The means by which they had discovered radical Islam were considered: 37 per cent had attended local meetings, 27 per cent had learnt of the creed through their spouse, 15 per cent were converted by missionaries and 4 per cent experienced a conversion while in prison. Of this sample, 28 per cent belonged to the Tabligh group, 30 per cent to Salafist groups.[129]

Didier Lapeyronne made the obvious criticism of the 'Muslim takeover' thesis: this was a two-way process; the wider French society was also turning its back on the people of the *banlieues*. In the specific context of the *banlieues*, Islam was more likely to function as a form of moralization that pulled many out of delinquency.[130] One can also criticize the assumption that the existence of an Islamist group in a *banlieue* automatically means its domination of the area. In Nadia Kiwan's careful research on North Africans in the *banlieues*, she found that among her sample of twenty-one young men, only two had any connections to religious associations.[131] Furthermore, one notes how selling a type of food, offering hair dressing facilities and opening a mosque are all being equated in these reports as somehow similar: like Brenner, the police research seems to skid over concepts, listing new – and sometimes undesirable – features and simply assuming that these all add up to a single, new phenomenon with a single cause.

The police reports single out two groups: the Tabligh and the Salafists. Neither tendency has participated in the CFCM, and each merits some consideration.

The Tabligh are a pietist movement which originated in nineteenth-century India. They were formed in France in 1972, with the title 'Faith and Practice', and have become notorious for their extreme moralism, dividing the world into the forbidden (haram) and the permitted (halal).[132] One convert explained to a reporter the effects of joining the group: 'I don't drink anymore, I don't smoke anymore, and I've stopped running after the girls.'[133] They avoid political activities, and seek to live in harmony with the French. In general, parents are relatively unconcerned by the activities of this inward-looking group.[134] Desirable or not, it is hard to imagine that this rigorous and demanding form of Islam could be the basis of any viable mass movement in the *banlieues*.

Salafism began in the nineteenth century as one of many movements that sought to reform Islam in the face of the West's growing political, cultural and economic domination of Muslim countries. Salafists criticized both the Ottomans and the Sufis for having betrayed the original message of Islam, and for failing to combat the West's advances. In the twentieth century this message encountered a sympathetic reception from the Saudi monarchy, the rulers of one of the rare Muslim countries which was never colonized by Western forces. In this form, the movement lost much of its original reforming and educational drive, and became 'puritan and backward-looking'.[135] While Salafism remains marked by different tendencies – some call for armed struggle, some for blind obedience to the Saudi monarchy, and some still discuss means by which to reform Islam – the groups in France are most noted for their ultra-strict, literal reading of the Koran.

Police reports suggest that the influence of Salafists is growing in the *banlieues*, particularly as the UOIF grows more bourgeois, more concerned with extending its influence into government and less concerned about building up associations in deprived areas. In 2003, it was estimated that Salafists controlled 22 mosques or prayer rooms around Paris; in 2004, they controlled 32 out of a total of 373.[136] Laurent Lévy, a veteran anti-racist campaigner, estimates that there might be 5,000 members of Salafist groups in France.[137] In local areas they can successfully create dedicated and separate micro-communities co-ordinated around small businesses and other facilities. However, the last word which should be applied to such activities is *communautarisme*. Joining a Salafist organization usually involves a rupture with one's family, neighbourhood and community.[138] It forms 'an Islam of the excluded', condemnatory and hate-filled. Here, one can find attitudes such as those deplored by Fadela Amara: such Muslims despise the 'depraved' girls of their areas. But their movement is hardly a convincing base for the subversion of French society. They do not vote, they do not organize demonstrations, they boycott the CFCM and they live within their tiny, pure, micro-communities.[139]

Conclusion

The material surveyed in this chapter suggests another aspect of the importance of our four thinkers and activists. French Muslims still have no viable form of representation. The CFCM is working less effectively each year, and therefore has less and less legitimacy. It still remains true that many French Muslims have never heard of it. In the absence of an effective, autonomous, democratic, representative structure, individual thinkers can have far greater influence than might be expected.

There are many aspects of the ethics and political culture of the UOIF, the Tabligh and the Salafists which might cause concern. However, the common objection that they are all fundamentalist groups directing French Muslims into the subversion of French society is nonsensical. The dominant tendency among French Muslims is to seek to find their place, not to try to destroy France. Their rituals and views vary: many are perfectly compatible with the norms of French culture; some may be eccentric, some may suggest legitimate criticisms and some may be unpleasant: however, a nation is not a closed community in which all are required to think the same, but something more resembling a family, in which the various relations do not always agree. The principal weakness of the various groups and organizations considered in this chapter is *not* that they are the vehicles of fundamentalist subversion, but that they have failed to represent their communities effectively within wider debates.

Chapter Five
Tariq Ramadan: an Islamic Liberation Theology

My aim is to affirm the absolute legitimacy of the statement 'I am French and Muslim'.

Tariq Ramadan, 2005[1]

In reality, nothing is fixed.
Tariq Ramadan, 2005[2]

May 2005: another edition of the ninety-minute-long television discussion programme *Culture et Dépendances*, this time on the provocative theme of anti-white racism. Alain Finkielkraut is, of course, present. Thirty-five minutes into the programme and he is in fine form. He orates, rather than speaks, with force and clarity, his voice rising and falling with his words, sometimes almost shouting and then speaking quietly and slowly, illustrating his arguments with dramatic, concentrated gestures of his arms and hands. One has to concede that it is an impressive performance. Opposite him, four opponents. As he speaks, three of them signal their opposition: they look horrified at his words, they sigh, they roll their eyes – this is all part of the ritual drama of a televised debate. The fourth, however, seems different. As the camera moves past, he seems smaller than the others, neatly (rather than smartly) dressed, with a well-cut, tidy beard. Something extraordinary is happening here, so extraordinary that the camera misses it: he is listening, intently, to Finkielkraut. And not 'listening' in the chess-game strategy style of these debates, waiting for his opponent to make the anticipated error, and then taking the opportunity to launch his counter-attack. No, the fourth opponent is *actually listening*, showing every sign of genuine interest in Finkielkraut's words. The fourth man is Tariq Ramadan. Curiously, this quiet, scholarly man has become a figure of hate in France.

In one of the very few French-language essays that present a reasonable, level-headed analysis of Tariq Ramadan, Sadri Khiari states – accurately – that Ramadan has become 'public enemy number one' in the French world of ideas.[3] In 2003–4, during the 'war of the veil', Ramadan was regularly denounced in the French press as an anti-Semite and an Islamist.[4] There was a string of accusations, articles and books on the theme of his 'double language', arguing that Ramadan spoke like a Western liberal in front of the television camera and like a fundamentalist fanatic when he addressed Muslim audiences. Three leading Socialist Party members co-authored an article entitled 'Ramadan cannot be one of us'.[5] Articles on Ramadan carried accusatory headlines such as 'The European Prophet of Muslim *communautarisme*' and 'The man who wants establish Islamism in France'.[6] When the French journalist Ian Hamel was given a contract to write a book on Ramadan, he was amazed by the pressure on him to produce a negative, damning picture.[7]

Like Chahdortt Djavann, Ramadan was frequently on French television, appearing on no less than fifteen programmes between September 2001 and December 2004, and he was also the subject of fifteen other television documentaries. Unlike Djavann, these were nearly universally critical of his ideas, and he faced extremely tough questioning from interviewers and other debaters, including a memorable television confrontation with Sarkozy in November 2003. One small indication of the hostility with which he was met occurred in a programme on 18 October 2003, when the journalist Claude Askolovitch spoke of him in the third person, termed his thinking 'fascistic' and refused to shake his hand.[8] Unlike Djavann, Ramadan has proved to be extremely resilient: he is an eloquent, charismatic speaker, even when faced with hostile questions, and it seems to be precisely his articulate arguments and his calm under pressure that has most infuriated his critics.

Ramadan is therefore quite different from our other three thinkers. First, he is not French: he was born in Switzerland in 1962. His father was an exiled member of the Egyptian-based Muslim Brothers. Arabic was the first language of his family but, as he was living in a French-speaking area, he quickly learnt to express himself in French. Ramadan studied for an MA and Ph.D. in Switzerland, where he studied the ideas of Descartes, Kant and Nietzsche: figures who have helped form his thinking.[9] He then attended the Al-Azhar Islamic University in Cairo in 1991–2. He has taught in a college and a university in Switzerland, and currently works in St Antony's College in Oxford. In 1995 he was briefly banned from entering France, and in July 2004 he was banned from entering the USA. Why does he feature in this work on French Muslims? Because, to date, his most extensive audience has been in France and, in turn, French political cultures have had a decisive influence on his thinking. French is the language in which he writes most frequently, although he has also published in Arabic and English. The second important difference between him and our other three thinkers is that while they are all activists, and have subsequently expressed themselves in writing, Ramadan is principally an intellectual. Following his studies at Al-Azhar, he has written more than 20 full-length works, over 800 shorter essays, articles and commentaries, and released countless audio cassettes of his talks.

Ramadan has been the subject of a near-relentless barrage of criticism since 1993. The ideas of his French critics are not original: they repeat the defence of *laïcité* and the suspicion of Muslim initiatives analysed in chapters one and four. Ramadan himself has described one of these attacks as 'a panoply of innuendos, pernicious phrases and untruths'.[10] Unfortunately, this is an accurate judgement. Surveying this stream of criticism will not advance this book's principal purpose, which considers the thinking and political cultures of French Muslims. For this reason, this chapter will concentrate on presenting and analysing Ramadan's ideas, and will not review in detail the points made by his critics.

Muslims in France

The two epigraphs at the head of this chapter introduce the broad themes of Ramadan's work. His first concern is with the Muslims who are now long-term residents in France and other European countries. As was shown in the last chapter, many commentators have noted their 're-Islamization': the immigrants' difficult reassessment of Islamic thinking. For some, this represents a step backwards from the earlier expectations that an increasingly secular group would grow more integrated into the structures of French *laïcité*. For others, it represents a type of rational choice, in the face of the twin impossibilities of a 'return' to an increasingly distant homeland and of a real integration into an increasingly hostile host nation. Ramadan presents this shift in identity cultures in more positive terms, as the development from the condition of being 'Muslims without Islam' to a 'rediscovery of their origins and their religion'. 'For the best educated, this does not mean practising the Islam of rural Morocco, Algeria or Pakistan, but they claim a return to the basic principles of Islamic teaching through an immediate contact with the sources of the Koran and the Sunna'.[11] This renewed, original faith has the potential to be the basis for a real intellectual revolution, with the capacity to transform both European countries and Muslim societies.[12] One first consequence to be drawn from this situation is the irrelevance of the ancient Islamic distinction between the *Dar al-Islam*, the realm of Islam, and the *Dar al-Harb*, the rest of the world, the realm of war. Ramadan points out that, in reality, independent scholars like him are actually safer in the West than they are in the dictatorships that dominate the Islamic world. In place of the *Dar al-Harb*, Ramadan proposes the concept of the *Dar ash-Shahada*, the realm of witness.

The fact that we are living in the West, helps us to come back to this deep understanding of what are the Islamic principles ... My living in a secular society in the West helps me to understand the universality of my message, the common values [I share] with my fellow citizens. This is a complete shift in our perception of our new societies.[13]

Secondly, however, there is the comment that 'nothing is fixed'. It must be acknowledged that this is a chance comment within a longer analysis by Ramadan that criticizes an accepted Islamic tradition through which women's status as witnesses in a court is only worth half that of men's. In citing this phrase, I certainly do not wish to imply that Ramadan is some type of moral relativist: anyone who has read a page of his writing will realize that his thinking is informed by a strong, clear sense of right and wrong. Yet this little phrase still seems to indicate something distinctive about Ramadan, perhaps relating indirectly to his attitude or his situation rather than to his thinking. Can one imagine Chahdortt Djavann or Fadela Amara uttering the same phrase? Our previous two thinkers live in worlds of absolute political and moral certainties: the tasks and agendas are more than clear, they are *fixed*; disagreement and debate seem either unnecessary or – in the case of Djavann – actually unwelcome. In one television programme, Amara repeated three times the phrase 'you must not mix things up'.[14] Ramadan inhabits a different world. Identifying the right action, arriving at the correct perspective is, for Ramadan, a difficult and always provisional task. The laborious, intricate structures of his analyses – from Koranic sources, through scholarly exegeses to commentary – involve the frequent turning-round of opinions, a dialectical journey through contraries to arrive at progression.[15] This awkward process inevitably provides hostile critics with plenty of ammunition: when Ramadan refers, with respect or affection, to an older Islamic custom, the critic can always cite this phrase, and then claim 'But he says', 'But he really believes that'. Yet even in the face of a decade and a half of sustained, hostile commentary, Ramadan is still reiterating that there must be dialogue and even more: that it is actually the duty of Muslims to debate, and that one of the greatest dangers they face is becoming isolated within their own communities.[16] One could also read this chance statement as an expression of regret: given the confusion of religions, cultures and ideas that the (post?) modern world faces, perhaps things ought to be fixed. Elsewhere, Ramadan sums up one theme in his project for contemporary Muslims: 'it concerns putting things back in their place, in the right order.'[17] We will return to the themes of the fixed and the mutable in the second half of this chapter. Let us now turn to consider how Ramadan's thinking developed in relation to France.

Religious themes dominate Ramadan's writing. This means that, in turn, he is less forceful when he addresses social or political issues: in his writing, such points tend either to be assumed or to be evoked in passing, rather than addressed through detailed, empirical studies. Thus, in one of his earlier works he simply states that there are 15 million Muslims living in Europe, while making little effort to differentiate between them according to national traditions (whether of host-nation or nation of origin) or social class.[18] He does, however, note generational differences. As second- and third-generation Muslims search for their identity, they first define themselves negatively, against what they are not. Even before they see themselves as Muslims, observes Ramadan, they find that they are being defined by others as Muslims, often against their own will.[19] In a sense, this is not surprising. Ramadan writes eloquently of this curious, paradoxical situation. 'Never has so much been said about Islam as in the last few years', he observes.[20] But these studies and commentaries tend to work in one particular manner: they are works by outsiders, who present Islam as a problem, a threat or a peril. For the majority of the French population, Islam is 'a strange, obscure universe, the cross-roads for a thousand fantasies, a symbolic landscape for all forms of revulsion'.[21] In discussions on Islam, everything is cited: religion, *laïcité*, integration, *communautarisme*, Islamism, radicalism, women, immigration, delinquency, unhappiness, soul-sickness and even hopes. 'As for us [Muslims], we are left annoyed or disappointed, just seeing our suspicions confirmed; most of the time we watch the sad spectacle of our religion, our faith, our spirituality daily being denied, simplified and/or reduced to the most vulgar of caricatures. Sensing racism, we grow obsessed.'[22] These passages demonstrate some of the strengths of Ramadan's writing: it is at once eloquent, clear and quite personal. When writing short pieces of Islamic commentary in French, Ramadan will frequently address his reader as *tu*, suggesting an intimacy between author and reader, but also implying a rather avuncular quality, as if he is giving advice to someone younger and less well educated.

These new generations of Muslims, argues Ramadan, then make their first attempts to find out what it really means to be a Muslim. At first, Islam seems to be a series of rules, prohibitions and bans, perhaps justified as a means of defence against an environment which appears at once too permissive and too hostile.[23] There is a confusion between rituals which are actually national or cultural in origin, and those which are genuinely Islamic.[24] There is also an important difference in attitude between the Muslims of the first generation who learnt the hard way that the best way to survive was by being discreet, almost invisible, and the second and third generations who wish to assert their rights and their presence.[25] Ramadan anticipates one possible, mistaken response to this situation: the temptation to think as a minority.

> *The minority syndrome begins when all the texts, all the regulations, all the acts are done with the aim of protecting oneself, preserving oneself and ulti-mately distinguishing oneself through opposition and retreat. In the long run, 'protecting oneself' builds the walls of a real mental and social ghetto.*[26]

In particular, Ramadan explicitly and firmly warns against the influ-ence of the Saudi-financed Wahabis, a form of the Salafism discussed in the last chapter. They promote a simple message: 'everything that is Western is against Islam' – a good example of a self-constructed ghetto.[27] How, then, are these new generations to live their faith? We will return to this question in the next section. First, let us survey further Ramadan's analysis of the French-Muslim experience in the 1990s.

Having returned from Al-Azhar University in 1992, Ramadan gave a speech at the UOIF congress at Le Bourget in 1993. Among his audience were a small group of young Muslims from Lyon, whose suburbs were already acquiring an unwelcome reputation as the one of the most troublesome and desperate areas of all the French *banlieues*. They belonged to a local association entitled the Union des Jeunes Musulmans (UJM – Union of Young Muslims).[28] They then contacted Ramadan following his speech. The journey from Geneva to Lyon is an easy one: Ramadan visited the city and the UJM frequently in the next twelve years (with the brief break caused by his ban from entry into France in 1995). One point needs to be stressed here: while there is frequently an avuncular, scholastic tone to Ramadan's writing, he was not searching for disciples. Ramadan would probably be willing to acknowledge that he learnt as much from the UJM as they learnt from him: they showed him the housing estates, they spoke of their experiences in prison.[29] Ramadan learnt that the problems of the young in the *banlieues* could not be reduced to a single issue: 'the problem is more complex, mixing social division, chronic unemployment, exclusion, plus religious and cultural factors'.[30] More importantly, the UJM also gave him a concrete lesson about the failure of existing attempts to represent their voices within French society.

As was described in chapters one and three, it was from Lyon that the movement exemplified in the Marche des Beurs originated in 1983. By the mid-1990s, the original optimism that the movement had inspired had worn thin. Despite the proliferation of associations, despite the construction of SOS-Racisme and its strategy of building up links to the Socialist Party, there were very few real successes. The UJM consciously set itself up as alternative to SOS-Racisme, whose faults now seemed obvious. The older organization had reduced Muslim culture to a colourful folklore, to be expressed in festivals.[31] Its representatives would only be heard if they spoke in the dominant paradigm, according to which it was because the Muslims of the *banlieues* had refused to integrate, that there had been no progress.[32] Ramadan's observations about SOS-Racisme are often surprisingly sharp and even cynical. Discussing Malik Boutih, the president of SOS-Racisme, Ramadan comments: '[Boutih] has used the *banlieues* far more than he has served them. No one is fooled.'[33] Boutih is useful to the Socialist Party because of his name, which sounds Arab.[34] Ni Putes ni Soumises is treated equally sharply, although Ramadan accepts that it has successfully raised some crucial questions about sexual discrimination and sexual violence.[35] With reference to both movements, Ramadan argues that the real problem is not so much that their programmes are wrong, as that they have allowed possibly worthy programmes to be exploited by a group of 'representatives' who serve outside political parties.[36]

The experience of these two failed movements also demonstrated a more serious point about French society: there was a systematic failure to listen to Muslim groups. When Muslims said 'citizenship', the French heard '*communautarisme*'; when they said 'reformism', the French heard 'fundamentalism'; when they said 'liberty', the French heard 'tyranny'.[37] For radicals like Ramadan, the constant referral back to the issue of integration was a diversion, which could be promptly dismissed. 'Muslims are *already* integrated', Ramadan curtly told one interviewer: the real problem that they faced was that the social institutions which at one time had sustained integration were no longer operating.[38] The ineffective, confused manner in which so many French commentators considered Islam was more than an expression of ignorance: French society was gripped by fear of Islam. Particularly after 9/11 and during the 'war of the veil', there was a tendency by many French people to retreat into 'the bunker of *laïcité*'.[39] Given the repeated failure of earlier initiatives, how were young Muslims to be heard?

One answer to this question is through the religious associations that made up the CFCM, in particular the UOIF. Ramadan has not had a close relationship with the UOIF. His first significant speech in France was given to the UOIF congress at Le Bourget in 1993. He retained contact with the organization afterwards, but – as seems to be a constant pattern in his interaction with other groups – he grew distant from them. The evidence is not clear, but it seems likely that between 1993 and 2008, he did not speak again at their congresses.

He encouraged the UJM to turn away from the UOIF.[40] Ramadan did, however, retain closer contacts with the UOIF youth wing, the JMF. In 2003 he echoed one of the obvious criticisms of the UOIF: it still relied too much on foreign activists to fill key posts in its structures.[41] During the crisis over the veil in 2003–4, both the UOIF and Ramadan seem to have been uncertain how to react. However, while the UOIF eventually chose a formal stance of rather weak, perfunctory opposition, Ramadan worked with existing contacts to create a new platform for protest, the Une école pour tou-te-s group (see chapter four). There is at least some reason to think that the UOIF resented this, and saw Ramadan as a potential threat to their claim to represent French Muslims.[42] Ramadan produces a more sophisticated argument to explain his distance for the UOIF. He cites the organization as an example of 'minority thinking' (we will return to this point later).[43] More speculatively, one wonders whether Ramadan's highly idealistic interpretation of Islam could ever be integrated within the politically orientated structures of the UOIF.

Thus, when Ramadan came in contact with the UJM in Lyon, he was not looking for disciples; he accepted that they were right to be sceptical of organizations such as SOS-Racisme; and he was not going to recommend that they should join the UOIF. What could he suggest to them?

Ramadan's first attempt to produce a synthesis of his interpretation of Islam and French political realities was through the structures of what is normally known in Britain as the anti-globalization movement, but which in France is more accurately termed the alter-globalization movement. Ramadan's point of entry was a shared apprehension concerning the culture industry. This flood of films, songs, music and other artistic commodities, structured around a culture which privileged profit and money above all morality, had a terrifying power to transform societies.[44] What was still more frightening was the prospect that this massive, global industry would soon dominate even Muslim countries. The ancient Islamic prohibition of earning interest from financial transactions was commonly being flouted by Muslims. From this simple premise, Ramadan drew a number of conclusions. The first was critical of existing Muslim governments and cultures: the vision of the ulamas was too fixed (figée) to be able to resist incorporation of their countries into the neo-liberal global market. Secondly, once again,

Ramadan pointed to the unique potential of Muslims living in the West: here the confrontation between marketplace logic and Islamic morality was at its most extreme. In a characteristically Ramadan-ian turn, he then presented this dilemma as an advantage: at least Muslims had a system of morality to which they could refer. Because of this, they could be in the forefront of the struggle against neoliberalism, an objective ally of the South and of all the dispossessed. 'To be the voice of the voiceless is, today, a moral imperative.'[45] Muslims could lead the 'resistance against the blind interests of the great powers and the multi-nationals'. They even had an advantage over the older leftist organizations, who were confused by the decline of their ideals into justifications for dictatorship. Islam, on the other hand, demanded dignity, justice and pluralism.

This was certainly a radically new vision of Islam, and Ramadan deserves credit for the originality of his thinking. At first sight, his analysis may appear unconvincing: however, on consideration, one realizes how firmly it is based in the lived reality of second- and third-generation immigrants. They were acutely aware of the shifts in global capitalism, and their cultural and religious links to the extra-European world sustained and developed this sensibility. Moreover, the alter-globalization movement threw its energies into building alliances between unlikely partners: illegal immigrants in Europe, radical Catholics in Latin America, landless peasants in Brazil, American radical intellectuals, ecological activists from Europe's cities, alternative medias and Polish workers could (might?) be united into a new type of democratic, international, pluralistic, anti-capitalist activism.[46] Was it not possible for Muslims to join the party? On the other hand, one can also note the limitations of Ramadan's argument. There was something 'free-standing' about his case: very little reference to any concrete economic or ecological situation, and little attempt to engage in any economic analysis, beyond the rather disappointing reference to the traditional Islamic ban on interest and usury.

Nonetheless, it was through this issue that Ramadan briefly acquired a terrible notoriety in France. Perhaps pursuing the idea of Muslims as a new kind of 'universal class', fit to represent the globalized society of the twenty-first century, Ramadan turned to criticize a strand of thinking which inspired some of his opponents. The result was an essay entitled 'Critique des (nouveaux) intellectuels communautaires': turned down by *Le Monde* (for reasons of lack of space) and *Libération* (due to concern about its political implications) it was eventually published by the independent Muslim website *www.oumma.com* in October 2003, at the same time as the expulsion of the two veiled Levy sisters from their school in Aubervilliers was making the headlines and as the Stasi Commission was conducting its interviews.[47] Ramadan's 'Critique' is not typical of his writing. First, it is an aggressive criticism of others: most of Ramadan's writing is clearly intended to 'accentuate the positive'. Secondly, the essay is bereft of all reference to Koranic thinking. The text lacks a clear focus and has a type of 'work-in-progress' feel to it. However, it could be summarized thus: a certain strand of French thinkers is more than willing to accuse others of anti-Semitism, and to claim that they alone represent the universal values which constitute the quintessence of French philosophy. The accusation of anti-Semitism is often made tactically, to de-legitimize critical voices. But these same thinkers are also more than willing to throw themselves into campaigns whose true aim is to shore up support for Israel, even at the expense of French interests. Prominent public intellectuals such as Bernard Kouchner, André Glucksman and Bernard-Henri Lévy therefore supported the American–British invasion of Iraq. Who, then, are the real defenders of universal values, and who are the *communautaristes*?

One mistake of the essay is its use of the term 'Jewish intellectuals'. In general, French public opinion is extremely wary of making public use of racial categories, partly out of commitment to the blind universalism implied in Republican patriotism, and partly because of the memory of the dreadful years of the German Occupation, in which the collaborationist Vichy government used existing censuses and other data to identify and to round up Jews for deportation to German death camps. France, therefore, has become the land of the euphemism. Common euphemisms for the social groups that this book discusses are 'issus d'immigration' and 'd'origine immigrée': respectively those who are descended from immigrants, and those who are of immigrant origin. (Ramadan himself notes how ridiculous these terms are: third-generation children, born in France, French speaking, with no knowledge of Arabic and little contact with Arab countries, are still being defined by their grandparents! When will these people become classified as 'French'?)[48] 'Noir' appears to be just about acceptable to designate people with an African origin, but even here it is noticeable that many French people actually prefer to use the English-language term 'black' instead of 'noir'. Thus France's World Cup winning football team in 1998 was hailed as a 'Black, Blanc, Beur' team. Also acceptable is 'Maghrebian', or North African. One reason for the brief success of *beur* was precisely that it was a way of indicating Arab without pronouncing the A-word. Ramadan's simple and explicit classification flew in the face of this taboo, and therefore automatically made many French readers suspect the worst of him. Perhaps more seriously, his list of Jewish intellectuals included the right-wing philosopher André Taguieff who cannot possibly be described as Jewish, no matter what definition of Jewishness one uses. Hostile critics could argue, with some legitimacy, that Ramadan was using the term as a catch-all pejorative.

Following the publication of this essay, the media turned against him, making him 'public enemy number one' in Khiari's words. Malik Boutih, the head of SOS-Racisme, referred to Ramadan as a 'little Le Pen'.[49] There was even the televised debate with Sarkozy, more akin to a duel, in which the Minister of the Interior uttered what was obviously intended to be a killer blow: 'Your article wasn't clumsy, it was wrong.' Sarkozy's next phrases also gave some indication of the state of mind of Ramadan's opponents: 'Ask the Muslims who listen to you not to wear the veil to school, not to ask for female doctors in hospital, and not to ask for women-only sessions in swimming pools! Ask them to try to integrate, and you will prove that you are a moderate!'[50] Once again, Sarkozy's words suggest some vast conspiracy of fanatical Muslims, drilled and coordinated by the too eloquent Ramadan, waiting on his words to know what they should wear to school tomorrow. Having been taught that there was a conspiracy against the Republic, French people were now being told who was the mastermind behind it: Tariq Ramadan. There were repeated calls for him to be banned from the second meeting of the European Social Forum in November 2003: to their credit, the organizers refused to do this, and Ramadan spoke.

Ramadan was unrepentant. But by 2004 he appeared less in public. In the Une école pour tou-te-s organization, he was careful not to be seen as one of its leaders: this would have had the effect of compromising the group. By 2005, his name was being used to stigmatize and de-legitimize protests. This was most obvious in some of the hostile reactions to the Mouvement des Indigènes de la

République, as will be seen in the next chapter. For example, the anarchist weekly *Monde libertaire* stated that their manifesto was 'the voice of Ramadan's friends', as if this quality alone was sufficient to invalidate it.[51] One Communist municipal councillor, Clémentin Autain, initially supported the movement, until she learnt that Ramadan had signed its *Appel*. She then promptly asked for her name to be withdrawn.[52]

In late 2003 and early 2004, the problem of the status of Islam in the Republic seemed to have been resolved. Sarkozy had pushed through the construction of the CFCM, which certainly did not lead any active opposition to the March 2004 law on religious symbols in schools. During the hostage crisis of August and September 2004 the CFCM seemed to give all the necessary signs of its loyalty to France (see chapter four). What role was left for an independent radical like Ramadan?

The answer lies with the three million or so French Muslims who were not represented by the CFCM. By 2005 it was obvious that the CFCM was working extremely ineffectively. Ramadan's distance from the body and his public criticisms of it began to win more sympathetic attention. He argued that while the Socialist Party relied on its organizations – SOS-Racisme, Ni Putes ni Soumises – to win the *beur* vote, the right had sought to create the CFCM as its alternative: 'each have their pawns, each have their strategies'.[53] The delegates who had been elected to the CFCM bureau simply were not legitimate representatives of French Muslims.[54] They were merely 'duty Muslims, always ready to obey the prince, to flatter him and to bow'.[55]

Civic Islam

French policies towards Muslims have developed through several stages over past decades. The government's initial, post-1945 assumption was that Muslims could be integrated into a modern, forward-looking France.[56] In the process, their religion might be smoothed over and rationalized, but there was still a confidence that integration would take place, almost as an automatic by-product of a wider process of modernization. As was outlined in the introduction to this book, the debacle of French Algeria did not lead to a sustained questioning of these policies: indeed, there was a surprising continuity.[57] When, in the 1980s, it became clearer that the process of integration was going to be more problematic than expected, the first response by many French political leaders was to try to give modernization a push by creating organizations such as SOS-Racisme which would act rather like the old local associations of the Communist Party: they would teach a loyalty to French values, even while criticizing them. The CFCM was a second attempt at the same type of policy: to create institutions which would act as conduits through which integration would take place.

Ramadan's thinking operates a type of Copernican revolution on this thinking. In place of pushing Muslims through French-designed structures, he asks instead that Muslims become active in their own right. I will term this type of thinking 'civic Islam.'

There are some precedents for interpretations of religious faith like those presented by Ramadan. One would be the radical, critical movements led by Marc Sangnier (1873–1950), first in the form of the Sillon, a social Catholicism within the Church, and then in 1912 as an independent movement outside the Church, Jeune République (Young Republic). Sangnier's Jeune République was the only Catholic-based organization to support the left-wing Popular Front coalition in 1935–6.[58] Rather less radical, but still innovative, were the various movements spearheaded by the Jeunesse Ouvrière Chrétienne movement (JOC – Christian Worker Youth), created in Belgium in 1925, which inspired a series of similar organizations in France for workers, young women, peasants and students. The importance of these movements is that they broke with much of the paternalistic, top-down management structures which had characterized previous attempts by the Church to communicate to workers and peasants.[59] These new groups at least spoke about the need to form judgements, to make criticisms and to achieve the empowerment of their target groups. It is easy to draw a link between Ramadan's contacts with the UJM and these earlier groups. To develop the comparison, one could cite the activities of the radical community priest, Father Delorme, who was working with Muslim families in the Lyon *banlieues* in the 1980s and 1990s, and who initially welcomed Ramadan's presence. However, it is open to question the extent to which Ramadan himself was aware of these older initiatives, and it seems unlikely that he was consciously inspired by them.[60]

A more useful comparison can be gained by considering
'Liberation Theology', a term first used in 1968 by Gustave Gutiérrez,
a Peruvian priest: this is of particular interest in view of the declaration by Ibrahim M. Abu-Rabi', a distinguished historian of ideas in
the Arab world, who bluntly states that there is no Muslim Liberation
Theology.[61] The Liberation Theology formulated by Gutiérrez had a
strong, explicit concern with poverty and the poor, which recalls the
frequent stress in the Biblical gospels on the poor.[62] Gutiérrez even
coined the short phrase 'the best choice for the poor' as a simple definition of his belief.[63] Poverty is understood by Gutiérrez as a material
and a spiritual condition.[64] His theology was intended to awaken the
poor, to create structures of solidarity for them, rather than to offer
them a political programme. Once again, there is little evidence that
Ramadan drew direct inspiration from this movement, but there are
some scattered examples that show that he is aware of it.[65]

Ramadan refers infrequently to poverty in his work. However, he
is more concerned by marginalization and discrimination, and he
does consider means by which Muslims in Europe can combat these
pressures. Here he is at his most original, in warning against 'the
minority condition' ('the minority syndrome' might be a clearer
translation of the point he is making). Obviously, there is a demographic reality: no matter how one conducts one's enquiry, it is
impossible to calculate that Muslims make up more than a tenth of
the French population. However, argues Ramadan, Muslims have
no need to act *as if* they are a minority. One reason for this is the
negative example of Salafi sects: walling oneself up in a little anti-
Western ghetto is not an example of liberation. It is not even
effective as a counter to Western influences, for one's position and
activities remain defined by the exterior culture: all that has been
produced is merely a 'negative mirror' of Western culture.[66] The
same criticism can be made of the 'binary' thought of Sayyed Qutb,
the principal thinker of the Muslim Brothers during Nasser's rule,
who defined Islam *against* the West.[67] Ramadan even criticizes
certain British schools in which – according to legend – 99 per cent
of the pupils are Pakistani: children need to experience social
mixing, he argues.[68] Above all, Muslims must resist the reduction of
their faith to a dreary dispute endlessly debating that which is halal
(permitted) and that which is haram (forbidden). In this way 'an
ethic which should guide is mutilated [until it becomes] an ethic
that stifles and ossifies the heart and the mind'.[69]

By rejecting their 'minority condition', Muslims in Europe can benefit from the many positive advantages to Western lifestyles and cultures: an aspect of Ramadan's thinking which most critics ignore. One obvious point here is that, in the last analysis, Ramadan retains a confidence in a liberal concept of the public sphere as a zone of free debate and real progress. This explains why, despite the constant denigration of his work, he has returned, again and again, to debate publicly with opponents. Ramadan also states quite clearly that there is nothing in the constitutions of the various European states which are actually hostile to Islam, although – on the other hand – sometimes the social context in which Muslims live make it difficult for them to live their faith.[70] Rather than supporting the establishment of a specific form of sharia law for Muslims in Europe (a proposal backed by the UOIF), Ramadan would prefer to use this situation as an opportunity in which sharia law itself should be debated.[71] There are also Western films, books and music to which the young should have access, and which have obviously had a profound effect on them: attempting to ban everything, to switch off all televisions and radios, throw away all papers and magazines, avoid all cinemas, theatres and exhibitions is frankly 'a bit mad' as a proposal.[72] And here, Ramadan is at his most sensible and most avuncular: 'Banning everything is like blinding yourself, allowing everything, is like losing yourself.' The key point is to make a critical selection.[73]

Instead of becoming a minority, instead of turning their backs on Western society, European Muslims must go out into it. They must leave the ghettos, both real and symbolic; they must bear witness to their faith in the civic context of European society. This is an act that, in reality, many mainstream political parties fear:[74] despite the frequent condemnations of *communautarisme*, most of them would really prefer Muslims to be kept in reservations, homelands and settlements, rather than being active in the wider society. This constitutes the first example of a refusal to think like a minority. As Ramadan constantly reiterates, he is not asking for special rights for Muslims, but for their liberation through their full participation in French society *as Muslims*. His attitude can be compared to some of the most original and daring initiatives of the last years of the twentieth century. One could cite the insurgent Zapatistas in Chiapas, Mexico, who despite being largely based on an indigenous population which had been suffering exclusion, discrimination and

exploitation for centuries, did not launch their campaign in order
to fight for special privileges. In the words of their most celebrated
speaker: 'We want a world in which many worlds fit. The nation that
we construct is one where all communities and languages fit, where
all steps may walk, where all may have laughter, where all may live
the dawn.'[75] Closer to home, one could also cite the insurrectionary
Berber movement in Kabylia, which constantly refused the Algerian
state's offers of new (limited?) tolerance for Berber language and
culture, and instead demanded real democracy for the entire
nation.[76]

Lastly, however, one can wonder whether Ramadan's insistence
that Muslims should not think as a minority is not a response to
French political culture. Given the dominant paradigm, which so
heavily emphasizes national unity over almost all other forms of
identity, it would be difficult to establish Muslims in France as a
distinct, autonomous, lobbying group. Demanding that they
become full, active members of the majority is more in tune with
the norms of French political culture.

However, in order to operate this Copernican revolution, French
Muslims first need to know who they are. Ramadan sums this up in a
pithy phrase: 'This simple truth is the essence of my message to
Muslims throughout the world: Know who you are, who you want to
be, and start talking and working with whom you are not.'[77] But the
process of the second and third generations' rediscovery of Islam
leads to some strange contradictions: 'we repeat slogans but we
don't know exactly what they mean'.[78] As has been seen, Ramadan
strongly warns against the reduction of Islam to a set of empty
rituals. (One interesting point here is that – to my knowledge –
Ramadan has never written with real emotion about the fate of
veiled schoolgirls in France. While he was certainly deeply
concerned about what 'the war of the veil' indicated about the state
of French culture, and while he clearly upheld the right to wear the
veil, he never seems to have considered that the wearing – or not –
of a veil was a vital, existential issue for Muslims in Europe.)

What then, for Ramadan, is the truth of Islam? One could start to
answer this complex question by citing the epigraph that crowns
Ramadan's website: 'Verily, in the creation of the heavens and the
earth, and in the succession of night and day, there are indeed signs
for those who are endowed with insight.'[79] The fascinating point
about this passage is its rationalistic qualities: it is a call for the study

of the world. It does not cite either a god or a prophet. This is typical of Ramadan's writing: references to God or to Mohammad are very infrequent. This is quite different from the Christian Liberation Theologians, who can – for example – read the Bible for evidence that 'God is liberating mankind from all that enslaves us'.[80] The first principle of Ramadan's Islam is a rational quest for the truth, solidly based on Koranic sources, but making full use of *ijtihād,* the tools of interpretation and debate. Through Ramadan's works, one gains a vision of Islam as a religion without any central council, without even a church in any substantial sense of the word, but with multiple debates and divergent scholars.[81] Ramadan's extensive and laborious rehearsals of Islamic debate are therefore perhaps more important than they might seem to the non-Muslim reader: they are examples of the means by which Islam is consti-tuted, and they also serve a means to demonstrate his authoritative status to the Muslim reader. It is through this status that he can act as a bridge between the more conservative Muslims in the estab-lished Islamic institutions of the East and the more fully educated Muslims of the West who are less familiar with Islamic learning.[82] This status can reassure the sceptical, and give him the authority with which to criticize the backward-looking, enclosed sects like the Wahabis.

On the other hand, there are limitations to this discursive strategy. It is worth reminding readers at this point that the Koran has a different ontological status in Islam than that of the Bible in Christianity. For Muslims, the Koran is the direct, revealed word of God, not an account by people who may have witnessed the actions of God's representatives on earth.[83] As the direct word of God, it cannot be contradicted: indeed, Muslims are often proud of the clarity and simplicity of their faith, which contrasts with the nebu-lous and contradictory strands of Christian biblical narratives. Ramadan accepts this: as a sincere Muslim, he believes that some miraculous revelation was experienced by an obscure seventh-century Arab trader, and the echoes of that miracle are still ringing through the world. However, through *ijtihād,* the Koran can be *inter-preted* and contextualized. On the one hand, these moral and intellectual structures empower and inspire Ramadan's thinking; on the other hand, they also set certain boundaries. Some of the most vigorous criticisms of Ramadan's thinking relate to these boundary points. Sarkozy, in their famous television duel, referred to one: the established regulation that permits the stoning to death of adulterous women. Ramadan has been quick to correct some of the first impressions about this. First, the punishment by stoning is not to be found in the Koran, but in the *hadith*, the sayings attributed to the Prophet: they are therefore less central to Islam, less well established than hostile critics claim. Secondly, in context, this is presented as a punishment for all adulterers, not specifically female adulterers.[84] Nonetheless, given that this is a horrific punishment for what is a human failing, one would then expect a humanitarian person – as Ramadan undoubtedly is – simply to condemn the practice. Sarkozy himself flung this challenge at Ramadan in their debate.[85] Ramadan responded with the unexpected proposal of a moratorium on the practice. He explained this by pointing out that he was not only debating with the French Minister of the Interior, but with 'Muslims of the entire world'. If he proposed, quite simply, to abolish the practice, he would be ignored as arguing against Islam (in one of its current interpretations). No lives would therefore be saved. By arguing for a moratorium, he is far more likely to be heard, and therefore have a practical effect in saving lives. His long-term strategy is that a wider and fuller education concerning the true nature of the Islamic texts would persuade the Muslim societies to drop the practice altogether.[86]

Similar problems arise with the issues of the status of homosexuals and concepts of male–female equality. Like many Christians, Ramadan cannot accept homosexuality as acceptable behaviour for a believer. He is swift to add that he does not condemn homosexuals, and given that he is specifically considering the situation of gay Muslims in France, it is hard to see what practical application this criticism could have.[87] Certainly, however, Ramadan would vote against proposals which would give homosexuals united through civil partnership the same status as a married couple – while, paradoxically, he cites French civil partnership as closer in spirit to the Islamic concept of marriage.[88] Male–female equality is genuinely a more confused issue. Certainly, Ramadan is opposed to all legislation which specifically discriminates against women's rights: he therefore opposes the reactionary Family Code introduced in Algeria, and accepts that women have a right to work.[89] He cites the Koranic injunction that both sexes should dress modestly but, wisely, refuses to specify certain garments, arguing that it is for individual Muslims to decide how they should interpret this requirement.[90] However, his concept of male–female equality is more based on 'complementarity' than 'similarity'.[91]

These examples show the limitations of Ramadan's Koranically based universalism. It appears that, sometimes, 'things are fixed'. On the one hand, his learning does give him access to the peoples who comprise one of the world's great religions, and allows him to advise them and even to participate in their liberation. On the other hand, there are limits: points at which the debates and discussions seem to stop, and where Ramadan just states: 'The text is explicit.'[92] Here, we can see how closely Ramadan resembles other religious thinkers: there will always be points at which the religion structures or confines the thought of even the most creative and subtle thinker.

Thus far, the matters discussed may well have appeared rather vague. Readers may still be wondering what Ramadan *really* stands for. This is probably the wrong question to ask. Ramadan is not a politician, and has refused to stand for election. He reveals that he tends to vote for left-wing parties, but does not speak about this at length.[93] While he did commit himself to the alter-globalization movement, his involvement always remained 'limited and cautious', observes Sadri Khiari.[94] In this respect, he resembles the Christian Liberation Theologians: he does not have a political programme. Gutiérrez has stated: 'Liberation Theology does not propose a social, economic or political path. Its aptitude is of another world. Theology is a reflection on faith, and faith is that which motivates people to change.'[95] Rather more prosaically Ramadan makes the same point: 'I don't have a list.'[96] He adds one surprising proviso: he seeks to avoid provocation.[97] For him, the great task is to make Muslims into the subjects of their own lives and politics.[98] Once they have achieved this transformation, it is for them to decide how to live their lives – within certain limits.

Before the conclusion, let us cite one further, remarkable observation by Ramadan concerning his work and its context.

Slander, exaggeration, lies: anything can be used to avoid seeing these revelations of new times and those individuals who are the precursors of a vast movement of affirmation and growing autonomy by 'those Arabs' or 'those Muslims'. At the same time, more seriously, people are becoming incapable of

understanding, or even of trying to understand, 'that Arab, that Muslim', as
so much passion and collective hysteria seems to be drowning out reason,
wisdom and dialogue.[99]

The public hounding of this original, humanitarian, liberal thinker
by some of the most prominent intellectuals in France ought to be
seen as a national disgrace.

Conclusion

At the start of chapter two, reference was made to Bhabha's concept
of the 'Third Space'. Obviously, neither Djavann nor Amara could
be seen as representatives of this 'Third Space': the force of their
thought is to promote the full assimilation of immigrants, minorities and Muslims into the political, social and cultural structures of
French society. Ramadan is clearly proposing something different,
and perhaps his call to Muslims to enact their faith within European
society is a better example of what 'Third Space' thought might
look like. One lesson we can gain from Ramadan is that this is a *difficult* space: one can see how Ramadan's thought inhabits a strange
area between the reified, ossified versions of Islam represented by
groups like the Wahabis, the close-minded centralism of French
Republicanism and a happy postmodern relativism, in which all
cultures are equally grey. Ramadan is an ethical, emancipatory
thinker: like the earlier Liberation Theologians, his overriding
concern is to assist the self-emancipation of the powerless. Of the
thinkers we have considered so far, Ramadan is undoubtedly the
most ambitious, the most demanding and the most original. It
remains open to question whether French Muslims' disillusion with
pseudo-representative structures like the CFCM will translate into a
larger audience for Ramadan's civic Islam.

Chapter Six
Houria Bouteldja: a Native in the Republic

France is no longer what she thought she was. She's slowly discovering her new identity.

Sadek Hajji and Stéphanie Marteau, 2005[1]

We share the same citizenship, or at least the same identity card, and yet we are not equals.

Houria Bouteldja, 2006[2]

Houria Bouteldja is the co-founder of the Mouvement des Indigènes de la République (MIR: Movement of the Natives of the Republic) and is one of their most prominent speakers. She has attracted much hostile criticism. Reactions to her speeches and interventions often range from the angry, through the offensive, to the quite unacceptable. A typical example was a viewer's reaction to the *Culture et dépendances* programme in January 2006, in which Bouteldja faced Chahdortt Djavann (described at the beginning of chapter two). Entitled 'A Rat', it describes Bouteldja as

> *dripping with hatred for our land, for the average Frenchman, for our society and people … She keeps her eyes lowered, so as not to look others in the face, with her teeth clenched with rage, her face twisted in contempt. She utters incoherent, bitter words, and looks offensively at the others. She is aggressive and spiteful, permanently exuding venom for our land, poisonous in her reactions, snakelike in her responses … A real example of a wicked thinker from the* banlieues, *educated at great expense from our taxes, and who now turns up to spit in our soup and rot our daily life, all thanks to positive discrimination.*[3]

A second description of her, on a website for the 'republican left', describes her participation at a public meeting in April 2007. She was 'unleashed and incapable of a single coherent phrase. All was hate and revenge: after four centuries of colonialism France, meaning of course the white French, must now pay'.[4]

This type of language is revealing: it tells us that that the topics under discussion have caused a deep emotion in viewers and readers. This emotionality has been a theme in many of the topics discussed in this book. In the first chapter, it was noted how the promoters of *laïcité* and the Republic were convinced that their beliefs and institutions were under attack, and that therefore pre-emptive strikes or counter-attacks were justified. This stance gave their writing a distinctively passionate edge, and suggested a type of Republican revivalism, as they appealed to the people of France to return to their 'true' identities and traditions. In this chapter, which analyses Houria Bouteldja and the movements with which she is associated, it is as if the lid has finally burst from the bottle, and we get to see raw passions previously left hidden by the idealistic references to French universalism and *laïcité*. Rather than the veil covering a mysterious Islamist conspiracy to subvert the Republic, here it appears in a different manner, more akin to a screen on which all the hidden tensions and unspoken fears of a modern nation are projected.[5]

In this chapter we will first briefly discuss Bouteldja's entry into political life, and then consider the MIR, the group with which she is most closely associated.

Houria Bouteldja

Bouteldja was born in 1974 in Algeria. While there is no doubt that her political values flow from her personal experience, Bouteldja has never sought to present a political analysis through an autobiographical account of her life: in this respect her approach to politics is quite different from that of Djavann and Amara. In the absence of a full narrative, one can only gather a few details. She grew up in a poor district in Lyon, and had a difficult time at school: while gifted enough to leave with the qualification that allowed university entry, Bouteldja remembers her school years as a time of humiliation.[6] Her family kept in contact with their Algerian relatives, and Bouteldja grew up knowing two cultures, French and Algerian. She records that she broke, very early in her life, with some key elements of her parents' culture: 'religion, virginity, ramadan'. Bouteldja was too young to participate in the Marche des Beurs of 1983 or the subsequent SOS-Racisme movement. She was, however, aware of these political movements affecting her immediate environment, and she reacted forcefully against the creation of Ni Putes ni Soumises in 2003. For Bouteldja, Ni Putes ni Soumises constituted a type of betrayal of her Algerian heritage, and she joined a much smaller, rival group, the Blédardes (the term is based on the Arabic word meaning countryside: it could be translated at 'the girls from the country').[7] In Lyon, she seems to have come into contact with some of the groups previously discussed: the UJM that Ramadan visited, Palestinian solidarity movements, and the Islamic groups which were growing in the 1990s. However, it was the 'war of the veil' which first inspired her into political action. Despite her personal lack of religious commitment, in 2003–4 she considered that the proposed law on religious symbols at school was a menacing development.

In the weeks between the publication of the Stasi Report in December 2003 and the vote on the law in March 2004, scattered initiatives were taken to organize opposition to the proposed law. On the one hand, Muslims experimented with forms of protest to represent their concerns to the wider French public (see chapter four); on the other hand, some secular, leftist and feminist organizations also attempted to frame their concerns. Bouteldja was part of this shifting coalition of forces. She joined Une école pour tou-te-s when it was created in January 2004. For all its political failures, the organization did achieve one major success: it marked the creation of a type of post-Muslim culture. While its members were portrayed in the press as fundamentalists, about 90 per cent of the people who joined were actually convinced atheists, according to one activist.[8] Bouteldja was one of four co-authors of an angry text – 'A New Dreyfus Affair?' – which probably predated the creation of the organization, but which expresses some of its distinctive themes.[9] This text defined a different kind of opposition to the law, one which was not based on religious commitment, but on a defence of civil liberties for Muslims, including the right to veil: it did not defend the veil in itself. The text on 'the New Dreyfus Affair' explained this point: what concerned the authors was the manner in which the so-called 'debate' on the veil was leading to 'a climate of mistrust, fear and rejection towards the North African and/or Muslim population'. It contributed to a 'cultural racism', according to which Muslims were defined as 'unassimilable'. In reality, what worried the prohibitionists – those who opposed the presence of the veil in the schools – was the open, confident presence of veil-wearing girls in the schools. In March 2004 Bouteldja wrote another short, angry text that circulated on anti-law websites. Entitled 'Feminism or Maternalism?' this criticized the media-star feminists who voiced their support for the new law. Bouteldja asked whether such women could really be presented as models of liberty. The glossy magazines to which they contributed led women into unhealthy, obsessive relationships with their own bodies. 'What is the real difference between a woman who is obliged to cover her body and one who is forced to undress?'[10] These stars' pronouncements about liberation were hypocritical and resembled the older colonialist justification for the French presence in Algeria: that French power would liberate Algerian women.

Bouteldja clearly made an impression in the overlapping groups and improvised discussion circles of the anti-law protests. Despite the ridiculous and grotesque descriptions given of her by the commentators cited at the beginning of this chapter, she is a powerful speaker, who presents her arguments with intensity and passion, and who can be a persuasive and eloquent advocate of her cause. An American visitor who attended a discussion at which Bouteldja spoke found her 'quite brilliant and radiant'.[11]

As was seen in chapter four, the initiatives in 2003–4 to organize opposition to the proposed law were clearly unsuccessful. The majority of the French population was convinced by the case put forward by Stasi; Tariq Ramadan was easily dismissed as an anti-semitic crypto-fundamentalist; and the Muslim groups were divided among themselves, inexperienced and unable to devise a clear, common message that would resonate with the public. On the other hand, for some this period was a political turning point. One militant who has worked with Bouteldja later explained: 'That was the trigger: the absence of any reaction to the law against the veil.'[12] For Bouteldja herself, the turning point may have come a few months later, in August 2004. She was perplexed and worried by the false accusations made by 'Marie L.' concerning the violent anti-semitic attack on her, and by the related press reactions to her story. For Bouteldja, this incident seemed to encapsulate some key issues. Many had been sceptical about the story when they had first heard it: no matter how violent the criminals in the *banlieues* might be, few of them are Nazi sympathizers. According to one account, when

Bouteldja heard that the police had established that Marie's accusations were false, she immediately said 'this just isn't possible: they
really do think we're *indigènes*'.[13]

And so, the word was uttered. It was later to acquire notoriety,
and Bouteldja has strongly defended its usefulness: 'The term
"indigène" has destroyed a myth: that of the universal and egali-
tarian Republic.'[14] In a second interview from 2006, she gives a
longer and revealing explanation:

> *We'd been discussing questions about immigration for a long time, and we
> kept hitting the same problem: what name should we give to ourselves? There
> was everything: Arabs, Muslims, Africans, Blacks, immigrants, children of
> immigrants, people descended from immigrants, I don't know what ... But I
> was never satisfied, and I always said that it was the name that was going to
> determine everything else ... For example, 'descendants of immigration': well,
> it's too much, there are now four generations, and we're no longer descen-
> dants of immigration, so that's no good ... Muslim: that asserts an identity,
> but is it always relevant? It's restrictive, because not everyone is a Muslim,
> and not everyone defines themselves as Muslims ... and so, well, we had to
> find a political term, and the term indigène came up because, finally, we had
> to give a name to reality. And in reality, we'll never be French, because to be
> French you have to belong to a sort of caste. It's a type of honour, and not
> everyone who wants to be French can have it. It's just like Le Pen said: 'To be
> French, you have to deserve it!' Le Pen said it, but the whole society thinks it.
> As for us, we can't claim this because we're too brown, and we'll never be
> white enough to be French, whatever one says. We're systematically forced to
> give proofs that we're really civilized, that we deserve to be French, and so on.
> Nothing works, and you can have all the identity cards you like, we have
> bodies and faces that stigmatize us, because French nationality is ethnic. It's
> ethnic.[15]*

What, exactly, does *indigènes* mean in this context? The most
simple meaning of the term could be translated as 'native', in the
sense of 'indigenous'. The Larousse dictionary of 1914 cited as its
definition as *indigène*: person native to a land. However, it also
included a reference to the more abstract quality of the *indigénat*
and used the following sentence to explain the term: 'The *indigénat*
of Algeria is governed by special laws.'[16] As has so often been the
case in this book, we need to explain France by turning to Algeria,
for this single word sums up the history of French–Algerian relations

over two hundred years. During the nineteenth century, those French experts who considered the future of the colonized peoples in the French Empire talked of the long-term goal of 'assimilation': those who were colonized would eventually grow to resemble the French. In reality, of course, this was largely an ideological proposition. Few seriously imagined that Algerians, Syrians and Indo-Chinese would really become French. Some questioned the wisdom and viability of the proposal. So, whether as a stop-gap or as a substitute, the ideal of 'association' became more commonly discussed in the twentieth century. This suggested the parallel development of the two groups and – most importantly – allowed for specific legislation to be applied to subject groups.

In Algeria, this process started as early as July 1865, and was then rationalized and codified in a series of laws known as the 'Code de l'Indigénat', in 1881–7. While formally defining *all* the inhabitants of Algeria as French citizens, it placed severe restrictions on the lives of Algerian Muslims, limiting – for example – their right to hold meetings, placing obstacles that prevented their registration as voters, demanding their formal respect for all French colonial officials and aiding the longer process of the French seizure of Algerian lands. The ultimate consequence of this process was the creation of two electoral colleges in 1947, one for the indigenous majority and one for the colonial minority. Patrick Weil's study of this legislation concludes: 'The Republican regime never established as deep a chasm between its words and its acts as it did in Algeria: it emptied all meaning from terms such as "nationality" and "equality".'[17]

This term 'indigène' is therefore a word with several dimensions. At first, it was a relatively innocent means of identifying a person by where they lived. But, as the colonisation of Algeria progressed, the *indigénat* became more than a mark of political and ethnic inferiority: it was a key symbol of the manner in which colonialism worked in practice, of how it twisted and betrayed apparently worthy causes for its own ends. The term recalls a painful memory: why would anyone wish to revive it? In her reaction to the news concerning 'Marie L.', Bouteldja's first use of the term suggested a recognition of the failure of the French Republic to institute meaningful equality. Black people and Arabs were second-class citizens, still there to be used as 'the usual suspects' in criminal cases involving violence. When the truth of the case became known, many sections of the press were embarrassed by their earlier reports of the case, but several papers simply refused to apologize. This added to her anger: her first, spontaneous use of the term was a bitter de-mystification. But Bouteldja's choice of words also represented a type of *détournement* just as militant gay groups have used the word 'queer' and African-Americans have taken the term 'nigger', Bouteldja was also taking a pejorative term and turning it into a source of identity and pride. Moreover, as shown in the long quotation given above, it was also a politically expedient word that ended the etymological cycle outlined by Alima Boumédienne-Thiery (cited in the introduction), from *indigènes*, through foreign workers, immigrants, descendants from immigration, *beurs*, North Africans, Muslims, to end, once again with the term *indigènes*, this time chosen and applied by the subject population to describe their experience and status. More importantly, however, than all these points, the word sustained an analysis.

Interval: a dialogue of the deaf

There is a neat French expression for a failed discussion, *un dialogue des sourds*, a dialogue between two deaf people. In a sense, a dialogue of this sort lies at the root of the various social problems and issues considered in this book. The dialogue has been running for many decades and it could be summarized thus:

A. The French Republic offers all its citizens liberty, equality and fraternity.

B. Wonderful! This is just what I've been waiting for!

A. Find yourself a job, a house, and then come back and talk.

B. Look, this is proving a bit more difficult than I expected.

A. Well, you've got to make an effort. Learn how to speak French properly, and smarten yourself up a bit. You'll soon find that people will accept you.

B. Yes, I really do want to settle here.

A. Speaking personally, I've got nothing against Muslims. But they always seem to make heavy weather …

B. I'm not a Muslim. But I keep finding people talking to me like that, and I still can't get the job that I'm qualified for.

A. This sounds serious. France has promised you equality, and I won't rest until we've achieved this. There's no place here for racism!

B. Good, but look, I'm not the only one having problems. A lot of people I know seem to be in the same situation. We need your help.

A. Well, don't just sit there. Join one of the associations that's campaigning for equality. Isn't there one in your neighbourhood?

B. There's not much at all in my neighbourhood. Maybe I could form an association of my own?

A. That might be a good idea. But, mind you, no *communautarisme*!

B. What's that?

A. You've got to remember you're a French citizen, first and foremost. If you start to form a little group of your own, you and the other Muslims …

B. I'm *not* a Muslim!

A. If you start to form a little group of your own, you're in danger of putting your own narrow, sectional, particular interests over the general interests of the nation.

B. But all we want to do is to organize a group that will help us join the nation that you talk so much about.

A. Who's this 'us' that you're speaking about? You see, you're beginning to do it, just thinking about your own petty little interests, and forgetting the universal interests that you have in common with all the other citizens of the nation.

B. But I share something in common with my neighbours: they can't get jobs either. It's really quite important to us.

A. I'm sure it's not as bad as you're making out. You're exaggerating, just a bit, aren't you?

B. Why don't you investigate?

A. It's not as easy as you might think. You see, as our Republic is based on universal rights, so our government agencies refuse to discriminate between the various groups present in the Republic. As soon as we start to investigate the problems that – for example – the Muslims face, then every other group, from the hunters to the vegetarians would start to demand a special status.

B. Well, if you're not prepared to do anything, we'll have to do it ourselves.

A. Can't you see? Once you start to engage in *communautarisme*, then that's the end to the equality that the nation guarantees for you.
B. What equality? I can't see much sign of equality here.
A. The French laws that proclaim the equality of all citizens are the envy of the world, and have served as model for the constitutions of many nations.
B. Great! That's just what we're campaigning for in my group.
A. You won't get equality by turning your back on the nation, and by adopting this pointlessly aggressive attitude to your fellow citizens.
B. Who's being aggressive?
A. That sort of cheap sarcasm that is just so typical of you Muslims.

Some points about this dialogue need to be clarified. First, the defenders of the Republic are absolutely sincere when they state that they are anti-racists. They are horrified by the success of Jean-Marie Le Pen, mortified by the memory of the Vichy years and embarrassed when observers point to a congruity of their secularist, republican discourse with the anti-immigrant polemics of Le Pen and De Villiers. Secondly, the dilemma that the dialogue poses, between universal rights and particular identities, is a real one: there is no easy solution, and this type of conflict is repeated in different forms on a global scale. Thirdly, to date, very, very few French voices have dared to question the basic conceptual framework created by republic, anti-*communautarisme* and *laïcité*. When required to do so, even radicals like Tariq Ramadan will pronounce the necessary homage to the Republican principles, stating that that they are active republicans who seek to help the Republic refind its pride.[18] The first public declaration by Une école pour tou-te-s included the argument that it was promoting the principles of *laïcité* by defending the right of veiled girls to attend school.[19] A leaflet by a Rennes-based branch of the organization repeated one of its common slogans: 'Yes to laïcité! No to exclusionary laws!'[20] The political importance of the Mouvement des Indigènes de la République is that, cautiously and gradually, they have begun the process of breaking this political consensus.

A protest

The summer of 2004 was a tense, difficult period. After the vote for the law on religious symbols in state schools (March 2004), there was then the dramatic case of 'Marie L.' (August 2004), followed by the apparent victory of the Republican state in September 2004 when the new law met with little open opposition. Discussions and contacts continued among the radicals who had tried to campaign against the law. Bouteldja was prominent in these. The exact chronology of events over the next months is not clear, but it is known that various draft versions of a collectively written text were circulating, carrying the provocative title 'We are the *indigènes* of the Republic!' It was finally published on 20 January 2005 through two websites, the independent Muslim website *www.oumma.com* and the libertarian leftist discussion site 'Les mots sont importants' ('words are important'), run by the radical teacher Pierre Tevanian. The exact purpose of the tract was unclear: ostensibly, it was to publicize a conference to be held in Paris in April 2005 to assess and debate anti-colonialism and post-colonialism in France. The tract, however, seemed to acquire a momentum of its own. It was initially signed by twelve organizations (including the Blédardes) and thirty-three individuals (including Bouteldja).[21] Commentators – particularly hostile commentators – struggled to see what had brought these diverse groups together.

The events of 2003–4 had linked previously divergent groups around a common set of concerns. Many of those who signed the *Appel* had been active in Palestinian solidarity groups. All of them had been concerned about the implications of the March 2004 law, and all wanted to present something other than a religious defence of the veil. All were disillusioned by the performance of the various groups linked to the Socialist Party, specifically SOS-Racisme and Ni Putes ni Soumises, who – in the eyes of these new radicals – constituted an anti-model. The *Appel* brought together some small, locally based groups constituted by immigrants, such as the Mouvement autonome de l'immigration du Nord (the Autonomous Movement of Immigrants of the Department of the Nord), some small research and activist groups (such as the Blédardes), plus some dissident feminist and leftist militants, such as Christine Delphy and Pierre Tevanian. In the following weeks, new individuals signed the *Appel*. They represented a broad range of experiences and positions: among others, one could cite Nacira Guénif-Souilamas, a sociologist; Corinne Angelini, a Communist municipal councillor from Saint-Denis; Alima Boumediene-Thiery, the Green senator; Vincent Geisser, a sociologist working for the prestigious CNRS research centre; Sylvestra Jaffard, a member of the Trotskyist LCR; Larisse Chamous-Agathe, a member of an association for Muslim women in Rennes; Jérôme Perret, a member of an anti-unemployment campaigning group; Yasmina Kherfi, a video producer; François Tarot, a musician; and Aïcha Touati, a member of the long-established Ligue des Droits de l'homme. Some tendencies among the *Appel*'s supporters are clearly observable: simply by considering the rather basic evidence of their names, one can surmise that the majority of the people who signed the *Appel* came from immigrant families. Secondly, approximately half the signatures came from women: a surprisingly large proportion when one considers the near-universal domination of French political organizations by men, who – in 2005 – formed 87.7 per cent of the deputies and 83 per cent of the senators.[22] Thirdly, one notes a certain social status. The mass of people who signed the *Appel* in 2005 were hardly the kids from the *banlieues*: they were a micro-elite of professional people and association organizers who were closely connected with *banlieues* and their problems.

Let us examine the substance of the *Appel*. It began by noting forms of discrimination in France against 'people from the colonies', in areas such as jobs, housing, health, education and leisure facilities: these groups formed the 'first victims' of social exclusion. Such groups were concentrated in the *banlieues*, which constituted *indigène* zones within the Republic, whatever the actual ethnic origin of the inhabitants. In these zones, people suffered provocations, persecution and police brutality: all evidence of a legal double standard. When such issues were discussed by France's authorities, it was the parents who were blamed: in contrast, the *indigènes* argued that 'we know of their sacrifices, the efforts they took, the suffering they endured'. (This theme of the silent suffering of the first immigrant generation has become extremely important within French immigrant culture.) The CFCM would do nothing to relieve these problems: it was another example of a colonial mechanism, controlled by the Minster of the Interior. The *Appel* then referred to the 'anti-headscarf law' in a single sentence, dismissing it as discriminatory, sexist and racist. The political rights of the descendants of the colonised and immigrants were denied:

their representatives were forced into the roles of 'duty black' or 'duty *beur*'. Authorizations were denied to the illegal immigrants who came to France to work. France had been a colonial state, participating in the slave trade and guilty of many colonial atrocities, and France remained a colonial state. Even within France, colonial practices continued to be implemented: in effect, the status of the *indigène* was still being recreated and enforced by the French state. Colonial thinking continued to ruin French intellectual and political life: it drew many intellectuals into supporting Bush's wars, it encouraged the accusation of anti-Semitism to be made against the young people of the *banlieues*, it stigmatized Africans, north Africans and Muslims as 'fundamentalists', and it exploited the themes of *laïcité*, citizenship and feminism to reactionary ends. Even French progressive opinion had been ruined. There was no Republican equality. Towards the end of the *Appel* there was an important experiment in self-definition:

> We, the descendants of African slaves and deportees, the sons and daughters of the colonized and the immigrants, we, French and non-French people living in France, male and female militants fighting against the oppression and the discriminations produced by the post-colonial Republic.

The *Appel* ended by inviting participation at the forthcoming conference and announcing a protest demonstration on 8 May 2005: a highly significant date, as it commemorated both the sixtieth anniversary of the ending of the Second World War in Europe, and the horrific cycle of violence in Sétif, Algeria, where – following the illegal unfurling of the Algerian national flag at VE day celebrations – tens of thousands of Algerian Arabs were massacred by French military forces.

This short, dramatic, lyrical text broke a number of taboos. First, one must appreciate that the assertion that a systematic form of discrimination existed in France was one that shocked and horrified many Republicans: partly because many still wished to believe that racism in France was a tragic exception to the rule, but also simply because the act of speaking about such issues so openly seemed outrageous. It was for these reasons that Alain Finkielkraut described the *Appel* as 'detestable' and would later refer it as 'vile' (*indigne*) in his television confrontation with Bouteldja.[23] One of the first critical reactions came from Jean-François Chalot, president of a *laïcist* organization in the Seine-et-Marne. His text clearly demonstrates the incompatibility between the *indigènes'* appeal and mainstream Republican patriotism. Chalot was concerned about the provenance of the *Appel*: he was puzzled that leftist militants, from the Communist Party, the Greens and the JCR, could be associating with those 'from the other side', in other words, Muslims, represented by what Chalot inaccurately described as the 'fundamentalist' website *www.oumma.com*. The only common point of concern seemed to be the issue of the veil. Chalot summed up the message of the *Appel* as 'immigrants you are, and immigrants you will stay!' In other words, Chalot considered that as soon as one raised the issue of the rights or interests of subordinate groups, one was therefore locking them into a *communautarisme*, and so their liberation or advancement would be impossible. The various supporting associations were merely 'an agglomeration of groups that shared nothing but their hatred of the Republic, of feminism and of the rights of man'.[24] Chalot, writing on 25 January 2005, seems to have gathered his thoughts within hours of the *Appel*'s publication. Following his vigorous denunciation, there was then something of a silence in the media. Interviewed on 10 February 2005, Boumedienne-Thiery talked of her frustration with the French Senate, and mentioned her support of Une école pour tou-te-s, but said nothing about the *indigènes*.[25] During this period it appears that the news of the *Appel* was circulating by word of mouth and through website contacts. It was not until 22 February 2005 that *Le Monde* published a short article, presenting a reasonably accurate summary of the *Appel*, which noted that the text was 'striking and provocative'.[26] By that time more than a thousand people had signed the *Appel*.

By March 2005, the orthodox left was beginning to react. In general, they were sharply critical. *Lutte ouvrière* (Workers' Struggle), the more hard-line daily paper of France's two main Trotskyist groups, published a stern critique rebuking the *indigènes* for ignoring the importance of class, and for trying to fight racism with *communautarisme*.[27] A second leftist critique was published on 16 March, making similar points concerning the *indigènes'* ignorance of class divisions *within* the *banlieues*.[28] A denunciation of the *Appel* as a crypto-islamist text, inspired or directed by Tariq Ramadan, was published in *Le Monde libertaire* in April 2005.[29] Dominique Sopo, a veteran anti-racist campaigner and leading member of SOS-Racisme, later cited the *indigènes* as a regrettable example of the cult of the victim and denounced their intellectual poverty.[30] Of the various left-wing organizations, it was noticeable that the Communist *L'Humanité* took a more neutral line, refusing to condemn the *Appel* while noting its limitations.[31]

In the same months, signatures continued to come in. By November 2005, roughly 2,500 people had signed, and 33 associations had signalled their support; by January 2006, there were 4,000 signatures.[32] The original authors of the *Appel* were surprised by this, and moved by the emotion and identification which these new allies expressed. There were people who said 'that *Appel*, it hit us in the heart, it's our life, and we were never able to say it'.[33] The profile of the *Appel*'s supporters grew clearer. Bernard Dreano, a member of the alter-globalization movement, gave an interesting account of his reasons for supporting it. It outlined what may well have been a typical itinerary: his frustration with constant denigration of all Muslims as subversive barbarians that developed during the 'war of the veil', his experience of attempting to organize opposition to the proposed law and, finally, a sense that signing the *Appel* was an appropriate way of registering a protest.[34] Dreano gives little impression that he considers that he is joining a movement; he sees the *Appel* as a means of provoking debate: 'the only goal of the *indigènes* is to raise questions.' Salah Amokrane, a community activist from Toulouse, applauded the *Appel* for calling attention to the racial divide that was poisoning French society, and noted that Jules Ferry was as proud of the French Empire as he was of France's schools.[35] Tariq Ramadan's cautious support – he explicitly signalled his distance from some of the *Appel*'s phrases – could be read in the same manner: it was just a means to register a protest.[36] There was also a tactical way in which the *Appel* could be used: moderate, apolitical, local Muslim associations, worried that they were being outflanked by the radical appeal of Salafist groups, could sign the *Appel* to signal that they too had radical ideals, they were critical of the Republic, and were concerned about the place of Muslims in France.[37]

There was also a growing – if measured – historians' interest. By coincidence, the *Appel* was circulating at the same time as a law, passed on 23 February 2005, demanded that history classes in school should teach the positive role played by colonization and should acknowledge the achievements of those who returned to France from Algeria in 1962.[38] (Some key articles of this law were rescinded in January 2006.) For historians concerned by the law's implication, reference to the *Appel* was a means by which to construct a wider context within which to criticize the law, although this tended to be accompanied by a distancing from the *Appel*, which was usually considered as too literal in its approach.[39] Thus an article in *Le Monde* criticized the *Appel* for its emotional excesses, but also criticized the chauvinistic implications of the February 2005 law.[40]

The *indigènes'* demonstration took place on 8 May 2005. A thousand people, maybe two thousand, attended: for hostile critics this was proof that the movement was just hot air, and that its time had passed. For others, however, drawing together a thousand or so people without the support of any major political party or organization was an achievement to be celebrated. Moreover, some of the slogans at this demonstration were quite radically distinct. 'Don't liberate me, that's my job', they shouted.[41] Referring back to the old SOS-Racisme badge 'Don't touch my mate', the *indigènes* chanted 'we're not your mates' ('On n'est pas vos potes').[42]

Who are 'we'?

With references to the achievements of the *Appel*, Bouteldja considered that 'to say "we" is the first step'.[43] Sadri Khiari, a leading member of the Mouvement des Indigènes de la République (MIR), was later to argue in similar terms that 'the first step towards emancipation is to know who we are, to achieve our auto-definition'.[44] Certainly, there was a crying need for this type of discussion: one could cite Boumédienne-Thiery's earlier, desperate question 'do we have to put on a headscarf to show that we want to exist, with all our rights and differences?'[45] Nacira Guénif-Souilamas, a signatory to the *Appel*, had voiced similar frustration that 'a unified and unifying republicanism ... claims to tolerate diversity and difference but in fact imposes a code of invisibility of specific and constructed groups ... in the name of so-called Jacobin universalism'.[46] It is also clear that one factor in the relative success of the *Appel* was the sense of self-recognition that readers felt when they read its words. The *Appel* seemed to break the taboos, to say the un-sayable. A text from May 2005 which claimed to explain the *Appel*'s arguments applauded its clarity and refusal of qualifications.[47] One can question, however, how successful the *Appel* was in constructing a solid identity for subject groups. One important issue that it sidestepped was ethnic identity.

The statements by the movement's speakers often only seemed to confuse the real significance of the term *indigène*, for they repeatedly insisted that it should be understood as a political category.[48] Thus, in June 2005, a first meeting of MIR militants assured *Le Monde*'s reporter that they sought to create a political movement, not a *communautarist* one. 'The "we" of the *indigènes* is neither religious nor ethnic, but political' stated Said Bouamama.[49] The *Appel* made reference to the poor whites who lived in the *banlieues*, to stigmatized religious minorities, to political militants who fought against discrimination, to descendants of colonized minorities and to descendants of immigrants. Could these various peoples really be proposed as a single 'we'? With specific reference to the *indigènes*' appeal to immigrants, it should be noted that while they have had some success among Arabs and Muslims, Asians have been largely indifferent to their themes.[50] The final impression was, therefore, confusing: the precise nature of the *indigènes*' identity remained unclear in 2005. The criticism that the movement was held together only by a common sense of victimhood does make some sense. Robine also suggests another dimension: in a ghostly echo of the colonial experience, in which national liberation movements were largely led by frustrated sub-elites who were never allowed access to the structures of metropolitan power, so the MIR also seems to be based on a type of educated *banlieues* petty-bourgeoisie, similarly denied access to jobs and positions.[51]

In considering these points, however, one should take into account the context within which the *indigènes* were operating: the legacy of the forceful attempts by the French state to deny the validity of identities based on ethnic criteria.

The authors of the *Appel* had not initially expected that their words might be the beginning of a political movement. Indeed, many signatories did not think of their adhesion in this sense. The creation of permanent structures proved difficult. During 2005, some signatories complained that the original authors were adopting an ultra-sectarian line. The creation of the Conseil Représentatif des associations noires (the Representative Council of Black Associations) in November 2005 suggested another manner in which the *Appel* might be interpreted: this organization recognized something specific about black people's experience in France, but dropped the flamboyant ultra-radicalism of the *Appel*.[52] A protest petition about the evolution of the MIR, signed by nineteen of the *Appel*'s signatories, circulated in January 2006. One of the protestors explained 'Many of us signed the *Appel* without being fully in agreement with some of the approximate formulas and rough links that it contained, nor with its passionate tone. We thought that it was time to re-focus'.[53] These protestors demanded that the struggle for equality should henceforth be the movement's priority.

Defining an organization

In order to explain the subsequent development of the MIR, it makes sense to compare the movement with some rival political formations and initiatives.

One example was that exemplified by Azouz Begag. By exploiting the opportunities offered by the mainstream parties' new interest in 'diversity', individual Muslims and Arabs could make their way close to positions of power in government. However, as Begag's *Un Mouton dans le bagnoire* revealed, in practice such experiences were frustrating, and while offering a single, celebrated representative a brief moment of fame, such practices did little or nothing to further the collective emancipation of minorities within French society.[54] In fact, the practice may well have a negative effect, as it has left many with a deep scepticism about the usefulness of isolated Arabs or black people in ministerial positions.

The second example is that provided by the ideas of Tariq Ramadan. Here, the relationship between the two initiatives is more complex. Bouteldja has stated that she considers Ramadan as the 'prototype' of the *indigènes*.[55] One can also trace a political heritage, from Ramadan's cautious, non-provocative seminars during the 'war on the veil', to the creation of Une école pour tou-te-s, and finally to the *Appel*. When Ramadan finally signed the *Appel* in February 2005, many hostile critics assumed that this proved that he was 'really' the mastermind behind it. Bouteldja noted 'Our enemies only see him!'[56] Certainly, there is a close similarity between Ramadan's calls for empowerment and liberation through self-activity, his refusal of assimilation as a model, and the MIR's assertion of a collective self-worth. On the other hand, as noted in chapter five, Ramadan's thought is firmly based on religious principles, while the *indigènes* refuse to found their political values on this type of thinking. Here, they are quite subtle. Khiari specifies that:

> *the assertion of Islam, today, functions as the re-affirmation (or re-invention)*
> *of a stigmatized culture, just as the demand for the republic's recognition of*
> *Islam is a means to protest against political, social and cultural discrimin-*
> *ation. Choosing to accept Islam is also a way of noting the illegitimacy of the*
> *established political framework and of leaving it.*[57]

In other words, while the MIR welcomes Muslims into their ranks, and while they sympathize with those who work for a reassertion of the value of their Muslim identity, the MIR is not a Muslim organization, nor is it religious in any sense of the term. This is very far from Ramadan's thinking, which places Islam at the centre of the identity of the subordinate groups with which he is concerned.

There is also a more profound political difference. In the last analysis, Ramadan was demanding entry into the Republic. The *indigènes*, on the contrary, refuse to play this game. Asking whether she considers herself a republican, Bouteldja snorts with derision, and replies that she is 'neither republican nor anti-republican'. Is she proud of being French? 'For me, being French is just a question of chance ... anyone who lives here is French', she replies, to the horror of her listeners.[58] Once again, it has to be stressed how unusual such thoughts are in the French media, and how genuinely shocking they sound to many French people. This leads to a political position and a public stance quite distinct from that taken by Ramadan. Bouteldja defines her movement as:

> *exactly the opposite of Tariq Ramadan, who thinks that you can debate and*
> *discuss. He thinks that he's in a system that offers these possibilities, he thinks*
> *that we're in a democratic system ... We don't believe this, so we decided to*
> *construct a project of political rupture, a project which is not based on the*
> *strategy of discussion with the dominant powers, of debate with them: we talk*
> *to the people who are involved in our project ... with a message for the*
> *powerful, obviously ... We're trying to change the framework, we're no longer*
> *on the same planet, and we don't speak the same words.*[59]

When reading these words, I was reminded of a maxim which has circulated in Israel in recent years: 'If you refuse to negotiate with

Fatah, you'll have to negotiate with Hamas.' By refusing to listen to Ramadan, by stigmatizing him as a crypto-fundamentalist, the French media effectively prevented the functioning of one potentially important channel of communication between French Muslims and the French state. The people who later joined the MIR took an important message from this experience: public dialogue was nearly always a worthless experience for French Muslims.

There was also a third group with which the MIR could be compared, despite the bitter rivalry between them: Ni Putes ni Soumises. Both attempt to construct political projects on the base of the social experience of those living in the *banlieues*. The differences between the two groups are obvious: the first is linked to the French Socialist Party, and has benefited financially from this position. Ni Putes ni Soumises appeals to the authorities for recognition, and thus is proud of its contacts with – for example – President Chirac. The MIR, on the contrary, makes a virtue out of its distance from the centres of power. Yet both have a claim specifically to represent the *women* of the *banlieues*. To an extent, this was forced on the MIR by the prior existence of the older group. One obvious point of difference emerged during the 'war of the veil': while Fadela Amara eventually came to support the banning of religious symbols in the schools, the people who joined MIR were drawn from the minority of the French population who could not accept this law. The first clash between the two currents came at the Women's March on 8 March 2004, where a section of the Une école pour tou-te-s contigent marched under a banner declaring that they were 'real bitches and very veiled' ('Nous, on est très putes et très voilées').[60] Bouteldja herself contributed a strongly argued text, analysing Ni Putes ni Soumises as a continuation of the colonialist policies which had produced a compulsory de-veiling ceremony in Algiers in 1958.[61]

Two months after the *Appel*, the MIR began to discuss a new section of '*indigènes* feminists'. An '*Appel des féministes indigènes*' was issued in January 2007. One strand here was simply the criticism of performance of Ni Putes ni Soumises, stressing that this organization had no right to claim to represent all women of the *banlieues*, and criticizing the stance of Amara, who seemed to consider that 'she was the Republic herself'.[62] Ni Putes ni Soumises reduced all the problems of sexism to the sexism of North African men; 'above all it implicitly presented white people as "better" on the question of male–female equality'.[63] As readers will have gathered, relations between the two movements are extremely bad. In 2007, after Amara joined the right-wing government, there was a split in Ni Putes ni Soumises, and a new section took the name 'Insoumis-es' (see chapter three): one might have expected that the *indigènes* might at least consider the possibility of a *rapprochement*. Instead they issued a bitter, sarcastic text, suggesting that the new group might be better called 'the amputated', and referring to their services in the 'wogs' section' of the Socialist Party.[64] What else could the *indigènes* feminists offer? An extended and revealing interview with Bouteldja in *Nouvelles Questions Féministes* provided some answers.

In this text Bouteldja stresses the inspiration that she has drawn from Algeria – not from its government, but from its people and, above all, from its liberation struggle. This is quite distinct from Amara, whose main political inspiration is clearly a variant of the French republican tradition. Bouteldja dismisses Amara's political ideals in an aggressive and possibly offensive passage. '[Amara] endlessly sings the Republic's praises. Well, it's not the Republic that has given her liberty and dignity, it's the liberation wars by the ex-colonized peoples, our parents ... Without these national liberation struggles for independence, she'd just be a wog, she'd still be an *indigène*.'[65] Bouteldja considers the situation of girls growing up in the *banlieues*. She notes how social pressures push them into a negative image of themselves and of Algeria, until they develop a form of self-hatred. To her credit, she also speaks of the harassment and even violence that *banlieue* women face from their brothers and male neighbours. The difference between her analysis, and that provided by Amara, is that Bouteldja considers that the young men and young women are caught in this situation together. Ni Putes ni Soumises offers one solution: 'leave the Arab areas'. This is utopian. 'This is a delusion, because French society doesn't offer any means by which girls can quit the estates: just as for the boys, they won't find jobs because of the discrimination against them.' In brief, devastating phrases Bouteldja explains: 'Not everyone can leave ... [The girls] do not want to leave their parents, because they love them despite the conflicts. French feminists just do not understand this. This lack of understanding really hurts us.' (One might also point to a wider context: at a time when jobs are scarce, family and family connections are one of the few resources that these young women can exploit. Leaving the *banlieues* also means leaving this potentially vital resource.) Bouteldja notes one use of the veil in this context: it is a means of negotiation, it is a form of proclaiming loyalty to the family while also gaining a degree of liberty. Bouteldja also goes beyond the simple recognition of male violence and harassment to a more sophisticated attempt to understand its causes. She notes how the young men are stuck, jobless, in the *banlieues*. 'They turn against women because they cannot direct their anger anywhere else ... If their women leave, they are reduced to nothing.' It is therefore the young women of the *banlieues* who pay for the stigmatization of young men by the wider French society.

For Bouteldja there are therefore two socio-political priorities: to rehabilitate the young men of the *banlieues*, and to re-found a new feminism based on the Arab values inherent in 'our culture'. She concedes that this is not an 'ideal feminism', it is a *bricolé*, do-it-yourself feminism for the women of the *banlieues* who have never read de Beauvoir, a pragmatic, paradoxical feminism based on the solidarity of the young men and young women of the *banlieues*. She feels strongly, passionately about these matters, and states openly that it was anger that drove her to participate in the creation of the MIR. Their *Appel* was a last cry to France, specifically to the left. The interview ends on a chilling note. 'Soon, it will be too late. Whites won't be able to enter the estates, as is already the case for the leftist organizations. They have to prove themselves, and they're always suspected of paternalism.'

This long, powerful interview illustrates the MIR's priorities. They attempt to build an autonomous feminist current. The *indigènes* feminists do not accept that *laïcité* is a necessary part of feminism, and they have grown tired of 'the requirement to deny Islam as a proof of good behaviour' in order to get a good job or position.[66] They note that despite the frequent protestations in favour of sisterhood, there seem to be significant limitations to feminist solidarity. French feminists only seem to feel solidarity with women 'whose daily language, whose appearance, whose clothes, whose patterns of consumerism, are similar'.[67] Rather than demanding the assimilation of Islam to French norms, the group – like Tariq Ramadan? – searches for initiatives from Muslims to reform Islam.[68] This also means a refusal of Islamist projects, which offer no space for women's autonomy.[69]

In its first three years, the MIR developed a distinctive political profile, which was often defined by negatives. Despite the support of many local associations run by Muslims, they were not a lobbying organization, seeking finances from the powerful groups in French society. Despite the presence of many militants from left-wing and far left-wing groups, they did not define themselves as socialist: indeed, their impression of socialism resembles that of many Arab people, for whom socialism is simply nationalism with a welfare state and a corporatist workers' movement. While they claimed inspiration from the many anti-colonial struggles, particularly that of the Palestinians, they did not accept any of the ex-colonial states as positive political models. Lastly, while not hostile to Islam, and while recruiting many French Muslims, this was also clearly a secular group. During 2005, the neologism 'islamo-leftist' (islamo-gauchiste) was coined by far-right wing groups as an insult to apply to left-wing individuals who had opposed the law on religious symbols. If the term is taken to mean a crossroads, where people from different tendencies met to debate common themes, then it could well be applied to the MIR.[70]

Developing an organization

The new organization faced a crucial test in October and November 2005 as riots developed in the *banlieues*. One would have expected MIR to be gripped by these events: after all, these were the people they claimed to represent, taking action that threw them in direct confrontation with the police authorities which the *Appel* had denounced. In fact, like all French political groups, the *indigènes* were stunned by the events. They only issued two texts concerning the events, and were unwilling to state a position of support.[71] Two and a half years later, Khiari would finally refer to the riots as possessing the substance of a protest and an anti-colonial revolt.[72]

However, in other fields, the MIR were developing a stronger organization. A website was created early in 2006: by mid-2008 it had evolved into a genuinely informative archive of struggles and debates. The contrast between the Ni Putes ni Soumises website and that of the *indigènes* is revealing. The Ni Putes ni Soumises site clearly benefited from financial support: it is stuffed with videoclips (none of which were working in 2008). There are some documents, but one notes that – first – all the available documentation is curiously bland, and – secondly – much of it seems to have been written by the same person. While there are references to twenty-two local committees, few of these seem to be active. The MIR website has –

without exaggeration – hundreds of documents, most with strings of replies attached to them. New messages arrive every day. Debate is lively, sometimes furious. The movement claims four sections: in Paris, Lyon and Lille-Roubaix (all of them places in which French Muslims are concentrated), plus a fourth section for teachers. It is hard to provide any estimate of numbers of members from this information: it is quite possible that there may only be a hundred hardcore militants in the MIR. However, to date, its importance has been more as a forum to debate ideas rather than as a group which organizes events, and it is probable that its influence stretches far more widely than its dedicated members. A magazine, the *Indigène*, was launched in March 2007, and twelve editions had been published by August 2008. Certainly, the number of their publications, in both electronic and paper forms, is growing each week.

Bouteldja seems to be writing less, but has acquired public prominence as a speaker for the MIR. She still has the capacity to infuriate French public opinion. One incident which would be amusing, if all concerned did not take it so seriously, occurred in June 2007 on the television channel France 3. It relates to a question already raised in this chapter: who are 'we'? Bouteldja attempted to answer this question by naming the 'other'. One way of doing this was by reusing a concept originally devised by the conservative French sociologist, Frédéric Le Play (1806–82), who admired the solid domestic virtues and large families of those he termed 'les français de souche': French people of old stock. The racist implications of the term are obvious, and have more recently been exploited by Le Pen. Bouteldja, talking spontaneously, argued that it was 'they' who needed educating, the privileged people of France, those 'de souche' – and then, she turned the phrase into a neologism, and referred to the *souchiens*. Unfortunately, in French, the term also sounds like *sous-chien*, literally under-dog, but understood in the sense of sub-dog. As is nearly always the case with Bouteldja's public appearances, press comment was extremely unfavourable. The left-of-centre weekly magazine *Marianne* accused her of proposing a programme of re-education by racism, and of being as racist as Le Pen.[73] Elsewhere, offensive, ugly remarks circulated about her, such as: 'Of North African heritage, she appears to be completely unhinged.'[74] Bouteldja did reply. First, she pointed out the racist insults that North Africans and others have had to put up with: they are the *sidis*, *bougnoles*, *rats*, *ratons*, *crouilles*, *melons*, *bicots* and *gris* of

French society.[75] *Marianne* really did seem to be extremely sensitive to the use of one word, of a respectable sociological heritage, which – at worst – was a bad pun. Instead, quipped Bouteldja, they should accept the term 'as the first contribution by an *indigène* to the enrichment of the language of Paradise'.

Important questions remained concerning the MIR's political strategy: many of these still centred on the awkward issue of 'who are "we"?' In February 2008, Sadri Khiari gave a paper to the MIR – 'The construction of an autonomous anticolonialist political organiza-tion' – which began to address this point, and which can be read as summarizing three years of political debates. The paper began by re-stating the MIR's basic principles: the formal end of colonialism had not ended all colonialist practices. The ex-colonial countries were not models of freedom. Racism persisted in France, not as a regret-table exception to the rule, but as an integral part of a structure of domination. It was not a biological reality, but a social construct. This situation certainly did produce prejudice and anti-white racism among the dominated groups, but such sentiments were usually expressed by groups with no political power. De-colonization and defeat in the Second World War had created a crisis of national iden-tity, first resolved by De Gaulle, but now raised again by the long-term presence in France of black people, Arabs and Muslims. The declining lifestyles of those living in the *banlieues* were the most obvious sign of this crisis. 9/11 created a type of colonialist counter-revolution, termed the 'clash of civilizations', which aimed to combat Islam. It was appropriate to use words such as black, Arab and Muslim as terms to describe our identity, for these indicated a refusal to assimilate to the republican model but, argued Khiari, *indigène* was still the term which best expressed a position of struggle. 'The *indigène* sees the world from their position, the White, even when well-meaning, has a white vision.'[76] The implications of this sentence are important: Khiari is making increasingly explicit use of ethnic categories with which to explain his political goals, to the point where he is just one step away from an ethnic definition of a rebel identity. The organisation which he sought to create would still work with anti-colonial whites, but it would never accept their domination.

Khiari refused all concept of integration in a passage which seems to contain an implicit criticism of Ramadan's ideas. 'You can tell them: "I'm a Muslim, but apart from that, I'm like you. I share the same values as you. After all, your values are also an aspect of Islam."' Such forms of integration, in reality, would never function in French society. 'The nation which is the foundation of the Republic is both political and ethno-racial.' Real liberation would only come through the re-making of a new national community. Finally, almost at the end of the essay, Khiari utters the phrase that will horrify any Republican readers: it is time to re-think the whole notion of *communautarisme.*

This is a bold, forceful essay, which makes uncomfortable reading. Khiari is clearly inspired by American notions of black separatism. Such concepts would be difficult to apply to the intricate, overlapping, criss-crossing identities of the *banlieue* communities from which the MIR is drawn, but it is clear that their call for autonomy is increasingly being expressed in terms of exclusivity. Their discourse, which may at first sight appear incompetently or ambiguously vague, can also be seen as appropriately flexible, well-suited to the MIR's constituency. There remains one crucial weakness: while the MIR has come a long way in re-thinking ideas about identity, exclusion and autonomy, while they have actually grown and developed as a discussion group and activist organization, they are still very weak in presenting positive ideas. Ramadan was entitled to say 'I don't have a list' when asked the same question: he is a religious thinker, not a politician. But the MIR *is* a political group, and has to function in a political world. In order to continue to grow, it will have to develop a political programme through which to represent its supporters' interests.

Conclusion

Bouteldja is not a professional political philosopher. However, she is a forceful speaker and an imaginative polemist, who has contributed to the the necessary task of confronting and critiquing France's Republican political culture.

Arjun Appadurai notes that:

> no idiom has yet emerged to capture the collective interests of the many groups in translocal solidarities, cross-border mobilizations, and postnational identities ... Postnational or nonnational movements are forced by the very logic of actually existing nation-states to become antinational or antistate and thus

> *to inspire the very state power that faces them to respond in the language of counternationalism. This vicious circle can only be escaped when a language is found to capture complex, nonterritorial, postnational forms of allegiance.*[77]

This sums up the MIR's dilemma. Ramadan proposes a type of Copernican revolution, through which Muslims should become the subjects of their own history by entering the structures of French society without giving up their identities. The people who compose the MIR are proposing a yet more challenging task: they are questioning the very foundations of national identity, in the context of one of the most stubbornly old-fashioned state forms of the twenty-first century, doggedly loyal to nineteenth-century concepts of nation, culture and identity. The first step that the movement has taken has simply been to claim the right to exist within the political invisibility of the Republic. Can it oppose racism without merely proposing a counter-racism? Can it create a viable, post-national, post-colonial movement? Can it build liberation in this strange land?

Conclusion
After the Funeral

It will be an intelligent rebellion, without any violence, in which we'll all rise up, in order to be recognized. There's more to our lives than rap and football.
Faïza Guène, 2004[1]

an Escher universe, where no one, at no point, can tell the difference between a way uphill and a descending slope.
Zygmunt Bauman, 2004[2]

Culture et Dépendances, January 2006: we're now eighty-five minutes into the ninety-minute programme, and Finkielkraut is getting into his stride. Chahdortt Djavann and Houria Bouteldja have repeatedly clashed: their exchanges have been aggressive, bad-tempered and confrontational. The camera pans over the speakers, moving quickly. There is a brief shot of Djavann: she's holding her head in her hands. It's hard to see why: is she tired? Has she a headache? Or is she crying? The last is quite possible. It had been an emotional, exhausting quarrel: a fitting reflection of how the debate has progressed in France.

Too much emotion

While completing this book, I met another French academic at a conference in Britain. Cautiously, I began to talk about the themes of my research. He sighed, and then said one short phrase: 'too much emotion'. His words neatly sum up the feelings of many French people concerning the clashes of 2003–4.

The tensions created during the war of the veil are obvious. One television documentary provided a poignant illustration of this point: Leticia and Noëlle were both teachers in a school to the north-east of Paris in 2003–4. They had been good friends for years, and they were concerned by the issues raised by the war of the veil. But, to their surprise, they found they were on different sides. Leticia was concerned about humiliation suffered by girls who were forced to wear a veil by their parents. Noëlle could see this point, but raised the issue of the rights of those girls who chose to wear the veil. To her surprise, Leticia dismissed this as an issue of no importance. The two women argued bitterly. Noëlle explained to the interviewer 'you cannot question whether our educational system might be racist ... [and so] I lost a friend'. Leticia, interviewed separately, finishes by noting 'they end up defending the veil, of all things'. The contempt and anger she feels about this stance is clear as she speaks. As she completes the sentence, her eyes begin to fill with tears.[3] This type of angry, awkward exchanges typified the manner in which issues were discussed. Opponents and supporters of the law threw angry rhetorical questions to their respective audiences. Christine Delphy criticized feminists who supported the law: 'How can feminists, who denounce men's paternalism, not see that the same logic is at work in the claim to "save" women, despite and against their expressed wishes?'[4] Two feminists who supported the law argued: 'How have we come to doubt [those qualities which are] the backbone and the honour of our democracy?'[5] This cycle of rhetorical questions suggest a stark and absolute clash of two opposing paradigms.

In reality, however, a wide range of opinion exists in France concerning this issue. One can identify the following strands:

- A racist, anti-immigrant far right, once quite sceptical about *laïcité*, now using the term as a means to embarrass a republican centre.
- A parliamentary right-wing, concerned about the mass presence of Muslims in France and seeking to regulate and structure their lives: such people appreciated the law as a means of setting limits to Muslims' activities and influences.
- A parliamentary centre, sometimes Christian-Democrat in inspiration, sometimes secular-republican, genuinely concerned about national unity, and open to arguments that the law was a means to unify French society. (Stasi himself is the perfect embodiment of this attitude.) Many Muslims accepted such arguments.
- A left-wing, stretching from the old centrist Radicals, through the Socialists, various feminists, to elements in the Communist Party and Trotskyist groups, who see *laïcité* as an essential liberating component in the project of modernity, and who

therefore supported the law while retaining doubts about its failure to raise social or economic issues. Some Muslims were willing to accept such arguments.

- Left-wing, feminist and centrist defenders of *laïcité* who voiced a pragmatic opposition to the law, as they valued social unity over *laïcité*: how could one create unity through exclusion? If these girls are oppressed at home, then they must be allowed into the schools in order to be liberated. The ideas of this current were sometimes summed up in the slogan 'Ni voile, ni loi': 'Neither veil nor law'.
- Leftist, Green and feminist radicals who opposed the law *on principle*, seeing it as an expression of racist values. Such people worked with Muslim groups as equal partners in their opposition to the law; they were joined by Muslims who opposed the law on the grounds of a defence of Muslims' human rights to self-expression.
- Muslims who opposed the law on religious grounds.

This brief categorization also explains some of the tensions aroused by the debate. The French government were forcing some quite sophisticated political participants into a simple grid: yes or no.

The law was passed, but its victorious supporters remain uncomfortable about their victory, for the law has not produced the expected benefits. Some sincere supporters of the law really had imagined that Muslim parents and schoolgirls would be grateful, and that they would thank the legislators for their actions.[6] Many were led to support the law on the basis that it would end confusion, that it would clearly define 'a border, a limit' and that this would be a practical, common-sense, productive innovation in the schools.[7] Stasi himself had suggested that it would produce 'a comforting and encouraging calm' in the schools.[8] In reality, it has done nothing of the sort. Legislating on 'the veil' is, in effect, like trying to catch water in a sieve: in schools, black hijabs were banned, then all hijabs, then headscarves, then bandanas which covered the ears, then bandanas which left ears exposed, then berets, then baseball caps, then all head-coverings …[9] Some Muslim girls have left state schools, many now turn up bare-headed, some still sneak in with various permutations of bandanas and berets. In some schools *proviseurs* have proved to be surprisingly pragmatic and tolerant, in others they run a daily witch hunt for visible signs of Islam.[10] There is a strange irony operating in these last schools: the only other country which devotes so much fetishistic attention to what school-girls wear on their heads is Iran. Instead of a place of toleration and mutual respect, such actions suggest that the school is becoming a counter-church, and its *laïque* supporters are now demanding that it be accorded the same degree of respect for its sacred character as is given to a church.[11]

Many Muslims accepted the principles of *laïcité* before 2003: perhaps they are congratulating themselves on having made the right choice. It is equally likely that they might be having second thoughts. Who wants to be part of such a divided national community? The bitterness which this law has created among others is clear. In a collection of interviews, the 21-year-old Keltoum first names the *proviseur* of her school and then states: 'I hope, from the depths of my heart, that you might have just a milligram of regret for what you made me suffer – me and my comrades – during the 2004–5 school year. As for me, whatever happens, I will never forget it.'[12] Her comments are a fitting epigraph, a necessary counterpart to the distress felt by Leticia and Noëlle.

Integration and its discontents

Why has there been such a problem with Islam in France? Over centuries, other immigrant groups have arrived in France, bearing their own cultural and religious peculiarities, and have eventually merged into the national community. The creation of a strong French-Jewish culture is one clear example of such a process. But one could also consider the Italian immigrants to south-west France in the inter-war years who arranged their own Catholic processions, run by Italian Catholic priests, conducted in Italian. While there were some critics of this movement, in general it was welcomed by the French church.[13] Alongside the *beur* movement of the 1980s, Portuguese immigrants developed the *Thos* movement, asserting and popularizing their identity: this was normally interpreted as an instrument through which their integration into France would be achieved, and therefore met with a positive reception.[14] These three examples seem to trace out a variety of models of successful integration into French society.

Islam, however, seems to be different. Unlike Jewish minorities, unlike the Portuguese and Italian immigrants, the public presence of Islam recalls the unresolved issues left from French colonialism: it quickly became seen by some French people as a type of revenge for Empire, a reverse colonialism.[15] This meeting of the Republic and Islam also suffers in another way, because of the repeated citations of Catholicism as a precedent: the Republic's defenders always start from the position that they 'know' religion, including Islam, and that therefore they have nothing to learn from their opponents. The Mouvement des Indigènes de la République is a well-aimed response to this unique situation: its particular blend of Muslim sympathies, global sensitivity, historical vindication of the memory of the colonised and social assertion on behalf of the marginalized make it almost the ideal enemy for today's typical neo-republican patriot.

The 'debate' raised questions about the formation of the borders of nation-state in a globalized world. Obviously, the exclusionary and regulatory aspects of the law can be linked to similar moves at an international level to build a 'Fortress Europe' and to regulate entry into this space.[16] But borders in the modern world are constructed and maintained in other ways than simply by tracing a line around the edges of national territory.[17] While the British, Dutch, German and French governments each claim to be pursuing quite different social policies, the results of their initiatives are surprisingly similar: 'an invisible wall' has been built around certain minorities.[18] The 'war of the veil' shows these new frontiers both stretching deep within French territory and reaching out to more distant areas. Islam plays a unique, vital role here, as the medium through which global tension points are revealed. The list of global issues related to Islam is quite extraordinary. If one considers the world's energy needs, then the politics of Saudi petro-sheikhs must be considered. If international politics are discussed, reference has to be made to the increasingly bitter disputes in Israel/Palestine. If security is being considered, then Islamist terrorism will be on the agenda. If forms of faith are being debated, then most Western governments will need to consider the growing place of Islam within Western societies. If issues of social exclusion are raised, then the role of Islam as a religion of the European sub-proletariat must be discussed. If the politics of the family are considered, then the distinctive Muslim ideas about family life will deserve consideration.

And, lastly, if the construction of socially acceptable forms of femininity are raised, how can one ignore the veil? In these examples, Islam is not so much a fixed 'other' to Western liberalism, as the medium through which Western peoples learn of the greater and wider experience of non-Western peoples and cultures. The few hundred veiled schoolgirls in France in 2003–4 were just one small example of this greater global interchange.

But more importantly, the episode also raises some awkward question about the nature of nationalism in a globalizing world. Despite the repeated invocation of the quality of 'vivre-ensemble' (living together, or – perhaps – just getting on with each other) during the debates of 2003–4, the final consequence of the law has been to stigmatize certain forms of Muslim practice as not acceptable in France. Rather than uniting a society, it has divided and excluded. To achieve the type of national consensus that so many French politicians claim that they wish to achieve, the first, essential step must be a willingness to debate with the other, accepting them as approximate equals.

It was this unusual, powerful yet indirect challenge to the historic norms of the nation-state which has given the war of the veil its distinctive character. The rigidity of French state structures made apparent and public the tensions which other Western states have often absorbed or camouflaged, but rarely resolved. The political and ideological leaders of French society, trapped within neo-republican thinking, found it difficult to adapt to new circumstances. Just as republicans in 1898 were slow to appreciate the nature and importance of the new forms of anti-Semitism created during the Dreyfus Affair, so republicans in 2003–4 judged contemporary issues with concepts drawn from the 1905 law on the separation of the state and church, while still proclaiming their modernity, their knowledge and their commitment to progress. For this reason, the most articulate contributors to the debate have come from 'the *coulisses*'.

Djavann, Amara, Ramadan and Bouteldja do not conform to the typical patterns of French intellectuals: they lack connections with the prestigious Parisian academic institutions; each – in varied forms – has suffered ostracism; each has received, in different ways, provocations and inspirations from Muslim cultures; each evokes the trans-national frontiers described above. Djavann and Amara respond by trying to revive the nation-state form in this new context, while Ramadan and Bouteldja suggest reforms and critiques. Djavann is a successful author; Ramadan has pursued a successful academic and publishing career, but he has had to do this outside France – however, despite these sometimes impressive successes, each of these four thinkers are marked by their borderline status.

Above all, the 'war of the veil' has thrown women into the spotlight: this particular frontier dispute concerns the borders of socially acceptable femininity and – slowly, grudgingly – even the French media has come to realize that women may have something to say about this matter. Republicans particularly valued speakers like Djavann and Amara who seemed to emerge from the frontier zone to validate French neo-republican rhetoric. The particular context formed by French republicanism, Western Muslim culture and globalization has produced some articulate and arresting debates which illuminate the common dilemmas of Western states in the twenty-first century: it remains to be seen whether they represent a substantial shift in the structures of Western Muslim political culture.[19]

The French paradigm

In one sense, the 'war of the veil' did seem to produce a sense of clarity: it reduced this exhausting, complex debate to an apparently simple yes/no question: are you for or against 'the veil'? Obviously, this stark choice did not properly represent the range of opinions within French society. In particular, it ignored or caricatured liberal ideas which upheld the right of individuals to choose how to express their faith, while not necessarily approving of either the faith or the form of expression. Instead, the framework set by the Stasi Commission and the resulting law taught French people that there was a binary clash between two irreconcilable forces, between which no meaningful compromise was possible. But, in reality, this is not a clash between new and old, modernity and tradition, not even a clash between secularism and religion. The simplistic caricatures of Islam paraded by *laïque* polemists must be rejected: the dominant forms of Islam that are developing in the world's fifteenth Islamic power are usually rationalistic, forward-looking and respect human rights. The common slur that French Islam is *communautarisme* in practice is laughable: the debates considered in this work show that Islam has the potential to encourage French Muslims to learn one of the world's great global languages, to inspire them to feel solidarity with peoples across the world and to highlight the issues raised in some key conflict zones. To label this *communautariste* is a silly, sloppy caricature of reality.

The substance of this debate is not being played out on the centre of the stage. The Chiracs and Finkielkrauts strut there, occasionally assisted by Amara and Djavann. At times, they still look like world statesmen or profound thinkers, but in the transition from Chirac to Sarkozy we can see another significant step downwards in the stature of the president: from world statesmen to a Mr Fix-It with a dramatic, populist touch.[20] To understand the true nature of this debate, we must shift our focus from the stage to the *coulisses*, we need to listen to the voices at the peripheries.

Epilogue

Fatima was getting impatient. Her shift as a cleaner in the hotel would start in a couple of hours: she'd need to leave soon if she was to get there on time. But this strange, silent ceremony was dragging on. How long could a funeral for a dead tramp last? The president had stated that there would be no speeches: why did they stay? Fatima picked up her broom, and walked back to the bench, set with its back to the graves. She sat down carefully: sitting too far back would hurt her knee, sitting too far forward would strain her back. The sun was shining. It was not that murderous sun of a few weeks ago, but a pleasant, clear autumn sun. Few people looked at her: they rarely did. Even those who noticed her usually seemed to accept her. She recalled the old couple the other day, lost in the labyrinth of graves, who'd been so glad to see her, and had thanked with that peculiar warm, restrained politeness that the French did so well. Of course, not everyone was so nice. You still got those looks, sniggers and whispers. As she remembered, she grew worried: she knew where her thoughts were leading. A week ago, in the supervisor's hut, someone had asked why the Louis-Blanc Cemetery was employing an Arab woman as a cleaner. Octave had laughed, and said quite happily, 'At the rates the council pays, do you think we could afford anyone but an old ...' She stopped herself. That one bad word. It had hurt so much, that time. And it was silly: he hadn't been talking to her, he'd even been *defending* her ... But she knew what it meant, she wouldn't be able to stay here for long. Another lost job.

She'd lose the job at the hotel if they didn't hurry up. What were they doing? Of course, it had started late. Bernard and Emmanuel had been delayed, getting lost on the ring road: Emmanuel had been certain that the cemetery was in the west of Paris. Faïza still hadn't turned up. Chahdortt had been the first to arrive. When the president walked in, she curtsied obsequiously. Would she never learn? Then Fadela, in her new fur coat, looking quite smart. Tariq

had sent his apologies: he had said he was attending a conference
on post-theology in America, but here he was, just like all the others,
waiting with them. He was as elegant as ever, and quite silent, his
eyes darting over the scene. Maybe he'd even seen her. Even Houria
was there, looking daggers at everyone. If only she'd been her
daughter! Because, these days, you had to be like that, you had to
fight, or they'd crush you.

When were they going to finish? She shifted backwards a little,
closed her eyes, enjoying the feel of the cool, clear light on her face.
It wasn't like autumn at all, more like spring.

Notes

Epigraph

1 Cited in Ismahane Chouder, Malika Latrèche and Pierre Tevanian (eds), *Les Filles voilées parlent* (Floch: La Fabrique, 2008), p. 167.

Introduction

1 Christelle Hamel and Christine Delphy, 'On vous a tant aimé.e.s! Entretien avec Houria Boutelja', *Nouvelles Questions Féministes* 25:1 (2006), 122–35.

2 'Discours du Président avec les élèves de première et de terminale du lycée Pierre Mendès-France', *http://presidence-de-la-republique.fr/elysee/ elysee.fr/francais_archives/interventions/dialogues_et_debats/2003/rencontre -discussion_de_m_jacques_chirac_president_de_la_republique_avec_des_eleves _du_lycee_pierre-mendes-france-tunis.2510.html*, posted 5 December 2005, accessed 1 January 2006.

3 Interview with Jürgen Habermas, « El antisemitismo en Alemania es más peligroso que en el resto de Europa », *El País*, 31 January 2004; Rowan Williams, Christmas sermon, *http://www.archbishopofcanter-bury.org/1209*, posted 25 December 2003, accessed 1 January 2004; Human Rights Watch, 'France: headscarf ban violates religious freedom', *http://www.hrw.org/en/news/2004/02/26/france-headscarf-ban-violates-religious-freedom*, posted 26 February 2004, accessed 6 March 2004; Christine Delphy, 'La loi anti-voile: un aveuglement collectif', *http://oumma.com/article.php3?id_article=943*, posted 9 February 2004, accessed 10 February 2004.

4 Caitlin Killian, 'The other side of the veil: North African women in France respond to the headscarf affair', *Gender and Society* 17:4 (2003), 567–90; John R. Bowen, 'Does French Islam have borders? – Dilemmas of domestication in a global religious field', *American Anthropologist* 106:1 (2004), 43–55; Jane Kramer, 'Taking the veil', *New Yorker* 22 November 2004, 58–71; Emmanuel Terray, 'Headscarf hysteria', *New Left Review* 26 (2004), 118–27; Parvati Nair, 'Moor – veiled – matters: the *hijab* as troubling interrogative of the relation between the West and Islam', *New Formations* 51 (2004), 39–49. My own work was: Sharif Gemie, 'Stasi's Republic: the school and the "veil", December 2003–March 2004', *Modern and Contemporary France* 12:3 (2004), 387–97.

5 An estimate put forward in Sadek Hajji and Stéphanie Marteau, *Voyage dans la France musulmane* (Paris: Plon, 2005), p. 11.

6   Françoise Gaspard and Farhad Khosrokhavar, *Le Foulard et la République* (Paris: La Découverte, 1995) and Oliver Roy, *La Laïcité face à l'Islam* (Paris: Stock, 2005).

7   Jonathan Laurence and Justin Vaisse, *Integrating Islam: Political and Religious Challenges in Contemporary France* (Washington: Brookings Institution Press, 2006) and Franck Frégosi, *Penser l'Islam dans la laïcité: les musulmans de France et la République* (Paris: Fayard, 2008).

8   See Christopher Flood, 'National Republican politics, intellectuals and the case of Pierre-André Taguieff', *Modern and Contemporary France* 12:3 (2004), 353–70.

9   Régis Debray, *Ce que nous voile le voile: la République et le sacré* (Paris: Gallimard, 2004); Michèle Vianès, *Un voile sur la République* (Paris: Stock, 2004). To his credit, Debray later re-considered some of his more aggressive and dismissive pronouncements. See the interview with him, 'Plaidoyer pour le clair-obscur', *Nouvel Observateur*, 21 December 2006.

10 Rachid Benzine, *Les Nouveaux Penseurs de l'Islam* (Paris: Albin Michel, 2004).

11 Dounia Bouzar and Saïda Kada, *L'Une voilée, l'autre pas: le témoignage de deux musulmanes françaises* (Paris: Albin Michel, 2003).

12 Ismahane Chouder, Malika Latrèche and Pierre Tevanian (eds), *Les Filles voilées parlent* (Floch: La Fabrique, 2008).

13 Hajji and Marteau, *Voyage dans la France musulmane.*

14 *Quand al-Qaïda parle: témoignages derrière les barreaux* (Paris: Grasset & Fasquelle, 2006).

15 Trica Danielle Keaton, *Muslim Girls and the Other France: Race, Identity Politics and Social Exclusion* (Bloomington: Indiana University Press, 2006); Paul A. Silverstein, *Algeria in France: Transpolitics, Race and Nation* (Bloomington: Indiana University Press, 2004).

16 Thomas Deltombe, *L'Islam imaginaire: la construction médiatique de l'islamophobie en France, 1975–2005* (Paris: La Découverte, 2005).

17 Alec G. Hargreaves, *Multi-Ethnic France: Immigration, Politics, Culture and Society* (2nd edn) (New York and London: Routledge, 2007).

18 International Crisis Group, *La France face à ses musulmans: émeutes, jihadisme et dépolitisation* (Rapport Europe 172, 2006).

19 Vincent Geisser and El Yamine Saum, *Discriminer pour mieux régner: enquête sur la diversité dans les partis politiques* (Ivry-sur-Seine: Les Editions de l'Atelier/Editions ouvrières, 2008).

20 X... du Figaro, *Les Coulisses du Boulangisme* (Paris: Cerf, 1890).

21 François Maspero, *Les Passagers du Roissy-Express* (Paris: Seuil, 1990).

22 Azouz Begag, *Un Mouton dans le bagnoire: dans les caulisses du pouvoir* (Paris: Fayard, 2007).

23 Alima Boumédienne-Thiery, 'Musulmanes féministes: du paradoxe à la réalité', *http://www.oumma.com/imprimer.php3 ?id_article=998*, accessed 12 March 2004 (published 10 March 2004). On this point, see also the pertinent remarks by Alec G. Hargreaves on the 'verbal acrobatics' involved in the labelling of Arab Algerians in France: 'Algerians in contemporary France: incorporation or exclusion?', *Journal of Algerian Studies* 3 (1998), 31–47.

24 Joan Gross, David McMurray and Ted Swedenburg, 'Arab noise and

Ramadan nights: Rai, rap and Franco-Maghrebi identities' in Smadar Lavie and Ted Swedenburg (eds), *Displacement, Diaspora and Geographies of Identity* (Durham and London: Duke University Press, 1996), pp. 119–56.

25 Cited in Hajji and Marteau, *Voyage dans la France musulmane*, pp. 58 and 36.

26 Tariq Ramadan, *Être Musulman européen: Etude des sources islamiques à la lumière du contexte européen* (translated from the English by Claude Dabbak) (Lyon: Tawhid, 1999), p. 187.

27 'Plus pratiquants, les musulmans de France sont aussi mieux inté-grés', *Le Monde*, 5 October 2001; Laurence and Vaisse, *Integrating Islam*, p. 76.

28 On this episode, see Hargreaves, *Multi-Ethnic France*, pp. 4–5.

29 See 'L'Islam ne joue pas un rôle déterminant dans la propagation des troubles', *Le Figaro*, 11 November 2005.

30 See Geisser and Soum, *Discriminer*, p. 138.

31 See Robert Castel, *La Discrimination négative: citoyens ou indigènes?* (Paris: Seuil, 2007), p. 88.

32 Hajji and Marteau, *Voyage dans la France musulmane*, p. 12.

33 On the Jewish presence in Europe, see David Rechter, 'The Jews: a European minority' in S. Berger (ed.), *A Companion to Nineteenth-Century Europe* (Oxford: Blackwell, 2006), pp. 274–87; on the long-term effects of the ghetto see the perceptive comments in Alexander Stille, *Benevolence and Betrayal; Five Jewish Italian Families under Fascism* (Harmondsworth: Penguin, 1991), pp. 22–5.

34 On the history of Jews and French republicanism, see Pierre Birnbaum, *Les Fous de la République: histoire politique des Juifs d'Etat de Gambetta à Vichy* (Paris: Fayard, 1992), and the same author's percep-tive, incisive survey 'Grégoire, Dreyfus, Drancy et Copernic' in Pierre Nora, *Les Lieux de Mémoire Vol II* (Paris: Quarto – Gallimard, 1997), pp. 2679–719. See also Jacques Adler, 'The Jews and Vichy: reflec-tions on French historiography', *Historical Journal* 44:4 (2001), 1065–81.

35 Perrine Simon-Nahun, 'French Judaism', trans. by A. Goldhammer in A. Prost and G. Vincent (eds), *A History of Private Life, Vol. V* (Cambridge, Mass.: Harvard University Press, 1991), pp. 347–78. See also Michel Abitol, 'The integration of North African Jews in France', *Yale French Studies* 85 (1994), pp. 248–61.

36 See the considerations on this theme in Alain Finkielkraut and Benny Lévy, *Le Livre et les livres: Entretiens sur la laïcité* (Paris: Verdier, 2006), pp. 38–9.

37 On the interplay between French culture and black culture, see Petrine Archer-Straw, *Negrophilia: Avant-Garde Paris and Black Culture in the 1920s* (London: Thames and Hudson, 2000).

38 Geisser and Soum, *Discriminer pour mieux régner*, pp. 83, 117.

39 See Jim House and Neil MacMaster, *Paris 1961: Algerians, State Terror and Memory* (Oxford: Oxford University Press, 2006) for an informa-tive study on the manner in which Algerian colonialism was brought

back to France. Paul Henissart, *Wolves in the City: The Death of French Algeria* (London: Rupert Hart-Davis, 1970) remains the classic text on the depth of violence and hatred among colonists, hard-line officers and the French far right in the last years of French Algeria.

40   Martin Evans, *The Memory of Resistance: French Opposition to the Algerian War (1954–1962)* (Oxford: Berg, 1997), and Sylvain Pattieu, *Les Camarades des frères: trotskistes et libertaires dans la guerre d'Algérie* (Paris: Syllepsie, 2002). See also Akli Dahmani, 'Le Parti communiste français face à la guerre d'Algérie', *Cahiers d'histoire immédiate* 20 (2001), 27–68.

41   Marnia Lazreg, 'Gender and politics in Algeria: unravelling the religious paradigm', *Signs* 15 (1990), 755–80.

42   On the colonial legacy in France, see Nicolas Bancel, Pascal Blanchard and Sandrine Lemaire (eds), *La France coloniale* (Paris: La Découverte, 2005) and Benjamin Stora, *La Guerre des mémoires; la France face à son passé colonial, entretiens avec Thierry Leclère* (np: L'Aube, 2007), and the useful articles by Laurent Dubois, 'La République métisée: citizenship, colonialism and the borders of French history', *Cultural Studies* 14:1 (2000), 15–34 and by Hélène Gill, 'Hegemony and ambiguity: discourses, counter-discourses and hidden meanings in French depictions of the conquest and settlement of Algeria', *Modern and Contemporary France* 14:2 (2006), 157–72.

43   Geisser and Soum, *Discriminer pour mieux régner*, p. 88. See also 'On nous qualifie sans cesse d'Arabes et on prétend nous empêcher de nous situer par rapport à l'islam', *Le Monde*, 6 July 2004.

44   Nacira Guénif-Souilamas, 'The other French exception: virtuous racism and the war of the sexes in postcolonial France', *French Politics, Culture and Society* 24:3 (2006), 23–41.

45   Yann Moulier Boutang, *La Révolte des banlieues, ou: les habits nus de la République* (Paris: Amsterdam, 2005), p. 96.

Chapter One

1   For example, see 'Rétrocontroverse: 1989: la République laïque face au foulard islamique', *Le Monde*, 3 August 2007.

2   See the analysis of this affair in Martin Evans, 'The left, laïcité and Islam', *Modern and Contemporary France* 45 (1991), 8–15.

3   John R. Bowen, *Why the French Don't Like Headscarves: Islam, the State and Public Space* (Princeton: Princeton University Press, 2007), p. 92.

4   On the pre-history of French–Arab relations before the crisis of 1989 see Margaret A. Majumdar, 'Extra-European national minorities in France and the concept of European identity', *History of European Ideas* 19:4–6 (1994), 647–53.

5   On this point, see 'L'enseignement, débouche sans préjugés pour enfants d'immigrés', *Libération*, 16 January 2008. For a far more critical appreciation of the school's role, see Pierre Bourdieu, 'L'idéologie jacobine' in his *Interventions, 1961–2001* (Marseilles: Agone, 2002), pp. 55–61.

6   Emmanuel Brenner (ed.), *Les Territoires perdus de la République* (Paris: Arthème Fayard, 2004).

7   Ibid., p. 24.

8   Ibid., pp. 12, 83, 17.

9   As suggested in Alain Gresh, 'Les Faux-semblants de la Commission Stasi', *http://www.islamlaicite.org/article187/html*, posted 23 January 2004, accessed 5 March 2004.

10 Brenner, *Les Territoires*, p.59.

11 See the pertinent arguments by Laurent Bonelli, *La France a peur: une histoire sociale de « l'insécurité »* (Paris: La Découverte, 2008), pp. 55–61.

12 Yann Moulier Boutang, *La Révolte des banlieues, ou: les habits nus de la République* (Paris: Amsterdam, 2005), p. 40.

13 'Le bloc-notes d'Ivan Rioufol: Signes d'autorité', *Le Figaro*, 12 November 2004. See also 'La face cachée de l'UOIF', *L'Express*, 2 May 2005.

14 This point is discussed in a number of contemporary press reports. See, for example, 'Editorial: Riposte', *Libération*, 9 December 2003; 'Comment l'idée d'une loi s'est imposée', *Le Figaro*, 3 February 2004; 'Douze mois de débats passionnés', *Le Figaro*, 4 March 2004.

15 'Editorial: Désarroi', *Libération*, 9 December 2003.

16 Jane Kramer, 'Taking the veil', *New Yorker*, 22 November 2004, pp. 58–71.

17 Natalie Benelli, Ellen Hertz, Christine Delphy, Christelle Hamel, Patricia Roux and Jules Falquet, 'Editorial: De l'affaire du voile à l'imbrication du sexisme et du racisme', *Nouvelles Questions Féministes* 25:1 (2006), 4–11 (7).

18 See Jean Baubérot, 'La Commission Stasi vue par l'un de ses membres', *French Politics, Culture and Society* 22:3 (2004), 135–41.

19 'Trois questions à … Bernard Brandmeyer', *Le Monde*, 17 January 2004.

20 Baubérot, 'La Commission Stasi', 140, footnote 9.

21 See Elisabeth Badinter et Alain Touraine, 'Une France plurielle … ou éclatée?: Un débat', *Nouvel Observateur*, 19 June 2003.

22 Bernard Stasi with Olivier Picard, *Tous français: Immigration, la chance de la France* (Paris: Hugo, 2007), pp. 33–4.

23 Stasi, *Tous français*, p. 22.

24 Stasi, *Tous français*, p. 17.

25 On Stasi, see the revealing interview, 'Bernard Stasi, contre les racismes', *La Croix*, 7 January 2005.

26 Jacqueline Costa-Lascoux, 'La loi des hommes contre la loi divine', *Le Monde de l'éducation* 321 (January 2004), 28–31.

27 'Bernard Stasi: "La escuela no puede ser escenario de lucha religiosa"', *El País*, 21 December 2003. This image of the islamicized suburbs has been challenged: see, for example, Nadia Kiwan, 'Managing marginalization: young French North-Africans and local associations', *Modern and Contemporary France* 13:4 (2005), 465–81.

28 'Membre de la Commission Stasi, Alain Touraine raconte sa conversion au principe d'une loi', *Le Monde*, 18 December 2003.

29 'Revue de la presse sur la remise du rapport Stasi au Président de la République', CRIF, *http://www.crif.org/impr.php?id=2110&type=Comm entaires*, posted 15 December 2003, accessed 1 January 2004.

30 Patrick Weill, 'Lifting the veil', *French Politics, Culture and Society* 22:3 (2004), 142–9 (143).

31 Baubérot, 'La Commission Stasi', 139.

32 Bernard Stasi, *Rapport au président de la République* (np: no publisher, 2003), 57.

33 Gresh, 'Les Faux-semblants', is probably the best analysis of the Stasi Commission's dynamics.

34 Weill, 'Lifting the veil', 145.

35 Nicolas Weill, 'What's in a scarf? – The debate on *laïcité* in France', *French Politics, Culture and Society* 24:1 (2006), 59–73 (67).

36 Baubérot, 'La Commission Stasi', 139.

37 Bernard Stasi, cited in the 'Revue de la presse sur la remise de rapport Stasi au Président de la République', CRIF, *http://www.crif. org/impr.php?id=2110&type=Commentaires*, posted 15 December 2003, accessed 1 January 2004. See also Bernard Stasi, 'Laïcité: soignons notre copie' in Yves Charles Zarka (ed.), *L'Islam en France* (Paris: PUF, 2004), pp. 177–9.

38 'Voile: les états d'âme de quatre sages de la Commission Stasi', *Le Monde*, 2 February 2004.

39 'Les désarrois de l'élève Stasi', *Le Figaro*, 20 January 2004.

40 Pierre Tevanian, *Le Voile médiatique – un faux débat: L'affaire du foulard islamique* (Paris: Raisons d'Agir, 2005), p. 15.

41 'La querelle du voile', *Le Monde*, 24 October 2003.

42 'L'UMP et le PS ont voté la loi sur la laïcité', *Le Monde*, 11 February 2004.

43 Ismahane Chouder, Malika Latrèche and Pierre Tevanian (eds), *Les Filles voilées parlent* (Floch: La Fabrique, 2008), p. 12.

44 'Un long débat pour une courte loi', *La Croix*, 27 January 2004.

45 Information from *www.afp.com/francais/home*.

46 Tevanian, *Voile médiatique*, p. 19.

47 Ibid., pp. 87–8.

48 Ibid., p. 32.

49 Ibid., p. 79.

50 'Les musulmans et la laïcité', *http://www.csa-fr.com/dataset/data2004/ opi20040121b.htm*, posted 21 January 2004, accessed 28 July 2008.

51 'Editorial: Politique de la peur', *Le Monde*, 19 December 2003.

52 'Les trois présidents du Conseil d'Eglises Chrétiennes en France s'adressent au Président de la République au sujet de la laïcité', *http://www.cef.fr/catho/actus/txtoffic/index.php*, posted 8 December 2003, accessed 10 December 2003.

53 'Les principes de laïcité réaffirmés', *http://www.cfdt.fr/actu/imprimer/ presse/communique/commm_360.thm*, posted 12 December 2003, accessed 18 December 2003.

54 'Pour les valeurs de la République', *http://www.cgt.fr/03actual/actupg/ france/2003/12/valeurs.htm*, posted 17 December 2003, accessed 18 December 2003.

55 Cited in 'Réactions au rapport Stasi', *La Croix*, 11 December 2003.
56 'A Montreuil, le foulard déchire les profs', *Libération*, 8 November 2003.
57 See, for example, 'Foulard: les dégâts de l'islamophobie', *Le Figaro*, 18 October 2003; 'Les véritables défis de la laïcité', *Marianne*, 27 October 2003; 'Le racisme est un et indivisible', *http://www.mrap. asso.fr/imprimer.php3?id_article=620*, posted 15 November 2003, accessed 6 January 2004; 'Signes religieux et politiques à l'École: une loi dangereuse', *http://www.mrap.asso.fr/imprimer.php3?id_article=634*, posted 20 November 2003, accessed 6 January 2004.
58 'Affirmer la laïcité', *http://www.ldh-france.org/actu_print.cfm?idactu= 743&type=derniere&content=single*, posted 16 December 2003, accessed 6 January 2004; 'Intégrer ou exclure', *http://www.ldh-france. orgh/actu_print.cfm?idactu=751&type=derniere&content=single*, posted 19 December 2003, accessed 6 January 2004.
59 Bowen, *Why the French Don't Like Headscarves*, p. 109.
60 See Jacques Godechot (ed.), *Les Constitutions de la France depuis 1789* (Paris: Flammarion, 1979), pp. 391, 424.
61 See Kay Chadwick, 'Education in secular France: (re)defining laïcité', *Modern and Contemporary France* 5:1 (1997), 47–60.
62 Max Gallo, 'La supériorité de la laïcité', in Yves Charles Zarka (ed.), *L'Islam en France* (Paris: PUF, 2004), pp. 201–4 (p. 203).
63 Jacqueline Costa-Lascoux, 'Les échecs de l'intégration, un accroc au contrat social', *Pouvoirs* 111 (2004), 19–27.
64 Weill, 'What's in a Scarf?, p. 59.
65 Olivier Roy, *La Laïcité face à l'Islam* (Paris: Stock, 2005), pp. 29, 37. See also Bowen, *Why the French Don't Like Headscarves*, p. 29.
66 Soheib Bencheikh, *Marianne et le Prophète: l'Islam dans la France laïque* (Paris: Grasset, 1998), p. 20.
67 'Relatif au respect du principe de laïcité dans la République', *http://www.elysee.fr/cgi-bin/auracom/auraweb/search/file?aur_file=discours/2003/DO31217.html*, posted 17 December 2003, accessed 4 January 2004.
68 Christian Bourepaux, 'Un principe qui ne va plus de soi', *Le Monde de l'éducation* 321 (January 2004), 25–7 (26).
69 Anne Vigerie and Anne Zelensky, '"Laïcardes", puisque féministes', *Le Monde*, 30 May 2003.
70 Jean-Marc Ayrault, *Discours … prononcé lors de la discussion du projet de loi sur les signes religieux à l'école*, 3 February 2004. *http://www.assemblee-nationale.fr/12/cri/2003–2004/20040148.asp*, accessed 4 March 2004.
71 Christine Delphy, Alima Boumedienne-Thiery and Noël Mamère, 'Appel à mobilisation contre les lois d'exclusions à l'initiative du collectif *Une école pour tous-tes*', *http://www.lmsi.net/impression.php3?id_ article=212*, posted 23 January 2004, accessed 6 February 2004.
72 François Fillon, 'Circulaire du 18 mai 2004', *Journal Officiel*, 22 May 2004.
73 Jean-Pierre Raffarin, *Discours … prononcé lors de la discussion du projet de loi sur les signes religieux à l'école*. 3 February 2004. *http://www.assemblee-nationale.fr/12/cri/2003–2004/20040148.asp*, accessed 4 March 2004.

74 'Les trois présidents', 8 December 2003.
75 See, for example, Daniel Bensaïd, *Fragments mécréants: sur les mythes imaginaires et la république imaginaire* (Paris: Lignes, 2005), p. 35.
76 See Richard Sennett's incisive analysis of this apparently idealistic form of political speech in his *The Fall of Public Man* (London: Faber & Faber, 1986 [1977]), pp. 228–31.
77 On this point, see Raymond Huard, *La Naissance du parti politique en France* (Paris: Sciences-Po, 1996).
78 Christopher Flood uses the term 'National Republican' to identify this strand: see his 'National Republican politics, intellectuals and the case of Pierre-André Taguieff', *Modern and Contemporary France* 12:3 (2004), 353–70. On the political philosophy of republicanism, see Claude Nicholet, *L'Idée républicaine en France (1789–1924)* (Paris: Gallimard, 1994). See also Sharif Gemie, 'An extremism of the center: Jean-Pierre Chevènement, French presidential candidate, 2002', *French Politics, Culture and Society* 22:1 (2004), 76–97.
79 Ayrault, *Discours*: 'Chacun chez soi et Dieu pour tous!'
80 '"*La laïcité doit se décréter*": Interview avec Régis Debray', *L'Express*, 15 January 2004.
81 Jean Baubérot, 'Une "haine démocratique" et son dépassement. Du combat anticlérical à la loi de séparation de 1905', *Diasporas* 10 (2007), 26–49 (34). On this point, see also Isaiah Berlin's classic essay, 'Two concepts of liberty', in his *Four Essays on Liberty* (Oxford: Oxford University Press, 1984).
82 Fadela Amara and Mohammed Abdi, *La Racaille de la République* (Paris: Seuil, 2006), p. 102.
83 'Les trois présidents'.
84 On the politics of this moment, see the perceptive article by Isser Woloch, 'Left, right and centre: the MRP and the post-war moment', *French History* 21:1 (2007), 85–106.
85 Dr Abdullah, *Le Foulard islamique et la République française: mode d'emploi*, http://www.nassira.net, no date of publication [1994–5?] accessed 1 March 2004, p. 95. Abdullard is a Muslim convert: he often appears as a type of caricature fundamentalist in Republican loyalist discourse. In truth, he is more like a barrack-room lawyer, attempting to provide a users' guide to Republican legislation: his stance is impeccably legalistic.
86 Example cited in Dounia Bouzar and Saïda Kada, *L'Une voilée, l'autre pas: le témoignage de deux musulmanes françaises* (Paris: Albin Michel, 2003), p. 64.
87 Chouder, Latrèche and Tevanian, *Les Filles voilées*, p. 35.
88 Ibid., p. 67.
89 'Le témoignage d'une élève qui a retiré son voile'.
90 'Une jeune turque, faute de pouvoir porter le voile dans un lycée de Strasbourg, s'est rasé la tête', *Le Monde*, 1 October 2004.
91 Chouder, Latrèche and Tevanian, *Les Filles voilées*, p. 54.
92 Ibid., p. 78.
93 Ibid., p. 71.

94   Ibid., p. 103.
95   'Kholoud 12 ans', *Le Monde*, 20 October 2004.
96   Chouder, Latrèche and Tevanian, *Les Filles voilées*, p. 31.
97   'Une étudiante voilée exclue de cours', *Ouest-France*, 27 January 2004.
98   Régis Debray, *Ce que nous voile le voile: la République et le sacré* (Paris: Gallimard, 2004), pp. 18–19.
99   'Relatif au respect du principe de laïcité dans la République'.
100 Jean-Louis Debré, 'Rapport fait au nom de la mission d'information sur la question du port des signes religieux à l'école' *Assemblée Nationale* 1275 (4 December 2003), vol. I, 9.
101 Michèle Vianès, *Un voile sur la République* (Paris: Stock, 2004), p. 205.
102 Bernard Stasi, *Rapport au président de la République* (np: no publisher, 2003), p. 43.
103 On the political culture of the anti-Dreyfusards, see Sharif Gemie, *French Revolutions, 1815–1914* (Edinburgh: Edinburgh University Press, 1999), pp. 220–48.
104 Philippe de Villiers, *Les Mosquées de Roissy* (Paris: Albin Michel, 2006), pp. 103, 82.
105 On this form of 'anti-Establishment' politics, see the excellent analysis in Sennett's *Fall of Public Man*, pp. 277–87.
106 'La *laïcité* n'est athéisme', *Monde libertaire*, 2 June 2005. On this publication's disappointing response to the 'war of the veil', see Sharif Gemie, 'The trial of Fatima: anarchists, Muslims and the *Monde Libertaire*, 2003–5', *Anarchist Studies* 14:1 (2006), 9–19.
107 On this point, see Roy, *Laïcité*, p. 60.
108 Fadwa El Guindi, *Veil: Modesty, Privacy and Resistance* (Oxford: Berg, 1999), pp. 6–7.
109 Anne Vigerie and Anne Zelensky, '"Laïcardes", puisque féministes', *Le Monde*, 30 May 2003.
110 Vianès, *Un voile*, pp. 163–71.
111 'Editorial: Stigmatisées', *Libération*, 19 January 2004.
112 'La querelle du voile', *Le Monde*, 23 October 2003.
113 François Bayrou, 'Discours … prononcé lors de la discussion du projet de loi sur le port des signes religieux à l'école', 3 February 2004. *http://www.assemblee-nationale.fr/12/cri/2003–2004/20040148. asp*, accessed 4 March 2004.
114 UFAL, 'Pour un 6 mars féministe et laïque sans femmes voilées dans nos cortèges', *http://www.ufal.org/spip/article.php3?id_article=56*, posted 20 February 2004, accessed 9 March 2004.
115 'Les revenantes et le plafond de chiffon' *Le Monde*, 5 February 2004.
116 Martine Billard, *Débat "laïcité à l'école": cette loi ne résoudra ni les discriminations subies par les femmes, ni la montée des intégrismes religieux*, *http://martinebillard.org/article.php3?id_article=221*, posted 3 February 2004, accessed 21 March 2004.
117 El Guindi, *Veil*, p. 16.
118 Hervé Flanquart, *Croyances et valeurs chez les jeunes Maghrébins* (Paris: Complexe, 2003), p. 37.

119 Bouzar and Kada, *L'Une voilée*, p. 22
120 Ibid., p. 89.
121 Ibid., p. 123.
122 Sophie Bessis, 'Entrevista del grupo Eleuterio Quintanilla a Sophie Bessis', *www.equintalla.com/bessis.htm*, posted 25 October 2004, accessed 20 June 2007.
123 Sadek Hajji and Stéphanie Marteau, *Voyage dans la France musulmane* (Paris: Plon, 2005).
124 Françoise Gaspard and Farhad Khosrokhavar, *Le Foulard et la République* (Paris: La Découverte, 1995), p. 47.
125 Halima Zouhar, 'Le foulard islamique: choix ou soumission', *http://www.oumma.com/Le-foulard-islamique-ou*, posted 17 March 2007, accessed 23 March 2007.
126 Caitlin Killian, 'The other side of the veil: North African women in France respond to the headscarf affair', *Gender and Society* 17:4 (2003), 567–90 (572).
127 Lucette Valensi, 'Confrontations/contradictions', in Gabriel Martinez-Gros and Lucette Valensi, *L'Islam en dissidence: Genèse d'un affrontement* (Paris: Seuil, 2004), pp. 140–302 (p. 286).
128 Karin Ask and Marit Tjomsland, 'Introduction' to their edited collection *Women and Islamization* (Oxford: Berg, 1998), pp. 1–16 (p. 11).
129 Jenny B. White, 'The paradox of the new Islamic woman in Turkey', in Inger Marie Okkenhaug and Ingvild Flaskerud (eds), *Gender, Religion and Change in the Middle East* (Oxford: Berg, 2005), pp. 123–35.
130 'The invisible power of piety wearing stilettos', *Times Higher Education Supplement*, 2 November 2006.
131 Reina Lewis, 'Veils and sales: Muslims and the spaces of postcolonial fashion retail', *Fashion Theory* 11:4 (2007), 423–42.
132 'My years in a habit taught me the paradox of veiling', *Guardian*, 26 October 2006.
133 Jen'nan Ghazal Read and John P. Bartkowski, 'To veil or not to veil? – A case study on identity negotiation among Muslim women in Austin, Texas', *Gender and Society* 14:3 (2000), 395–417.
134 Bencheikh, *Marianne et le Prophète*, pp. 144–5.
135 'Leur voile, j'ai envie de l'arracher', *Libération,* 9 December 2003.
136 Abdelwahab Meddeb, *Face à l'Islam* (Paris: Textuel, 2004), pp. 197–9.
137 Chouder, Latrèche and Tevanian, *Les Filles voilées*, p. 53.
138 Debré, *Rapport*, p. 75.
139 Billard, *Débat "laïcité à l'école"*.
140 Stasi, *Rapport*, pp. 56–7.
141 See *The Headmaster and the Headscarves*, BBC2, 29 March 2005.
142 'Une collégienne exclue demande réparation', *Nouvel Observateur*, 26 October 2004.
143 Chouder, Latrèche and Tevanian, *Les Filles voilées*, p. 64.
144 On French social science and colonialism, see Patricia M. E. Lorcin, *Imperial Identities: Stereotyping, Prejudice and Race in Colonial Algeria*

(London: Tauris, 1999). There is some reason to argue that such attitudes are distinctively colonial: for a revealing comparison, see Chinua Achebe, 'Colonial Criticism', in Bill Ashcroft, Gareth Griffith and Helen Tiffin (eds), *The Post-Colonial Studies Reader* (2nd edn) (London: Routledge, 2006), pp. 74–8.

145 Julia Clancy-Smith, 'Le regard colonial: Islam, genre et identités dans la fabrication de l'Algérie française' translated by Françoise Armengaud, *Nouvelles Questions Féministes* 25:1 (2006), 25–40; Aïcha Touati, 'Féministes d'hier et d'aujourd'hui, ou le féminisme à l'épreuve de l'universel', *Nouvelles Questions Féministes* 25:1 (2006), 108–20.

146 Bouzar and Kaya, *Voilée*, p. 146.

147 'Straw gets the debate he wanted', BBC, *http://news.bbc.co.uk/1/hi/uk_politics/5413012.stm*, posted 6 October 2006, accessed 15 April 2008.

148 Azouz Begag, *Un Mouton dans le bagnoire: dans les coulisses du pouvoir* (Paris: Fayard, 2007), p. 118.

149 Chouder, Latrèche and Tevanian, *Les Filles voilées* p. 121.

150 Gaspard and Khosrokhavar, *Le Foulard*, p. 52.

151 Begag grew up close to this area: see his *Place du Pont, ou la médina de Lyon* (Paris: Autrement, 1997).

152 Fadela Amara with Sylvia Zappi, *Ni Putes ni Soumises* (Paris: La Découverte, 2003), pp. 26–8.

153 Thomas Deltombe, *L'Islam imaginaire: la construction médiatique de l'islamophobie en France, 1975–2005* (Paris: La Découverte, 2005), p. 61.

154 Robert Castel, *La Discrimination négative: citoyens ou indigènes?* (Paris: Seuil, 2007), p. 81

155 See David Blatt, 'Immigrant politics in a Republican nation', in A. G. Hargreaves and M. McKinney (eds), *Post-Colonial Cultures in France* (London: Routledge, 1997), pp. 40–55 for a good survey of this theme.

156 On the actions of the Socialist Party, see Serge Malik, *Histoire secrète de SOS-Racisme* (Paris: Albin Michel, 1990), pp. 72–3.

157 See Vincent Geisser and El Yamine Soum, *Discriminer pour mieux régner: enquête sur la diversité dans les partis politiques* (Ivry-sur-Seine: Les Editions de l'Atelier/Editions ouvrières, 2008), pp. 22–8 for a good summary of criticisms and complaints about the experiences of SOS-Racisme.

158 Ibid., p. 155.

159 Michèle Lamont, Ann Morning and Margarita Mooney, 'Particular universalisms: North African immigrants respond to French racism', *Ethnic and Racial Studies* 25:3 (2002), 390–414.

160 Bouzar and Kada, *Voilée*, p. 73.

161 My analysis of this incident is largely drawn from the article by Xavier Ternisien, 'Sortir du petit monde de Marie L', *Le Monde*, 8 August 2004.

Chapter Two

1 *Culture et Dépendances*, FR2, 27 January 2006.
2 W. J. T. Mitchell, 'Translator translated (interview with cultural theorist Homi Bhabha)', *http://prelectur.stanford,edu/lecturers.bhabha/interview.html*, originally published in 1995, accessed 18 June 2007. See also Jonathan Rutherford, 'The third space: interview with Homi Bhabha' in his *Identity: Community, Culture, Difference* (London: Lawrence and Wishart, 1990), pp. 207–21.
3 Arjun Appadurai, *Modernity at Large: Cultural Dimensions of Globalization* (Minneapolis: University of Minnesota Press, 1996), pp. 21–2.
4 On the long-term intellectual and cultural significance of the 1967 war, see Ibrahim M. Abu-Rabi', *Contemporary Arab Thought: Studies in Post-1967 Arab Intellectual History* (London: Pluto, 2004).
5 On the French reception of the Iranian Revolution, see the useful observations by Thomas Deltombe, *L'Islam imaginaire: la construction médiatique de l'islamophobie en France, 1975–2005* (Paris: La Découverte, 2005), pp. 15–33.
6 Chahdortt Djavann, *Je viens d'ailleurs* (Paris: Autrement, 2002).
7 Chahdortt Djavann, *Bas les voiles!* (Paris: Gallimard, 2003).
8 'L'écrivaine Chahdortt Djavann à la commission Stasi: « Le port du voile doit être considéré comme un acte de maltraitance »', 22 September 2003, *Libération*.
9 Deltombe, *Islam imaginaire*, p. 354.
10 Ibid., p. 352, footnote 47.
11 Mireille Duteil, 'Interview: Chahdortt Djavann', *Le Point*, 26 August 2004; Isabelle Rabineau, 'Dévoilez Chahdortt', *Topo* 11 (November 2004), 19–29.
12 'Le voile de la honte', *Le Monde*, 12 September 2003.
13 'Le cri d'une jeune iranienne: jeunesse voilée sous le voile', *Le Figaro*, 6 November 2003.
14 'Le Combat de Chahdortt Djavann: pour cette Française d'origine iranienne, le voile relève de la maltraitance', *L'Express*, 30 October 2003.
15 '"Une pudeur pornographique": Chahdortt Djavann', *L'Humanité*, 19 December 2003.
16 'Le voile n'est pas soluble dans l'anarchisme', *Monde libertaire*, 27 January 2005.
17 'Merci Chahdortt', *Le Figaro*, 19 January 2004.
18 'Le cri d'alarme d'une "dissidente" iranienne', *Le Monde*, 10 November 2007.
19 Djavann, *Je viens d'ailleurs*, p. 13.
20 Rabineau, 'Dévoilez Chahdortt', 26.
21 Djavann, *Bas les voiles!*, p. 9.
22 Chahdortt Djavann, *A mon corps défendant, l'Occident* (Paris: Flammarion, 2007), pp. 60–9.
23 Djavann, *Je viens d'ailleurs*, p. 12.

24 Djavann, *A mon corps*, p. 61.
25 Djavann, *Je viens d'ailleurs*, p. 11.
26 Ibid., p. 26.
27 Ibid., p. 29; *A bas les voiles*, p. 17.
28 Ibid., p. 48.
29 Ibid., p. 51.
30 Ibid., pp. 64–8.
31 Ibid., pp. 112–13.
32 Ibid., p. 113.
33 Djavann, *Comment peut-on être français?* (Paris: Flammarion, 2006), pp. 11 and 30.
34 Ibid., p. 20.
35 Ibid., p. 71.
36 'Comment peut-on être français?', FR2, 27 January 2006.
37 Djavann, *Comment*, p. 33.
38 Djavann, *A mon corps*, p. 308.
39 Ibid., pp. 200–3.
40 Rabineau, 'Dévoilez Chahdortt', 21.
41 Djavann, *Bas les voiles*, p. 11.
42 Djavann, *Je viens d'ailleurs*, p. 70.
43 Chahdortt Djavann, *Que pense Allah de l'Europe* (Paris: Gallimard, 2004), p. 23; Djavann, *A mon corps*, p. 146.
44 Djavann, *Bas les voiles*, p. 39.
45 Ibid., p. 25.
46 'Interview with photographer Shadafarin Ghadirian', *http://www3.estart.com/iran/women/shadafarin*, accessed 20 April 2005.
47 'Riverbend', *Baghdad Burning: Girl Blog from Iraq* (London: Marion Boyars, 2006), pp. 122–4.
48 Rosemary Bechler, 'Islam and democracy: an interview with Heba Ezzat', Open Democracy (*http://www.opendemocracy.net*), accessed 28 October 2008, posted 11 May 2005.
49 See the wide-ranging survey by Azadeh Kian-Thiébaut, 'L'islam, les femmes et la citoyenneté', *Pouvoirs* 104 (2003), 71–84.
50 Djavann, *Que pense Allah*, p. 23.
51 Djavann, *A mon corps*, p. 25. On the medieval Christian concept of Islam as simply a heresy, see John V. Tolan, *Saracens: Islam in the Medieval European Imagination* (New York: Columbia University Press, 2002), pp. 135–73.
52 Djavann, *A mon corps*, p. 29.
53 Ibid., pp. 29, 32; 'Voile: légiférer sur le port du foulard à l'école aidera-t-il à l'islam à s'adapter', *Le Figaro*, 6 January 2004.
54 Rabineau, 'Dévoilez Chahdortt', 23. This comment can only make sense if one accepts the veil as an example of pornography.
55 Djavann, *A mon corps*, p. 53; Djavann, *Que pense Allah*, p. 29.
56 Karen Armstrong, *Islam: A Short History* (London: Phoenix, 2001), p. 149.
57 Farzaneh Milani, 'On women's captivity in the Islamic world', *Merip* 246 (2008), *http://www.merip.org/mer/mer246*, accessed 4 June 2008.

58 Ayaan Hirsi Ali, *The Caged Virgin: A Muslim Woman's Cry for Reason* (London: Simon and Schuster, 2006), p. 13.
59 Oriana Fallaci, *The Force of Reason* (New York: Rizzoli, 2006), pp. 67, 35.
60 Oriana Fallaci, *The Rage and the Pride* (New York: Rizzoli, 2001), p. 83.
61 Ibid., p. 27.
62 Ibid., p. 58.
63 Benny Morris, 'On ethnic cleansing', *New Left Review* 26 (2004), 37–51 (49).
64 Robert Redeker, 'Face aux intimidations islamistes, que doit faire le monde libre ?', *Le Figaro*, 19 September 2006. On the nature of Islam, see Karen Armstrong, 'We cannot afford to maintain these ancient prejudices against Islam', *Guardian*, 18 September 2006.
65 See 'Affaire Redeker: « L'heure n'est pas à la lacheté »', *L'Express*, 3 October 2006, and 'Non aux propos stéréotypés', *Le Monde*, 6 October 2006.
66 'Le cri d'alarme d'une "dissidente" iranienne.'
67 Djavann, *A mon corps*, p. 119.
68 Samuel P. Huntington, *The Clash of Civilizations and the Remaking of the World Order* (London: Simon & Schuster, 1997), p. 47.
69 Ibid., p. 58.
70 Ibid., p. 217.
71 Djavann, *Je viens d'ailleurs*, p. 12; Djavann, *A mon corps*, p. 88.
72 Djavann, *A mon corps*, p. 40.
73 Djavann, *Je viens d'ailleurs*, pp. 80–7.
74 Djavann, *Comment*, p. 256.
75 Ibid., p. 105.
76 Rabineau, 'Dévoilez Chahdortt', 24.
77 Ibid., 24.
78 Ibid., p. 22; Djavann, *Que pense Allah,* p. 32.
79 Djavann, *A mon corps*, p. 49.
80 Stefan Durand, 'Fascisme, islam et grossiers amalgames', *Monde Diplomatique* (November 2006), 10–11.
81 Djavann, *Comment*, pp. 39–40; Alec Hargreaves, *Multi-Ethnic France: Immigration, Politics, Culture and Society* (2nd edn) (New York and London: Routledge, 2007), pp. 26–8; see also Graham Murray, 'France: the riots and the Republic', *Race and Class* 47:4 (2006), 26–45 for a clear condemnation of discriminatory practices in contemporary France.
82 'Votre ADN, s'il vous plaît', *Le Figaro*, 11 October 2007.
83 Djavann, *Bas les voiles*, p. 13.
84 Fadwa El Guindi, *Veil: Modesty, Privacy and Resistance* (Oxford: Berg, 1999), p. 121.
85 Djavann, *Que pense Allah*, p. 20.
86 Djavann, *Bas les voiles*, p. 7.
87 Djavann, *A mon corps*, p. 203.
88 Ali, *Caged Virgin*, pp. xvi and 14.
89 Ismahane Chouder, Malika Latrèche and Pierre Tevanian (eds), *Les Filles voilées parlent* (Floch: La Fabrique, 2008), p. 180.

90 Djavann, *Bas les voiles*, p. 41.
91 Ziba Mir-Hosseini, 'Is time on Iranian women protestors' side?', *Merip* (June 2006), *http://www.merip.org/mero/mero061606.html*. See also Haleh Esfandiari, 'The politics of the "women's question" in the Islamic Republic, 1979–99' in J. L. Esposito and R. K. Ramazani (eds), *Iran at the Crossroads* (New York: Palgrave, 2001), pp. 75–92. Djavann argues that this expansion in education is simply an example of the regime brain-washing the population: *A mon corps*, p. 258.
92 Shirin Ebadi (with Azadeh Moaveni), *Iran Awakening: From Prison to Peace Prize: One Woman's Struggle at the Crossroads of History* (London: Rider, 2006), pp. 20–33.
93 Ibid., p. 38.
94 Ibid., p. 72.
95 Ibid., p. 171.
96 Ibid., p. 122.
97 Ibid., p. 191.
98 Ibid., pp. 78–81.
99 Zygmunt Bauman, *Identity: Conversations with Benedetto Vecchi* (Cambridge: Polity, 2004), p. 12.

Chapter Three

1 Fadela Amara with Sylvia Zappi, *Ni Putes ni Soumises* (Paris: La Découverte, 2003), p. 19.
2 This occurred several times during the programmes 'Les religions sont-elles les ennemis des femmes?', *Culture et Dépendances*, FR2, 19 May 2005 and 'Itinéraire d'une révoltée', broadcast as part of 'Envoyé Spécial', FR2, 17 January 2008.
3 Fadela Amara and Mohammed Abdi, *La Racaille de la République* (Paris: Seuil, 2006), pp. 10–14.
4 Amara and Abdi, *Racaille*, p. 15.
5 Ibid., pp. 21–3.
6 Albert Jacquard and Fadela Amara, *Jamais soumis, jamais soumise* (Paris: Stock, 2007), p. 51.
7 Ibid., p. 97.
8 Amara and Abdi, *Racaille*, p. 35.
9 Amara, *Ni Putes ni Soumises*, p. 21.
10 Jacquard and Amara, *Jamais soumis*, p. 51.
11 Amara and Abdi, *Racaille*, pp. 24–5.
12 Ibid., p. 26.
13 Ibid., p. 31.
14 Jacquard and Amara, *Jamais soumis*, p. 15.
15 Laurent Bonelli, *La France a peur: une histoire sociale de « l'insécurité »* (Paris: La Découverte, 2008), p. 62.
16 Amara and Abdi, *Racaille*, p. 41.
17 Ibid., pp. 42–3.

18   Jacquard and Amara, *Jamais soumis*, p. 39.
19   'Débuts précurseurs de Fadela Amara dans la gestion du milieu associatif', *http://www.niputesnisoumises.com/mouvement.php?section=historique_2000*, undated, accessed 6 August 2008.
20   Robert Castel *La Discrimination négative: citoyens ou indigènes?* (Paris: Seuil, 2007), p. 17.
21   Bonelli, *La France a peur*, pp. 22–34.
22   Ibid., p. 26.
23   Ibid., p. 30; Castel, *Discrimination*, p. 19.
24   Olivier Masclet, 'Des quartiers sans voix: sur le divorce entre la Gauche et les enfants d'immigrés', *French Politics, Culture and Society* 24:3 (2006), 5–22 (13–15).
25   Castel, *Discrimination*, p. 19.
26   Abdelmalek Sayad, *L'Immigration ou les paradoxes et l'altérité, I: L'illusion du provisoire* (Paris: Raisons d'Agir, 2006), p. 25.
27   Sadek Sellam, *La France et ses musulmans: un siècle de politique musulmans, 1895–2005* (Paris: Fayard, 2006), p. 116.
28   Bonelli, *La France a peur*, pp. 73–5.
29   See Thomas Deltombe, *L'Islam imaginaire: la construction médiatique de l'islamophobie en France, 1975–2005* (Paris: La Découverte, 2005), pp. 38–47.
30   François Maspero, *Les Passagers du Roissy-Express* (Paris: Seuil, 1990), p. 216.
31   Maspero, *Les Passagers*, p. 242.
32   Castel, *Discrimination*, p. 28.
33   Ibid.; on the French problem with accurate statistics relating to minority ethnic populations, see Patrick Simon, 'The choice of ignorance: the debate on ethnic and racial statistics in France', *French Politics, Culture and Society* 26:1 (2008), 7–31.
34   Masclet, 'Des quartiers sans voix', 11–13.
35   Castel, *Discrimination*, p. 85.
36   Bonelli, *La France a peur*, pp. 91–6.
37   Jacqueline Costa-Lascoux, 'Les échecs de l'intégration, un accroc au contrat social', *Pouvoirs* 111 (2004), 19–27 (27).
38   Paul A. Silverstein, *Algeria in France: Transpolitics, Race and Nation* (Bloomington: Indiana University Press, 2004), p. 113.
39   Amara and Abdi, *Racaille*, p. 124.
40   Yann Moulier Boutang, *La Révolte des banlieues, ou: les habits nus de la République* (Paris: Amsterdam, 2005), p. 21.
41   Faïza Guène, *Kiffe Kiffe Demain* (Paris: Hachette, 2004), p. 13, p. 120.
42   Ibid., p. 22.
43   Ibid., p. 14.
44   Ibid., p. 19.
45   Ibid., p. 90.
46   Ibid., p. 159.
47   Ibid., p. 41.
48   Ibid., p. 20.
49   Paul Silverstein and Chantal Tetreault, 'Urban Violence in France',

Merip (November 2005), *http://www.merip.org/mero/interventions/silver-stein_tetreault_interv.htm.*

50   Boutang, *La Révolte*, p. 37.
51   'Paroles bruits d'émeutiers', *Le Figaro*, 14 November 2005.
52   'Une nuit avec des "émeutiers" qui ont "la rage"', *Le Monde*, 7 November 2005.
53   'Des religieux musulmans organisent des patrouilles de nuit pour tenter d'arrêter la violence', *Le Monde*, 9 November 2005.
54   Monique Boireau-Rouillé, 'La crise des banlieues, novembre 2005: entrevue avec Michel Pialoux', *Réfractions* 17 (2006–7), 132–8.
55   Castel, *Discrimination*, p. 24.
56   See Bernard Stasi with Olivier Picard, *Tous français: Immigration, la chance de la France* (Paris: Hugo, 2007), p. 111.
57   Boutang, *La Révolte*, p. 41.
58   Tariq Ramadan, 'C'est l'ensemble de la classe politique française qui se trompe ...' *http://www.saphirnews.com/C-est-l-ensemble*, accessed 14 November 2005 (published 9 November 2005).
59   Azouz Begag, *Un Mouton dans le bagnoire: dans les coulisses du pouvoir* (Paris: Fayard, 2007), p. 95, p. 101.
60   Boireau-Rouillé, 'La crise des banlieues', 137.
61   'Banlieues en crise ... "Il est important de noter l'absence des femmes au sein des dernières émeutes"', *DS*, February 2006.
62   'Des filles de banlieue lancent la première "marche des femmes"', *Le Monde*, 2 February 2003.
63   Ibid.
64   '2003', *http://www.niputesnisoumises.com/mouvement.php?section=histor ique_2003*, accessed 6 August 2008.
65   'La marche des Ni Putes ni Soumises a assuré le succès du cortège de la Journée des femmes', *Le Monde*, 11 March 2003.
66   'Le voile, c'est le sceau de l'humiliation des femmes', *L'Express*, 11 December 2003. See also Deltombe, *L'Islam imaginaire*, pp. 307–9.
67   On this point, see the excellent analysis by Nacira Guénif-Souilamas, 'The other French exception: virtuous racism and the war of the sexes in postcolonial France', *French Politics, Culture and Society* 24:3 (2006), 23–41.
68   'Fort de ses premiers succès, le mouvement Ni Putes ni Soumises interpelle le chef de l'Etat', *Le Monde*, 5 October 2003.
69   'Un "tour de France" des Ni Putes ni Soumises', *Le Monde*, 4 February 2004; *Rapport d'activité 2006*, PDF file at *http://www.niputesnisoumises. com/mouvement.php?section=historique_2006*; accessed 7 August 2008, p. 69.
70   'Ghetto Warrior', *Guardian*, 17 July 2006.
71   'Laïcité: Laurent Fabius reçoit le soutien de Fadela Amara', *Le Monde*, 11 October 2005.
72   Amara and Abdi, *Racaille*, p. 165.
73   Amara, *Ni Putes ni Soumises*, pp. 78–80.
74   'Dans *Elle*, un appel à M. Chirac de femmes favorables à une loi', *Le Monde*, 7 December 2003.
75   'Laïcité, ils ont dit', *L'Humanité*, 12 December 2003.

76 See Erwann Lecorre, 'La Marche de TOUTES les femmes? – A propos de la manifestation féministe du 6 mars 2004', *www.lmsi.net/article.php3?id_article=227*, accessed 12 March 2004 (published 8 March 2004).

77 'Ni Putes ni Soumises manifeste pour la "mixité" et "contre toutes formes d'intégrisme"', *Le Monde*, 8 March 2005.

78 '2005', *http://www.niputesnisoumises.com/mouvement.php?section=historique_2005*, accessed 6 August 2008.

79 As noted by the reporter from *Le Monde*: see 'La marche des Ni Putes ni Soumises'.

80 *Rapport d'activité*, p. 103.

81 Ibid., p. 7.

82 Ibid., p. 7.

83 Ibid., p. 8.

84 Amara, *Ni Putes ni Soumises*, p. 52.

85 Ibid., p. 50.

86 '2004', *http://www.niputesnisoumises.com/mouvement.php?section=historique_2004*, accessed 6 August 2008.

87 *Rapport d'activité*, p. 7; Amara and Abdi, *Racaille*, pp. 108–9.

88 Amara and Abdi, *Racaille*, p. 54.

89 Amara, *Ni Putes ni Soumises*, p. 45.

90 Ibid., p. 44.

91 Amara and Abdi, *Racaille*, p. 55.

92 Amara, *Ni Putes ni Soumises*, p. 75.

93 Amara and Abdi, *Racaille*, p. 49.

94 Amara, *Ni Putes ni Soumises*, p. 76.

95 Amara and Abdi, *Racaille*, p. 189.

96 Deltombe, *Islam imaginaire*, p. 308.

97 Sellam, *La France*, p. 114.

98 See, for example, the evidence in Farhad Khosrokhavar, *Quand al-Qaïda parle: témoignages derrière les barreaux* (Paris: Grasset & Fasquelle, 2006).

99 See 'Entretien avec Didier Lapeyronnie, professeur de sociologie à l'Université Victor-Segalen de Bordeaux', *Le Monde*, 6 July 2004.

100 See 'Ghetto Warrior'.

101 See, for example, Sadek Hajji and Stéphanie Marteau, *Voyage dans la France musulmane* (Paris: Plon, 2005), pp. 114–15; Christine Delphy, 'Antisexisme *ou* antiracisme? Un faux dilemme', *Nouvelles Questions Féministes* 25:1 (2006), 59–83; Christelle Hamel and Christine Delphy, 'On vous a tant aimé.e.s! Entretien avec Houria Boutelja', *Nouvelles Questions Féministes* 25:1 (2006), 122–35.

102 Fatima Ouassak, 'La stigmatisation du garçon arabe: Ni Putes ni Soumises', *http://www.indigenes-republique.org/spip.php?article524*, posted 1 November 2006, accessed 25 November 2006.

103 Deltombe, *Islam imaginaire*, p. 309.

104 See her contribution to 'Les religions sont-elles les ennemis des femmes?', *Culture et Dépendances*, FR2, 19 May 2005.

105 'Itinéraire'.

106 *Rapport d'activité*, p. 8.

107 Ibid., p. 107.
108 Ibid., pp. 24–7.
109 Ibid., p. 54.
110 Ibid., p. 7.
111 Ibid., p. 8.
112 Information from: 'La marche des Ni Putes ni Soumises'; '2004'; 'Ni Putes ni Soumises manifeste pour la mixité'.
113 Lecorre, 'La Marche'.
114 Deltombe, *Islam imaginaire*, p. 309.
115 Aziz Zemouri, *Faut-il faire taire Tariq Ramadan ? suivie d'un entretien avec Tariq Ramadan* (Paris: l'Archipel, 2005), p. 195.
116 *Rapport d'activité*, p. 75.
117 Amara and Abdi, *Racaille*, pp. 166–7.
118 'En banlieue, les associations saluent "l'ouverture à la diversité"', *Le Monde*, 21 June 2007.
119 Amara and Abdi, *Racaille*, p. 112.
120 'Ni Putes ni Soumises: Y a-t-il une vie après Fadela Amara?', *http://npnsmorbihan.canalblog.com/archives/articles_de_presse_/index.html*, posted 13 November 2007, accessed 6 August 2008.
121 'Démission de comités locaux de Ni Putes ni Soumises', *Le Monde*, 10 November 2007.
122 'Y a-t-il vie?'
123 '"Insoumis(es)" en rupture', *Le Monde*, 16 November 2007.
124 'Une militante des Insoumises agressée dans un contexte de tensions entre associations', *Le Monde*, 16 February 2008.
125 'Historique de l'association', *http://npnsmorbihan.canalblog.com/archives/historique_de_l_association_/index.html*, accessed 6 August 2008.
126 See *http://www.maitre-eolas.fr/2008/07/11/1030-faut-il-etre-francaise-pour-porter-l* for an analysis of the case.
127 'Refus de naturalisation d'une marocaine en burqa', *http://npnsmorbihan.canalblog.com/archives/articles_de_presse_/index.html*, posted 11 July 2008, accessed 6 August 2008.
128 Amara and Abdi, *Racaille*, pp. 83–4.
129 Zygmunt Bauman, *Identity: Conversations with Benedetti Vecchi* (Cambridge: Polity, 2004), p. 39.
130 On this point, see the still pertinent remarks by Frantz Fanon on racism and black identity in his *Peau noire, masques blancs* (Paris: Seuil, 1975 [1962]).

Chapter Four

1 Zadie Smith, *White Teeth* (Harmondsworth: Penguin, 2000), p. 327.
2 Soheib Bencheikh, *Marianne et le Prophète: l'islam dans la France laïque* (Paris: Grasset, 1998), p. 84; Neil MacMaster, 'Imperial facades: Muslim institutions and propaganda in inter-war Paris' in T. Chafer and A. Sackur (eds), *Promoting the Colonial Ideal* (Houndmills:

Palgrave, 2002), pp. 71–81 and his *Colonial Migrants and Racism: Algerians in France, 1900–1962* (Houndsmill: Basingstoke, 1997), pp. 105–6.

3   Data from Felice Dassetto, 'Islam et Europe: au défi d'une rencontre de civilisations' in C. Pailhe (ed.), *Europes et Mondes musulmans* (Bruxelles: Grip, 2004), pp. 143–64.

4   Juan Vernet, *Lo que Europa debe al Islam de España* (Barcelona: El Acantilado, 1999).

5   This is a point which has had a profound influence on Tariq Ramadan's thinking: see his *Être Musulman européen: Etude des sources islamiques à la lumière du contexte européen* (translated by Claude Dabbak) (Lyon: Tawhid, 1999). These arguments will be explored at greater length in the next chapter.

6   On this point, see the perceptive arguments in Olivier Roy, *L'Islam mondialisé* (Paris: Seuil, 2002).

7   'La difficile insertion d'une communauté multiforme: crise de crois-sance dans l'Islam de France', *Le Monde*, 11 May 1989.

8   'Mgr André Vingt-Trois appelle les catholiques à "rencontrer sans angoisse" les musulmans', *Le Monde*, 9 November 2007.

9   See Alain Boyer, 'La représentation du culture musulman en France', *French Politics, Culture and Society* 23:1 (2005), 8–22.

10 'Le bloc-notes d'Ivan Rioufol', *Le Figaro*, 17 October 2003.

11 On the change in Sarkozy's attitudes, see the useful interview with Vincent Geisser, 'Pour les politiques, l'objet "islam" est devenu un créneau', *Le Monde*, 23 February 2007.

12 'Sarkozy: TF1.fr joue à saute-mouton', *Nouvel Observateur*, 7 February 2007. (It was the reference to killing sheep in one's flat that inspired the title of Azouz Begag's *Un Mouton dans le bagnoire* (A sheep in the bathroom).)

13 'Islam: le temps de la Réforme', *L'Express*, 12 June 2006.

14 'Editorial: Procès d'un autre âge', *Le Monde*, 8 February 2007. For a rare defence of the CFCM's action, see Leila, 'La liberté d'expression à la sauce Sollers et autres intellectuels médiatisés', *http://www.oulala. net/Portail/imprimersans.php3?id_article=2852*.

15 'Communiqué de presse de Philippe de Villiers', *http://www.pourla france.fr/communique_detail.php?id=239*, posted 22 March 2007, accessed 23 March 2007. Philippe de Villiers, *Les Mosquées de Roissy* (Paris: Albin Michel, 2006), p. 29.

16 'P. de Villiers persiste à prêcher la haine', *http://www.uoif-online.com/ print.php?sid=441*, posted 27 April 2006, accessed 5 October 2006.

17 See Olivier Roy, *La Laïcité face à l'Islam* (Paris: Stock, 2005), p. 47.

18 'Les positions se durcissent autour du groupe scolaire musulman de Décines', *Le Monde*, 13 October 2006.

19 'L'extrême droite tente de retarder la construction d'une mosquée en Seine-Saint-Denis', *Le Monde*, 18 May 2007.

20 'Deux lieux de culte musulman incendiés dans l'agglomération d'Annecy', *Le Monde*, 22 February 2004.

21 'Nouvelle profanation de tombes musulmanes', *Le Monde*, 8 April 2008.

22 'Un collectif tente de dénombrer les actes "islamophobes"', *Le Monde*, 21 October 2004.

23 On this experience, see Michèle Lamont, Ann Morning and Margarita Mooney, 'Particular universalisms: North African immigrants respond to French racism', *Ethnic and Racial Studies* 25:3 (2002), 390–414. Bernard Stasi, *Rapport au président de la République* (np: no publisher, 2003), p. 47.

24 Thomas Deltombe, *L'Islam imaginaire: La construction médiatique de l'islamophobie en France, 1975–2005* (Paris: La Découverte, 2005), p. 103.

25 'Communiqué de EMF: d'un intégrisme à l'autre', *http://www.uoif-online.com/print.php?sid=150*, posted 11 December 2003, accessed 1 January 2004.

26 '53 per cent des musulmans sont contre la loi', *Le Monde*, 27 January 2004.

27 'Lettre ouverte aux responsables du CFCM', *http://www.oumma.com/Lettre-ouverte-aux-responsables-du*, posted 26 December 2003, accessed 31 December 2003.

28 'Communiqué du bureau de CFCM', posted 18 December 2003, *http://www.saphirnews.com/Communique-du-bureau-du-CFCM_a640.html*, accessed 31 December 2003.

29 'M. Sarkozy obtient l'appui de la plus haute autorité sunnite sur le voile islamique', *Le Monde*, 1 January 2004.

30 'A Strasbourg, les ultra-radicaux s'en prennent à Chirac', *Le Figaro*, 22 December 2003.

31 'Un défilé se voulant "citoyen"', *Libération*, 22 December 2003.

32 'Manifestation à Paris contre une loi "anti-voile"', *Le Monde*, 23 December 2003.

33 'Editorial: Détournement', *Libération*, 22 December 2003.

34 'Les revenantes et le plafond de chiffon', *Le Monde*, 5 February 2004.

35 'Un défilé se voulant "citoyen"', *Libération*, 22 December 2003.

36 'Ces imams radicaux qui enflamment les mosquées des cités', *Le Figaro*, 28 January 2004.

37 'Nord-Pas-de-Calais: Le Pen surfe sur l'affaire du voile', *Le Figaro*, 19 January 2004; 'Musulmans dans l'isolement', *Libération*, 19 January 2004. 'Enquête sur les ennemis de la République', *L'Express*, 26 January 2004.

38 'Une manifestation pas si spontanée', *Le Figaro*, 22 December 2003.

39 'La loi sur le voile a réuni 20,000 manifestants en France', *Le Figaro*, 18 January 2004.

40 'Je ne retirerai mon foulard', *Le Parisien*, 18 January 2004; 'Laïcité: la manifestation contre la loi n'a pas fait le plein', *Le Figaro*, 19 January 2004.

41 'Echec du rassemblement "pro-voile"', *Ouest-France*, 8 February 2004.

42 'A la rencontre des manifestants', *http://www.oumma.com*, 16 February 2004.

43 'Rassemblement contre le projet de loi', *http://www.ma-liberte.com/modules.php?name=News&file=article&sid=523*, posted 5 February 2004, accessed 5 February 2004.

44 Erwann Lecorre, 'La Marche de TOUTES les femmes ? – A propos

190 		*French Muslims*

de la manifestation féministe du 6 mars 2004', *http://www.lmsi.net/ article.php3?id_article=227*, posted 8 March 2004, accessed 12 March 2004.

45 	'La loi sur le voile a réuni 20,000 manifestants en France', *Le Figaro*, 18 January 2004.

46 	'Editorial', *Libération*, 22 December 2003.

47 	'Le double jeu de l'UOIF', *L'Express*, 15 January 2004.

48 	'Laïques et musulmans "hors intégrismes" tenter de manifester ensemble contre la loi antivoile', *Le Monde*, 15 February 2004.

49 	'Compte-rendu de la réunion à Montpellier', Une école pour tou-te-s, 6 February 2004, personal communication to author.

50 	'Appel à mobilisation contre les lois d'exclusions à l'initiative du collectif Une école pour tou.te.s', *http://www.lmsi.net/impression. php3?id_article=212*, posted 23 January 2004, accessed 6 February 2004.

51 	'Tract adressé aux lycéen.ne.s et aux étudiant.e.s', *http://ww.lmsi.net/ impression.php3?id_article=217*, posted 28 January 2004, accessed 6 February 2004.

52 	For information on its activities, see Ismahane Chouder, Malika Latrèche and Pierre Tevanian (eds), *Les Filles voilées parlent* (Floch: La Fabrique, 2008).

53 	'Présentation du comité 15 mars et Libertés', *http://www.uoif-online.com/print.php?op_article=249*, posted 30 August 2004, accessed 3 September 2004.

54 	'Les responsables musulmans français proclament leur solidarité avec le gouvernement', *Le Monde*, 31 August 2004.

55 	'Avec la crise des otages et la rentrée, le Conseil Français du Culte Musulman a assis sa légitimité', *Le Monde*, 4 September 2004.

56 	'Trois autres lycéennes exclues pour non-respect de la loi sur la laïcité à Mulhouse et dans l'Orne', *Le Monde*, 21 October 2004. Note to confused readers: this statement is ironic.

57 	Karen Armstrong, *Islam: A Short History* (London: Phoenix, 2001), p. 52.

58 	L. Carl Brown, *Religion and State: the Muslim Approach to Politics* (New York: Columbia University Press, 2000), p. 33.

59 	See Steve Benen's revealing interview with Tariq Ramadan, 'A man with a triangulation plan?', *http://www.salon.com/people/feature/2002/ 02/15/ramadan/print.html*, undated (2002?), accessed 26 August 2007.

60 	Soheib Bencheikh, *Marianne et le Prophète: l'islam dans la France laïque* (Paris: Grasset, 1998), p. 90

61 	On this point, see the intelligent and ambitious survey of Islamic history in Ira M. Lapidus, 'State and religion in Islamic societies', *Past and Present* 151 (1996), 3–27.

62 	MacMaster, *Colonial Migrants*, pp. 105, 109.

63 	Bencheikh, *Marianne et le Prophète*, p. 11.

64 	Yamina Benguigi, 'Le voile et la République' in her *Les Femmes d'Islam*, FR2, 1994.

65 	'Sondage IFOP: 5 millions de fidèles', *Le Monde*, 5 October 2001.

66 Ibid., 'Une laïcité de chanoine', *Le Monde*, 1 February 2008.
67 Information cited in Jonathan Laurence and Justin Vaisse, *Integrating Islam: Political and Religious Challenges in Contemporary France* (Washington: Brookings Institution Press, 2006), p. 83.
68 Information cited in Laurence and Vaisse, *Integrating Islam*, p. 83.
69 'Comment Jean-Claude Gaudin (UMP) a renoncé à son "grand projet"', *Le Monde*, 18 June 2004.
70 Franck Frégosi, *Penser l'Islam dans la laïcité: les musulmans de France et la République* (Paris: Fayard, 2008), p. 119.
71 'Plus pratiquants, les musulmans de France sont aussi mieux intégrés', *Le Monde*, 5 October 2001.
72 See Vincent Tiberj, 'Le vote des Français issus de l'immigration', *http://tns-sofres.com/interview.php?id=257*, posted 4 January 2007, accessed 28 June 2008.
73 'Les français musulmans aiment le président mais penchant gauche', *Le Figaro*, 17 December 2003.
74 'L'opinion des Français musulmans', *http://www.ipsos.fr/CanalIpsos/poll/7756.asp*, posted 7 April 2004, accessed 28 June 2008.
75 Vincent Geisser and El Yamine Soum, *Discriminer pour mieux régner: enquête sur la diversité dans les partis politiques* (Ivry-sur-Seine: Les Editions de l'Atelier/Editions ouvrières, 2008), pp. 33–5.
76 Geisser and Soum, *Discriminer*, p. 53.
77 A leading member of the Moroccan-linked FNMF, quoted in 'Les privilèges de la Mosquée de Paris de plus en plus contestée', *Le Monde*, 4 July 1995.
78 'La formation des imams, le nouveau défi de l'islam français', *Le Monde*, 1 July 2003.
79 Frégosi, *Penser l'Islam*, p. 232.
80 'Jean-Pierre Chevènement dessine les contours d'un islam à la française', *Le Monde*, 19 February 2000. On Chevènement's political values, see Sharif Gemie, 'An extremism of the center: Jean-Pierre Chevènement, French presidential candidate, 2002', *French Politics, Culture and Society* 22:1 (2004), 76–97.
81 'Ce savant dosage qui a mis d'accord l'islam de France', *Le Monde*, 22 December 2002.
82 'Désunion contre Sarkozy', *L'Express*, 11 February 2003.
83 Laurence and Vaisse, *Integrating Islam*, p. 99.
84 Tariq Ramadan, 'Il y a un vrai problème de liberté d'expression en France', *www.saphirnet.info/Tariq-Ramadan-il-y-a* , posted 17 October 2006, accessed 20 October 2006.
85 'Les instances de l'islam de France présentent un maigre bilan', *Le Figaro*, 27 May 2008.
86 Patrick Simon, 'The choice of ignorance: the debate on ethnic and racial statistics in France', *French Politics, Culture and Society* 26:1 (2008), 7–31.
87 Sadek Hajji and Stéphanie Marteau, *Voyage dans la France musulmane* (Paris: Plon, 2005), p. 79.
88 'L'opinion des Français musulmans', *http://www.ipsos.fr/CanalIpsos/poll/7756.asp*, posted 7 April 2004, accessed 28 June 2008.

89 Frank Peter, 'Leading the community of the middle way: a study of the Muslim field in France', *Muslim World* 96 (2006), 707–36.

90 Laurence and Vaisse, *Integrating Islam*, p. 105.

91 'UOIF: Un réseau eu quête de reconnaissance', *Le Monde*, 23 June 2006.

92 Laurence and Vaisse, *Integrating Islam*, pp. 108–9.

93 Claire de Galembert and Mustafa Belbah, 'Le Conseil Français du Culte Musulman à l'épreuve des territoires', *French Politics, Culture & Society* 23:1 (2005), pp. 76–86.

94 Julien Landfried, 'Réflexions sur le Conseil Français du Culte Musulman' (Interview with Hakim El Ghissassi), *http://www.communautarisme.net/Reflexions-sur-le-Conseil-Francais-du-Culte-Musulman_a77.html*, posted 9 July 2004, accessed 19 July 2004.

95 Mayanthi Fernando, 'The Republic's "second religion": Recognizing Islam in France', *Merip* 235 (2005), *http://www.merip.org/mer/mer235/fernando.html*, accessed 26 July 2007. Frégosi poses the same question: *Penser l'Islam*, p. 295.

96 Alexandre Caeiro, 'Religious authorities or political actors? – The Muslim leaders of the French representative body of Islam' in J. Cesari and S. McLoughlin (eds), *European Muslims and the Secular State* (Aldershot: Ashgate, 2005), pp. 71–84 (p. 74). See also Frégosi, *Penser l'Islam*, p. 325.

97 'Campagne électoral précoce au CFCM', *http://www.saphirnot.info/imprimer.phd ?id=309*, posted 21 September 2004, accessed 24 September 2004.

98 'La tentation de la sédition saisit le Conseil Français du Culte Musulman', *Le Monde*, 13 November 2004.

99 'On n'est pas au service du pouvoir', *Libération*, 7 May 2005.

100 Frégosi, *Penser l'Islam*, p. 308.

101 See, for example, 'L'instance représentative des musulmans est minée par de violentes querelles', *Le Monde*, 27 November 2005; 'Culte musulman: les raisons d'une crise', *Le Monde*, 11 May 2006.

102 Soroya Duval, 'New veils and new voices: Islamist women's groups in Egypt', in K. Ask and M. Tjomsland (eds), *Women and Islamization* (Oxford: Berg, 1998), pp. 45–72.

103 For a good example of a hostile critique of the UOIF along this line, see 'La face cachée de l'UOIF', *L'Express*, 2 May 2005.

104 'Enquête sur ces musulmans qui inquiètent l'islam de France', *Le Monde*, 13 December 2002.

105 Hajji and Marteau, *Voyage*, p. 75.

106 'Nicolas Sarkozy se pose en "ami exigeant" des musulmans', *Le Monde*, 22 April 2003.

107 'Enquête sur ces musulmans qui inquiètent l'islam de France', *Le Monde*, 13 December 2002.

108 'Les musulmans de France, entre affirmation identitaire et inquiétudes', *Le Monde*, 12 May 2002.

109 'La difficile insertion d'une communauté multiforme: crise de croissance dans l'Islam de France', *Le Monde*, 11 May 1989; 'La

consultation Chevènement en débat au rassemblement musulman du Bourget', *Le Monde*, 3 May 2000, and 'Au Bourget, les musulmans se mobilisent pour la Palestine', *Le Monde*, 2 May 2001.

110 See the interesting, if hyper-critical, account by 'Sappho', 'Among the believers', *http://www.sappho.dk/Den per cent20loebende/bourgetengelsk.html*; posted 1 June 2007, accessed 16 July 2008.

111 'Nicolas Sarkozy se pose en "ami exigeant" des musulmans', *Le Monde*, 22 April 2003.

112 'Sifflets pour M. Sarkozy et Mme Royal au congrès de l'UOIF', *Le Monde*, 17 April 2007.

113 'Les leaders viennent davantage de l'étranger que des cités', *Le Monde*, 13 December 2002.

114 'A propos de l'entretien de Monsieur Fouad Alaoui paru dans *Le Monde* du 1ᵉ décembre', UOIF, 1 December 2004, *http://www.uoif-online.com/print.php?sid=289*, accessed 9 December 2004.

115 'UOIF: Un réseau en quête de reconnaissance', *Le Monde*, 23 June 2006.

116 Fouad Alaoui, 'Le CFCM, réalité et conditions de réussite', *French Politics, Culture and Society* 23:1 (2005), 115–17.

117 'Pour l'UOIF, une participation très rare', *Le Monde*, 7 November 2004.

118 'Communiqué de l'UOIF concernant les troubles qui touchent la France', *http://www.uoif-online.com/print.php?sid=415*, posted 6 November 2005, accessed 14 November 2005. 'Des religieux musulmans organisent les patrouilles de nuit pour tenter d'arrêter la violence', *Le Monde*, 9 November 2006.

119 'Lettre de l'UOIF aux musulmans de France concernant l'application de le loi du 15 juin 2004', *http://www.portail-religion.com/encyclopedie/u/union_des_organisations_musulmanes_de_france_UOIF/2004–06 –29-lettre_aux_musulmans_loi_15_mars-2004.php*, posted 30 June 2004, accessed 22 September 2008.

120 'L'UOIF invite les musulmans à ignorer la loi interdisant le port du voile à l'école', *Le Monde*, 3 July 2004. See also the similar article 'L'UOIF au-dessus des lois', *Libération*, 16 July 2004.

121 'L'Islam à la table de la République', *L'Express*, 5 October 2006.

122 Bencheikh, *Marianne et le Prophète*, p. 178.

123 Aziz Al-Azmeh, *Islams and Modernities* (2nd edn) (London: Verso, 1996), p. 135.

124 Ayşe Saktander, *Living Islam: Women, Religion and the Politicization of Culture in Turkey* (London: Tauris, 2002), p. 15.

125 Roy, *Laïcité face à l'Islam*, p. 47.

126 The exact nature of this group in still subject to debate. On this topic, see the sophisticated analysis of Salima Mellah, 'Le mouvement islamiste algérien entre autonomie et manipulation', *Comité Justice pour l'Algérie* 19 (2004), 21–3; *http://www.algerie-tpp.org/ tpp/presentation/dossiers_presentes.htm*.

127 'Les RG constatent un phénomène de repli communautaire dans la moitié des quartiers sensibles surveillés', *Le Monde*, 5 July 2004.

128 'Les "barbus" dans le 9–3', *Le Monde*, 17 November 2006.
129 'Les conversions à l'islam radical inquiètent la police française', *Le Monde*, 13 July 2005.
130 'Entretien avec Didier Lapeyronnie, professeur de sociologie à l'Université Victor-Segalen de Bordeaux', *Le Monde*, 6 July 2004.
131 Nadia Kiwan, 'Managing marginalization: young French North-Africans and local associations', *Modern and Contemporary France* 13:4 (2005), 465–81.
132 Hajj and Marteau, *Voyage*, pp. 62–6.
133 'La difficile insertion d'une communauté multiforme: crise de croissance dans l'Islam de France', *Le Monde* 11 May 1989.
134 International Crisis Group (ICG), *La France face à ses musulmans: émeutes, jihadisme et dépolitisation* (Rapport Europe 172, 2006), p. 15.
135 ICG, *Understanding Islamism* (Middle East/North Africa Report 37, March 2005), p. 9.
136 'Les salafistes ont conquis de nouvelles mosquées en Ile-de-France', *Le Monde*, 22 February 2004.
137 Laurent Lévy, *Le Spectre du communautarisme* (Paris: Éditions Amsterdam, 2005), p. 63.
138 ICG, *La France*, pp. 15–16.
139 Hajji and Marteau, *Voyage*, pp. 42–4.

Chapter Five

1 Aziz Zemouri, *Faut-il faire taire Tariq Ramadan?* suivie d'un entretien avec *Tariq Ramadan* (Paris: l'Archipel, 2005), p. 113.
2 Ibid., p. 94.
3 Sadri Khiari, 'La pensée politique de Tariq Ramadan', *http://lmsi.net/spip.php?article256*, posted 29 May 2004, accessed 29 June 2004.
4 On this point, see Denis Sieffert, 'L'affaire Tariq Ramadan: l'ère du soupçon', *http://www.politis.fr/article716.html*, posted 16 October 2003, accessed 29 June 2004.
5 Jean-Luc Mélenchon, Vincent Peillon and Manuel Valls, 'Monsieur Ramadan ne peut être des nôtres', *Nouvel Observateur*, 23 October 2003.
6 Bernard-Henri Lévy, 'L'autre visage de Tariq Ramadan', *Le Monde*, 1 November 2003; 'Tariq Ramadan, prophète européen du communautarisme musulman', *Le Figaro*, 14 November 2003; 'L'homme qui veut instaurer l'islamisme en France', *L'Express*, 18 October 2004; Caroline Fourest, *Frère Tariq* (Paris: Grasset & Fasquelle, 2004).
7 Ian Hamel, 'Quand pourra-t-on critiquer honnêtement Tariq Ramadan?' *http://oumma.com/article.php3?id_article=1333*, posted 5 January 2005, accessed 14 March 2005.
8 Thomas Deltombe, *L'Islam imaginaire: la construction médiatique de l'islamophobie en France, 1975–2005* (Paris: La Découverte, 2005), pp. 331–2 (footnote 37).
9 'What you fear is not who I am', *Globe and Mail*, 30 August 2004,

http://www.theglobeandmail.com/servlet/story/RTGAM.20040830.wrama
ndan30/BNPrint/Front/, accessed 16 August 2008.
10 'Dr Jeckyll et M. Hyde ? – A Propos d'un pitoyable portrait dans *Le Monde*', *http://oumma.com/Dr-Jeckyll-et-M-Hyde*, posted 27 February 2006, accessed 2 March 2006.
11 Tariq Ramadan, *Être Musulman européen: Etude des sources islamiques à la lumière du contexte européen* (translated from the English by Claude Dabbak) (Lyon: Tawhid, 1999), p. 187.
12 Tariq Ramadan, *Peut-on vivre avec l'islam?* (Lausanne: Favre, 2004), p. 10.
13 See Steve Benen's revealing interview with Tariq Ramadan, 'A man with a triangulation plan?', *http://www.salon.com/people/feature/2002/02/15/ramadan/print.html*, undated (2002?), accessed 26 August 2007. After its rather simplistic, sensationalistic beginning – is Ramadan the new Luther? – this article presents the best English-language introduction to Ramadan's ideas.
14 'Il faut pas mélanger les choses' in 'Les religions sont-elles les ennemis des femmes?', *Culture et Dépendances*, FR2, 19 May 2005.
15 On Ramadan's method of analysis, see Zemouri, *Faut-il faire taire*, p. 67.
16 'Il y a un vrai problème de liberté d'expression en France', *www.saphirnet.info/Tariq-Ramadan-il-y-a*, posted 17 October 2006, accessed 20 October 2006.
17 Tariq Ramadan, *La Foi, la voie et la résistance* (2nd edn) (Lyon: Tawhid, 2004), p. 72.
18 Ramadan, *Être Musulman européen*, p. 23.
19 Zemouri, *Faut-il faire taire*, p. 72.
20 Ramadan, *La Foi, la voie*, p. 29.
21 Ramadan, *Peut-on vivre*, p. 17.
22 Ramadan, *La Foi, la voie*, pp. 29–30.
23 Ramadan, *Être Musulman européen*, p. 26.
24 Ibid., p. 311.
25 Ibid., p. 176.
26 Ramadan, *La Foi, la voie*, p. 7.
27 Benen, 'A man with a triangulation plan'.
28 Zemouri, *Faut-il faire taire*, p. 16.
29 Ibid., p. 32.
30 Ramadan, *Peut-on vivre*, p. 224.
31 Zemouri, *Faut-il faire taire*, p. 136.
32 Ibid., p. 193.
33 Ibid., p. 234.
34 Ibid., p. 176.
35 Ibid., p. 194.
36 Ibid., p. 15.
37 Ibid., p. 13.
38 Clémence Boulouque, 'Controverses autour du dernier ouvrage d'une figure de l'islam: Tariq Ramadan', *Le Figaro littéraire*, 27 February 2003.

39 Zemouri, *Faut-il faire taire*, p. 191.
40 International Crisis Group (ICG), *La France face à ses musulmans: émeutes, jihadisme et dépolitisation* (Rapport Europe 172, 2006), pp. 9–10.
41 Cited in 'Les leaders viennent davantage de l'étranger que des cités', *Le Monde*, 13 December 2002.
42 This argument is briefly considered in '4, 7 et 14 février: le calendrier des manifestations des opposants à la loi se précise', *Le Monde*, 4 February 2004.
43 Zemouri, *Faut-il faire taire*, p. 114.
44 Ramadan, *Être Musulman européen*, p. 344.
45 The most concise expression of Ramadan's ideas concerning globalisation are to be found in his 'Les musulmans et la mondialisation', *Pouvoirs* 104 (2003), 97–109. The points made in this paragraph have largely been drawn from this essay.
46 On the nature of the alter-globalisation movement, see the examples presented in Notes from Nowhere, *We are Everywhere: The Irresistible Rise of Global Anti-capitalism* (London: Verso, 2003).
47 Ramadan's essay remains available: *http://oumma.com/article.php3?id_article=719*, posted 3 October 2003, accessed 6 June 2007.
48 Zemouri, *Faut-il faire taire*, p. 196.
49 'Tariq Ramadan: le chantre de la citoyenneté musulman', *L'Express*, 26 January 2004.
50 'Face à Tariq Ramadan', *Le Monde*, 22 November 2003.
51 'L'Appel ... ou la voix des amis de Ramadan', *Monde libertaire*, 28 April 2005.
52 See Silvia Cattori, 'Nous sommes tous indigènes de la politique', interview with Julien Salingue, *http://www.oulala.net/Portail/article.php3?id_article=1818*, posted 25 May 2005, accessed 22 August 2007.
53 Ramadan, *Peut-on vivre*, p. 24.
54 Ibid., p. 226.
55 Zemouri, *Faut-il faire taire*, pp. 101–2.
56 On the origins of such thinking, see Stephen Tyre, 'From *Algérie française* to *France musulmane*: Jacques Soustelle and the myth and realities of "integration", 1955–62', *French History* 20:3 (2006), 275–96.
57 On this point, see Sadek Sellam, *La France et ses musulmans: un siècle de politique musulmans, 1895–2005* (Paris: Fayard, 2006).
58 On the politics of these movements, see Sharif Gemie, *Brittany, 1750–1950: the Invisible Nation* (Cardiff: University of Wales Press, 2007), pp. 125–7.
59 For an informative study concerning one of these groups, see Sarah Whitney, 'Gender, class and generation in interwar French Catholicism: the case of the Jeunesse Ouvrière Chrétienne Féminine', *Journal of Family History* 36:4 (2001), 480–507.
60 Zemouri does ask Ramadan one direct question about Sangnier's influence. Ramadan's response is to refer to wider issues; he speaks about the nature of faith in secular France. One is left with the impression that he has little interest in Sangnier. Zemouri, *Faut-il*

faire taire, p. 173. Ramadan also mentions the JOC in passing: see *Faut-il faire taire*, pp. 234–5.

61 Ibahim M. Abu-Rabi', *Contemporary Arab Thought: Studies in Post-1967 Arab Intellectual Theory* (London: Pluto, 2004), p. xiii.

62 Richard Harries, *Should A Christian Support Guerillas?* (Guildford: Lutterworth Press, 1982), p. 32.

63 See 'Entrevista al padre Gustavo Gutiérrez por Yolando Vaccaro', undated, *http://www.soldiaridad.net/imprimir712_enesp.htm*, accessed 22 August 2008.

64 Angel Darío Carrero, 'Entrevista exclusiva al padre de la teología de la liberación, Gustavo Gutiérrez, en su 80 aniversario', *http://es.geocities.com/fraternidadmaranatha/novedades/entrevGutierrez.html*, posted 21 July 2008, accessed 22 August 2008.

65 For example, see his 'The Call to Jihad', *http://www.tariqramadan.com/spip.php?article65*, posted 28 September 2004, accessed 27 August 2007.

66 Ramadan, *La Foi, la voie*, p. 38.

67 Tariq Ramadan, *Aux sources du renouveau musulman: d'al-Afghānā à al-Bannā; un siècle de réformisme islamique* (Lyon: Tawhid, 2002), pp. 416–29.

68 'Se puede ser musulmán y europeo', *El País*, 8 January 2006.

69 Ramadan, *La foi, la voie*, p. 8.

70 Ramadan, *Être Musulman européen*, p. 199.

71 'L'islam en France entre gauche et conservatisme', *Le Monde*, 1 March 2003.

72 Ramadan, *Être Musulman européen*, p. 328.

73 Ibid., p. 329.

74 Zemouri, *Faut-il faire taire*, p. 116.

75 Subcomandante Insurgente Marcos, 'Fourth Declaration of the Lacandon Jungle' (1 January 1996), *Our Word is Our Weapon: Selected Writings* (London: Serpent's Tail, 2001), pp. 78–81 (p. 80).

76 See Georges Rivière, 'The Libertarian insurrection of the "Arrooch" Assembly Movement in Kabylia (Algeria), 2000–2' translated by Sharif Gemie, *Anarchist Studies* 11:2 (2003), 102–10.

77 'What you fear is not who I am', *http://www.theglobeandmail.com/servlet/story/RTGAM.20040830.wramandan30/BNPrint/Front/*, posted 30 August 2004, accessed 24 August 2008.

78 Steve Benen's interview with Tariq Ramadan, 'A man with a triangulation plan?', *http://www.salon.com/people/feature/2002/02/15/ramadan/print.html*, undated (2002?), accessed 26 August 2007.

79 *http://www.tariqramadan.com/spip.php?lang=en*, accessed 24 September 2008. In passing, one notes that despite the Koran's status as a literary and even poetic masterpiece, English-language quotations from it still sound like they were written by a committee of health and safety officials.

80 Harries, *Should A Christian Support Guerillas?*, p. 32.

81 Ramadan, *Peut-on vivre*, p. 141.

82 Ramadan even defines himself as 'a bridge' in his interview with *El País*: 'Se puede ser musulmán y europeo', 8 January 2006.

83 Ramadan, *Peut-on vivre*, p. 44.
84 Zemouri, *Faut-il faire taire*, pp. 216–17.
85 See the extracts from their debate reproduced in Zemouri, *Faut-il faire taire*, p. 352.
86 See Tariq Ramadan, 'Pour un moratoire sur l'application de la charia dans le monde musulman', *Le Monde*, 1 April 2005.
87 Zemouri, *Faut-il faire taire*, p. 179; Ramadan, *Peut-on vivre*, p. 152.
88 Zemouri, *Faut-il faire taire*, p. 185.
89 Ibid., p. 81.
90 Ibid., pp. 207–8.
91 Ibid., pp. 54–5.
92 Benen, 'A man with a triangulation plan'.
93 Zemouri, *Faut-il faire taire*, p. 238.
94 Khiari, 'La pensée politique'.
95 Gustavo Gutiérrez, 'La pobreza significa muerte injusta y prematura', interview with the BBC, 12 May 2003, *http://www.soldiaridad.net/imprimir712_enesp.htm*, accessed 22 August 2008.
96 Benen's 'A man with a triangulation plan?'.
97 Ramadan, *Peut-on vivre*, p. 174.
98 Ramadan, *La Foi, la voie*, p. 32.
99 Zemouri, *Faut-il faire taire*, p. 313.

Chapter Six

1 Sadek Hajji and Stéphanie Marteau, *Voyage dans la France musulmane* (Paris: Plon, 2005), p. 11.
2 Houria Bouteldja, cited in Jérémy Robine, 'Les « indigènes de la République »: nation et question postcoloniale', *Hérodote* 120 (2006), *http://www.herodote.org/article.php?3id_article=211*. This article is undoubtedly the best study of the formation of the Mouvement des Indigènes de la République.
3 'Un raton', *http://forums.france2.fr/france2/livres/chahdortt-djavann-berberian-sujet_673_1.htm*, posted 27 January 2006, accessed 22 July 2008.
4 Mustafa Al Ayyubi, 'Rassemblement des indigènes de la République à Paris', *http://www.gaucherepublicaine.org/2,article,1202,,,,_Rassemblement*, posted 16 April 2007, accessed 22 July 2008.
5 This metaphor is used in Daniel Bensaïd, *Fragments mécréants: sur les mythes imaginaires et la république imaginaire* (Paris: Lignes, 2005), p. 27 and in Sadri Khiari, Laurent Lévy and Alix Héricord, 'Indigènes de la République, réponses à quelques objections…', *http://oumma.com/Indigenes-de-la-Republique*, posted 25 February 2005, accessed 10 March 2007.
6 Christelle Hamel and Christine Delphy, 'On vous a tant aimé.e.s! Entretien avec Houria Boutelja', *Nouvelles Questions Féministes* 25:1 (2006), 122–35 (125).
7 Hamel and Delphy, 'On vous a tante aimé.e.s', 122.

8 As recorded in Robine, 'Les indigènes de la République'.
9 Houria Bouteldja, Catherine Grupper, Laurent Lévy and Pierre Tevanian, 'Le Voile à l'école: une nouvelle affaire Dreyfus', *http://lmsi.net/spip.php?article214*, posted 26 January 2004, accessed 10 March 2007.
10 Houria Bouteldja, 'Féminisme ou maternalisme?', *www.lmsi.net/article.php3?id_article=225*, posted 8 March 2004, accessed 12 March 2004.
11 Karine Gantin, 'Who are the French "Indigenous Feminists"? – About an interesting debate that occurred during the Anticolonial Week in Paris, February 2007', *http://www.resistingwomen.net/spip.php?article116*, posted 19 November 2007, accessed 22 June 2008.
12 Silvia Cattori, 'Nous sommes tous indigènes de la politique', interview with Julien Salingue, *http://www.oulala.net/Portail/article.php3?id_article=1818*, posted 25 May 2005, accessed 22 August 2007
13 Robine, 'Indigènes de la République', 8.
14 'Interview de Houria Bouteldja', *Algérie News*, 7 June 2008, reproduced in *http://www.indigenes-republique.org/spip.php?page=imprimer&id_article=1458*, posted 13 June 2008, accessed 26 August 2008.
15 Chiara Bonfiglioli, 'Entretien avec Houria Bouteldja, porte-parole du Mouvement des Indigènes de la République', *www.indigenes-republique.org.spip.php?page=imprimer&id_article=599*, posted 10 December 2006, accessed 10 March 2007.
16 Claude Augé, *Petit Larousse illustré* (Paris: Larousse, 1914).
17 Patrick Weil, *Le Statut des musulmans en Algérie coloniale: une nationalité française dénaturée* (San Domenico: European University Institute, 2003), p. 17.
18 As happened during his intervention on 'Y a-t-il un racisme blanc?', *Culture et Dépendances*.
19 Christine Delphy, Alima Boumedienne-Thiery and Noël Mamère, 'Appel à mobilisation contre les lois d'exclusions à l'initiative du collectif *Une école pour tous-tes*', *http://www.lmsi.net/impression.php3?id_article=212*, posted 23 January 2004, accessed 6 February 2004.
20 'Tract adressé aux lycéen.ne.s et aux étudiant.e.s', *http://lmsi.net/article.php3?id_article=217*, posted 28 Jan 2004, accessed 10 March 2007.
21 'Nous sommes les indigènes de la République! – Appel pour des Assises de l'anti-colonialisme post-colonial', *http://lmsi.net.article.php3 id_article=356*, posted February 2005 (?), accessed 5 December 2006.
22 Valérie Amiraux, 'Representing difference', *http://www.opendemocracy.net/democracy-resolution_1325/difference_3026.jsp*, posted 15 November 2005, accessed 15 December 2005.
23 'J'assume', *Le Monde*, 27 November 2005, 'Comment peut-on être français ?', *Culture et Dépendances*, 27 January 2006.
24 'Des indigents de la pensée lèvent le voile', *http://www.ufal29, infini.fr/article.php ?id_article=183*, posted 25 January 2005, accessed 5 December 2006.
25 'Islamophobie: j'ai assisté à une forme de boycottage, aucun sénateur

n'a voulu entendre', *http://www.saphirmet.info/imprimer.php?id=1484*, posted 10 February 2005, accessed 21 February 2005.

26   'Des "enfants de colonises" revendiquent leur histoire', *Le Monde*, 22 February 2005.

27   'L'appel des "indigènes de la République": dénoncer le colonialisme ... ou renforcer le communautarisme ?', *Lutte ouvrière*, *http://www. lutte-ouvriere-journal.org/art_prt.php?LO-1910&ARTICLE=5*, posted 11 March 2005, accessed 5 December 2006.

28   Fabienne Messica and Serge Quadruppani, 'A propos de l'Appel "Nous sommes les indigènes de la République"', *http://quadru.free.fr/ article.php3?id_article=31*, posted 16 March 2005, accessed 5 December 2006.

29   'L'Appel ... ou la voix des amis de Ramadan', *Monde libertaire*, 28 April 2005.

30   Dominique Sopo, *SOS Antiracisme* (np: Denoël, 2005), pp. 31, 98.

31   'Les indigènes s'invitent dans le débat', *L'Humanité*, 21 March 2005.

32   Figures cited in Robine, 'Les indigènes de la République', footnote 4; 'Colonisés hier, immigrés aujourd'hui, citoyens demain', *Le Monde*, 21 January 2006.

33   Said Bouamama, cited in Robine, 'Les indigènes de la République'.

34   Bernard Dreano, 'Lettre d'un aborigine de la république (ou pourquoi je signe avec des indigènes)', *http://www.reseauipam. org/article.php3?id_article=364*, posted 15 March 2005, accessed 22 August 2008.

35   Salah Amokrane, 'L'appel "nous sommes les indigènes de la République" est utile, le débat qu'il engage, politiquement légitime', *http://oumma.com/spip.php?page=imprimer&id_article=1453*, posted 5 April 2005, accessed 5 December 2006.

36   As voiced during 'Y a-t-il un racisme anti-blanc?'.

37   Robine, 'Les indigènes de la République', 18.

38   On the implications of this law, see Benjamin Stora, *La Guerre des mémoires; la France face à son passé colonial; entretiens avec Thierry Leclerc* (np: l'Aube, 2007).

39   See, for example, Nicolas Bancel and Pascal Blanchard, 'Comment en finir avec la fracture coloniale', *Le Monde*, 17 March 2005.

40   'Le piège des mémoires antagonistes', *Le Monde*, 12 May 2005.

41   'Les "indigènes" à République', *L'Humanité*, 9 May 2005.

42   Cattori, 'Nous sommes tous'.

43   'Les indigènes s'invitent dans le débat', *L'Humanité*, 21 March 2005.

44   Sadri Khiari, 'Construire une organisation politique autonome anti-colonialiste', *http://www.indigenes-republique.org/spip.php?page=impr imer &id_article-1162*, posted 13 February 2008, accessed 26 August 2008.

45   Alima Boumédienne-Thiery, 'Musulmanes féministes: du paradoxe à la réalité', *http://www.oumma.com/imprimer.php3 ?id_article=998*, posted 10 March 2004, accessed 12 March 2004.

46   Nacira Guénif-Souilamas, 'The other French exception: virtuous racism and the war of the sexes in Postcolonial France', *French Politics, Culture and Society* 24:3 (2006), 23–41 (25).

47 Khiari, Lévy and Héricord, 'Indigènes de la République, réponses à quelques objections'.

48 Robine, 'Les indigènes de la République'.

49 'Les "indigènes de la République" veulent élargir leur base', *Le Monde*, 28 June 2006.

50 Robine, 'Les indigènes de la République'.

51 Ibid.

52 'Colonisés hier, immigrés aujourd'hui, citoyens demain', *Le Monde*, 21 January 2006.

53 'Quelques precisions ...', *http://www.pyepimanla.com/pye2/info/Les_indigenes_de_la_republique_0600306_005.html*, undated (March 2006?), accessed 22 August 2008.

54 See the convincing critique presented in Vincent Geisser and El Yamine Soum, *Discriminer pour mieux régner: enquête sur la diversité dans les partis politiques* (Ivry-sur-Seine: Les Editions de l'Atelier/Editions ouvrières, 2008).

55 Robine, 'Les indigènes de la République', footnote 12.

56 Cited in 'Les indigènes s'invitent dans le débat', *L'Humanité*, 21 March 2005.

57 Sadri Khiari, 'Les indigènes de la République: d'irrécupérables "islamo-gauchistes"', *http://www.indigenes-republique.org/imprimer.php3?id_article=49*, posted 16 March 2006, accessed 25 Nov 2006.

58 'Comment peut-on être français?'.

59 Robine, 'Les indigènes de la République'.

60 'La question du voile a divisé les manifestants en faveur des droits des femmes', *Le Monde*, 9 March 2004.

61 Houria Bouteldja, 'De la cérémonie du dévoilement à Alger (1958) à Ni Putes ni Soumises', *http://www.alterinfo.net/De-la-ceremonie-du-devoilement-a-Alger-1958-a-Ni-Putes-Ni-Soumises_a105.html?start_liste=50&paa=2*, posted 9 March 2005, accessed 21 May 2006. Several versions of this text are available; some are dated to 2004.

62 Lila Benzid-Basset, 'Féministes indigènes', *www.indigenes-republique.org/spip.php?page=imprimer&id_article=16*, posted 23 March 2005, accessed 17 August 2007.

63 Fatima Ouassak, 'La stigmatisation du garçon arabe: Ni Putes ni Soumises', *http://www.indigenes-republique.org/imprimer,php3?id_article=524*, posted 1 November 2006, accessed 25 November 2006.

64 'Ni Putes ni Soumises dans la tourmente', *http://www.indigenes-republique.org/spip.php?page=imprimer&id_article=1136*, posted 30 November 2007, accessed 7 December 2007. I regret the use of the term 'wog' here, but it is the most accurate translation of the common French term 'bicot'. In this context, it is being used with bitter irony: the MIR consider that the Socialist Party have exploited rather than liberated the Arabs, Asians and Africans who have joined them. Their use of the term is an indication of how charged the debate has become.

65 Hamel and Delphy, 'On vous a tant aimé.e.s', 130.

66 'Appel des Féministes indigènes', *http://www.indigenes-republique.org/*

spip.php?page=imprimer&id_article=667, posted 25 January 2007, accessed 10 March 2007; Dada Rahal-Sidhoum, 'Féministe et de culture musulmane dans la société française: une identité sans contrôle', *http://www.indigens-republique.org/spip.php?page=imprimer& id_article=680*, posted 5 February 2007, accessed 7 February 2007.

67 Rahal-Sidhoum, 'Féministe et de culture musulmane'. For a relevant discussion of the politics of feminist solidarity, see Chandra Talpade Mohanty, '"Under Western Eyes" revisited: feminist solidarity through anticapitalist struggles', *Signs* 28:2 (2002), 499–535.

68 For example, see Nathalie Dollé, 'Musulmanes et féministes', *http://www.indigenes-republique.org/imprimer.php3?id_article=64*, posted 16 March 2006, accessed 25 November 2006.

69 Rahal-Sidhoum, 'Féministe et de culture musulmane'.

70 See Sadri Khiari's comments on this theme: 'Les indigènes de la République: d'irrécupérables islamo-gauchistes'.

71 Robine, 'Les indigènes de la République'.

72 Khiari, 'Construire une organisation politique'.

73 'Petite leçon de racisme', *Marianne*, 28 June 2007.

74 'Les Souchiens', *http://galliawatch.blogspot.com/2007/08/les-souchiens. html*, undated, accessed 31 August 2008.

75 Houria Bouteldja, 'Petite leçon de français d'une sous-sous-chienne aux souchiens malentendants', *http://www.indigenes-republique.org/ spip.php?page=imprimer&id_article=920*, posted 5 July 2007, accessed 22 August 2007.

76 Sadri Khiari, 'Construire une organisation politique autonome anti-colonialiste', *http://www.indigenes-republique.org/spip.php?page=impr imer&id_article-1162*, posted 13 February 2008, accessed 26 August 2008.

77 Arjun Appadurai, *Modernity at Large: Cultural Dimensions of Globalization* (Minneapolis: University of Minnesota Press, 1996), p. 166.

Conclusion

1 Faïza Guène, *Kiffe Kiffe Demain* (Paris: Hachette Littératures, 2004), p. 193.

2 Zygmunt Bauman, *Identity: Conversations with Benedetto Vecchi* (Cambridge: Polity, 2004), p. 51.

3 *The Headmaster and the Headscarves*, BBC2, 29 March 2005. Noëlle speaks in English when interviewed, Leticia's words are translated.

4 Christine Delphy, 'Antisexisme *ou* antiracisme? Un faux dilemme', *Nouvelles Questions Féministes* 25:1 (2006), 59–83 (75).

5 '"Laïcardes", puisque féministes', *Le Monde*, 30 May 2003.

6 See the comments in Patrick Weill, 'Lifting the veil', *French Politics, Culture and Society* 22:3 (2004), 142–9 (146).

7 Nicolas Weill, 'What's in a scarf? – The debate on *laïcité* in France', *French Politics, Culture and Society* 24:1 (2006), 59–73 (67).

8   See Bernard Stasi with Olivier Picard, *Tous français: Immigration, la chance de la France* (Paris: Hugo, 2007), p. 148.

9   None of these examples are fictional: see the evidence in Ismahane Chouder, Malika Latrèche and Pierre Tevanian (eds), *Les Filles voilées parlent* (Floch: La Fabrique, 2008).

10 See information in Chouder, Latrèche and Tevanian, *Les Filles voilées parlent*.

11 See the observations by Hervé Flanquart, *Croyances et valeurs chez les jeunes Maghrébins* (Paris: Complexe, 2003), pp. 70–2.

12 Chouder, Latrèche and Tevanian, *Les Filles voilées parlent*, pp. 56–7.

13 Laure Teulières, 'Le "pèlerinage des émigrés": itinéraires de dévotion et missions catholiques italiennes dans la France du Sud-Ouest', *Mouvement social* 209 (2004), 53–70.

14 Jean-Baptiste Pingualt, 'Jeunes issus de l'immigration portugaise: affirmations identitaires dans les espaces politiques nationaux', *Mouvement social* 209 (2004), 71–89. On the experience of Portuguese immigrants, see also Marie-Christine Volovitch-Tavares, 'L'église de France et l'acceuil des immigrés portuguais (1960–1975)', *Mouvement social* 188 (1999), 89–102.

15 On this theme see Christopher Flood and Hugo Frey, 'Defending the empire in retrospect: the discourse of the extreme right' in T. Chafer and A. Sackur (eds), *Promoting the Colonial Idea* (Houndmills: Palgrave, 2002), pp. 195–210.

16 Carl Levy, 'The European Union after 9/11: the demise of a liberal democratic asylum regime?', *Government and Opposition* 40:4 (2005), 26–59.

17 On this point, see Hastings Donnan and Thomas M. Wilson, *Borders: Frontiers of Identity, Nation and State* (Oxford: Berg, 1999).

18 Robert A. Saunders, 'The ummah as Nation: a reappraisal in the wake of the "Cartoons Affair"', *Nations and Nationalism* 14:2 (2008), 303–21 (311).

19 See Rosi Braidotti, 'In spite of the times: the postsecular turn in feminism', *Theory, Culture and Society* 25:1 (2008), 1–24, for a relevant, rather pessimistic overview of some recent shifts in feminist politics. On French reactions to globalization, see Philip H. Gordon and Sophie Meunier, 'Globalization and French cultural identity', *French Politics, Culture and Society* 19:1 (2001), 22–42.

20 On this theme, see Perry Anderson, 'Dégringolade', *London Review of Books* (2 and 23 September 2004).

Select Bibliography

Abdullah, Dr, *Le Foulard islamique et la République française: mode d'emploi*, *http://www.nassira.net*, no date of publication [1994–5?] accessed 1 March 2004.

Abitol, Michel, 'The integration of North African Jews in France', *Yale French Studies* 85 (1994), 248–61.

Abu-Rabi', Ibrahim M., *Contemporary Arab Thought: Studies in Post-1967 Arab Intellectual History* (London: Pluto, 2004).

Achebe, Chinua, 'Colonial criticism' in Bill Ashcroft, Gareth Griffith and Helen Tiffin (eds), *The Post-Colonial Studies Reader* (2nd edn) (London: Routledge, 2006), pp. 74–8.

Adler, Jacques, 'The Jews and Vichy: reflections on French historiography', *Historical Journal* 44:4 (2001), 1065–81.

Al Ayyubi, Mustafa, 'Rassemblement des indigènes de la République à Paris', *http://www.gaucherepublicaine.org/2,article,1202,,,,_Rassemblement*, posted 16 April 2007, accessed 22 July 2008.

Al-Azmeh, Aziz, *Islams and Modernities* (2nd edn) (London: Verso, 1996).

Amara, Fadela and Mohammed Abdi, *La Racaille de la République* (Paris: Seuil, 2006).

Amara, Fadela with Sylvia Zappi, *Ni Putes ni Soumises* (Paris: La Découverte, 2003).

Amiraux, Valérie, 'Representing difference', *http://www.opendemocracy.net/democracy-resolution_1325/difference_3026.jsp*, posted 15 November 2005, accessed 15 December 2005.

Anderson, Perry, 'Dégringolade', *London Review of Books* (2 and 23 September 2004).

Appadurai, Arjun, *Modernity at Large: Cultural Dimensions of Globalization* (Minneapolis: University of Minnesota Press, 1996).

Archer-Straw, Petrine, *Negrophilia: Avant-Garde Paris and Black Culture in the 1920s* (London: Thames and Hudson, 2000).

Armstrong, Karen, *Islam: A Short History* (London: Phoenix, 2001).

Ask, Karin and Marit Tjomsland, 'Introduction' to their edited collection *Women and Islamization* (Oxford: Berg, 1998), pp. 1–16.

Bancel, Nicolas, Pascal Blanchard and Sandrine Lemaire (eds), *La France coloniale* (Paris: La Découverte, 2005).

Bauman, Zygmunt, *Identity: Conversations with Benedetto Vecchi* (Cambridge: Polity, 2004).

Baubérot, Jean, 'La Commission Stasi vue par l'un de ses membres', *French Politics, Culture & Society* 22:3 (2004), 135–41.

——— 'Une "haine démocratique" et son dépassement. Du combat anti-clérical à la loi de séparation de 1905', *Diasporas* 10 (2007), 26–49.

Begag, Azouz, *Place du Pont, ou la médina de Lyon* (Paris: Autrement, 1997).

——— *Un Mouton dans le bagnoire: dans les coulisses du pouvoir* (Paris: Fayard, 2007).

Bechler, Rosemary, 'Islam and democracy: an interview with Heba Ezzat', Open Democracy (*http://www.opendemocracy.net*), accessed 28 October 2008, posted 11 May 2005

Bencheikh, Soheib, *Marianne et le Prophète: l'islam dans la France laïque* (Paris: Grasset, 1998).

Benelli, Natalie, Ellen Hertz, Christine Delphy, Christelle Hamel, Patricia Roux and Jules Falquet, 'Editorial: De l'affaire du voile à l'imbrication du sexisme et du racisme', *Nouvelles Questions Féministes* 25:1 (2006), 4–11.

Benen, Steve, 'A man with a triangulation plan?' [interview with Tariq Ramadan], *http://www.salon.com/people/feature/2002/02/15/ramadan/print.html*, undated (2002?), accessed 26 August 2007.

Bensaïd, Daniel, *Fragments mécréants: sur les mythes imaginaires et la république imaginaire* (Paris: Lignes, 2005).

Benzid-Basset, Lila, 'Féministes indigènes', *http://www.indigenes-republique.org/spip.php?page=imprimer&id_article=16*, posted 23 March 2005, accessed 17 Aug 2007.

Benzine, Rachid, *Les nouveaux penseurs de l'Islam* (Paris: Albin Michel, 2004).

Berlin, Isaiah, *Four Essays on Liberty* (Oxford: Oxford University Press, 1984).

Billard, Martine, *Débat "laïcité à l'école": cette loi ne résoudra ni les discriminations subies par les femmes, ni la montée des intégrismes religieux, http://martinebillard.org/article.php3?id_article=221*, posted 3 February 2004, accessed 21 March 2004.

Birnbaum, Pierre, *Les Fous de la République: histoire politique des Juifs d'Etat de Gambetta à Vichy* (Paris: Fayard, 1992).

——— 'Grégoire, Dreyfus, Drancy et Copernic' in Pierre Nora, *Les Lieux de Mémoire Vol. II* (Paris: Quarto – Gallimard, 1997), pp. 2679–2719.

Blatt, David, 'Immigrant politics in a Republican nation' in A. G. Hargreaves and M. McKinney (eds), *Post-Colonial Cultures in France* (London: Routledge, 1997), pp. 40–55.

Boireau-Rouillé, Monique, 'La crise des banlieues, novembre 2005: entrevue avec Michel Pialoux', *Réfractions* 17 (2006–7), 132–8.

Bonelli, Laurent, *La France a peur: une histoire sociale de « l'insécurité »* (Paris: La Découverte, 2008).

Bonfiglioli, Chiara, 'Entretien avec Houria Bouteldja, porte-parole du Mouvement des Indigènes de la République', *http://www.indigenes-republique.org.spip.php?page=imprimer&id_article=599*, posted 10 December 2006, accessed 10 March 2007.

Boumédienne-Thiery, Alima, 'Musulmanes féministes: du paradoxe à la réalité', *http://www.oumma.com/imprimer.php3?id_article=998*, posted 10 March 2004, accessed 12 March 2004.

Bourdieu, Pierre, 'L'idéologie jacobine' in his *Interventions, 1961–2001* (Marseilles: Agone, 2002), pp. 55–61.

Boutang, Yann Moulier, *La Révolte des banlieues, ou: les habits nus de la République* (Paris: Éditions Amsterdam, 2005)

Bouteldja, Houria, 'Féminisme ou maternalisme?', *http://www.lmsi.net/article.php3?id_article=225*, posted 8 March 2004, accessed 12 March 2004.

——— 'De la cérémonie du dévoilement à Alger (1958) à Ni Putes ni Soumises', *http://www.alterinfo.net/De-la-ceremonie-du-devoilement-a-Alger-1958-a-Ni-Putes-Ni-Soumises_a105.html?start_liste=50&paa=2*, posted 9 March 2005, accessed 21 May 2006. Several versions of this text are available; some are dated to 2004.

——— 'Petite leçon de français d'une sous-sous-chienne aux souchiens malentendants', *http:www.indigenes-republique.org/spip.php?page=imprimer&id_article=920*, posted 5 July 2007, accessed 22 August 2007.

Bouteldja, Houria, Catherine Grupper, Laurent Lévy and Pierre Tévanian, 'Le Voile à l'école: une nouvelle affaire Dreyfus', *http://lmsi.net/spip.php?article214*, posted 26 January 2004, accessed 10 March 2007.

Bouzar, Dounia and Saïda Kada, *L'Une voilée, l'autre pas: le témoignage de deux musulmanes françaises* (Paris: Albin Michel, 2003)

Bowen, John R., 'Does French Islam have borders? – Dilemmas of domestication in a global religious field', *American Anthropologist* 106:1 (2004), 43–55.

——— *Why the French Don't Like Headscarves: Islam, the State, and Public Space* (Princeton: Princeton University Press, 2007).

Boyer, Alain, 'La représentation de la culture musulmane en France', *French Politics, Culture and Society* 23:1 (2005), 8–22.

Braidotti, Rosi, 'In spite of the times: the postsecular turn in feminism', *Theory, Culture and Society* 25:1 (2008), 1–24.

Brenner, Emmanuel (ed.), *Les Territoires perdus de la République* (Paris: Arthème Fayard, 2004)

Brown, L. Carl, *Religion and State: The Muslim Approach to Politics* (New York: Columbia University Press, 2000).

Caeiro, Alexandre, 'Religious authorities or political actors? – The Muslim leaders of the French representative body of Islam' in J. Cesari and S. McLoughlin (eds), *European Muslims and the Secular State* (Aldershot: Ashgate, 2005), pp. 71–84.

Castel, Robert, *La Discrimination négative: citoyens ou indigènes?* (Paris: Seuil, 2007)

Cattori, Silvia, 'Nous sommes tous indigènes de la politique', interview with Julien Salingue, *http://www.oulala.net/Portail/article.php3?id_article=1818*, posted 25 May 2005, accessed 22 August 2007.

Chadwick, Kay, 'Education in secular France: (re)defining laïcité', *Modern and Contemporary France* 5:1 (1997), 47–60.

Chouder, Ismahane, Malika Latrèche and Pierre Tevanian (eds), *Les Filles voilées parlent* (Floch: La Fabrique, 2008)

Clancy-Smith, Julia, 'Le regard colonial: Islam, genre et identités dans la fabrication de l'Algérie française' translated by Françoise Armengaud, *Nouvelles Questions Féministes* 25:1 (2006), 25–40.

Costa-Lascoux, Jacqueline, 'La loi des hommes contre la loi divine', *Le Monde de l'éducation* 321 (January 2004), 28–31.

—— 'Les échecs de l'intégration, un accroc au contrat social', *Pouvoirs* 111 (2004), 19–27.

Dahmani, Akli, 'Le Parti communiste français face à la guerre d'Algérie', *Cahiers d'histoire immédiate* 20 (2001), 27–68.

Dassetto, Felice, 'Islam et Europe: au défi d'une rencontre de civilisations' in C. Pailhe (ed.), *Europes et Mondes musulmans* (Bruxelles: Grip, 2004), pp. 143–64.

Debray, Régis, *Ce que nous voile le voile: la République et le sacré* (Paris: Gallimard, 2004)

'Débuts précurseurs de Fadela Amara dans la gestion du milieu associatif', *http://www.niputesnisoumises.com/mouvement.php?section=historique_2000*, undated, accessed 6 August 2008.

Delphy, Christine, 'La loi anti-voile: un aveuglement collectif'. *http://oumma.com/article.php3?id_article=943*, posted 7 February 2004, accessed 10 February 2004.

—— 'Antisexisme *ou* antiracisme? Un faux dilemme', *Nouvelles Questions Féministes* 25:1 (2006), 59–83.

Deltombe, Thomas, *L'Islam imaginaire: la construction médiatique de l'islamophobie en France, 1975–2005* (Paris: La Découverte, 2005)

Djavann, Chahdortt, *Je viens d'ailleurs* (Paris: Autrement, 2002).

—— *Bas les voiles!* (Paris: Gallimard, 2003).

—— *Que pense Allah de l'Europe* (Paris: Gallimard, 2004).

—— *Comment peut-on être français?* (Paris: Flammarion, 2006).

—— *A mon corps défendant, l'Occident* (Paris: Flammarion, 2007).

Donnan, Hastings and Thomas M. Wilson, *Borders: Frontiers of Identity, Nation and State* (Oxford: Berg, 1999).

Dreano, Bernard, 'Lettre d'un aborigine de la république (ou pourquoi je signe avec des indigènes)', *http://www.reseau-ipam.org/article.php3?id_article=364*, posted 15 March 2005, accessed 22 August 2008.

du Figaro, X..., *Les Coulisses du Boulangisme* (Paris: Cerf, 1890).

Dubois, Laurent, 'La République métisée: citizenship, colonialism and the borders of French history', *Cultural Studies* 14:1 (2000), 15–34.

Durand, Stefan, 'Fascisme, islam et grossiers amalgames', *Monde Diplomatique* (November 2006), 10–11.

Duval, Soroya, 'New veils and new voices: Islamist women's groups in Egypt' in K. Ask and M. Tjomsland (eds), *Women and Islamization* (Oxford: Berg, 1998), pp. 45–72.

Ebadi, Shirin (with Azadeh Moaveni), *Iran Awakening: From Prison to Peace Prize: One Woman's Struggle at the Crossroads of History* (London: Rider, 2006).

El Guindi, Fadwa, *Veil: Modesty, Privacy and Resistance* (Oxford: Berg, 1999).

Eleuterio Quintanilla, 'Entrevista del grupo Eleuterio Quintanilla a Sophie Bessis', *www.equintalla.com/bessis.htm*, posted 25 October 2004, accessed 20 June 2007.

Esfandiari, Haleh, 'The politics of the "women's question" in the Islamic Republic, 1979–99' in J. L. Esposito and R. K. Ramazani (eds), *Iran at the Crossroads* (New York: Palgrave, 2001), pp. 75–92.

Evans, Martin, 'The left, laïcité and Islam', *Modern and Contemporary France* 45 (1991), 8–15.

—— *The Memory of Resistance: French Opposition to the Algerian War (1954–1962)* (Oxford: Berg, 1997).

Fallaci, Oriana, *The Rage and the Pride* (New York: Rizzoli, 2001).

—— *The Force of Reason* (New York: Rizzoli, 2006).

Fanon, Frantz, *Peau noire, masques blancs* (Paris: Seuil, 1975 [1962]).

Fernando, Mayanthi, 'The Republic's "second religion": recognizing Islam in France', *Merip* 235 (2005), *http://www.merip.org/mer/mer235/fernando.html*, accessed 26 July 2007.

Finkielkraut, Alain and Benny Lévy, *Le Livre et les livres: Entretiens sur la laïcité* (Paris: Verdier, 2006).

Flanquart, Hervé, *Croyances et valeurs chez les jeunes Maghrébins* (Paris: Complexe, 2003)

Flood, Christopher, 'National Republican politics, intellectuals and the case of Pierre-André Taguieff', *Modern and Contemporary France* 12:3 (2004), 353–70.

Flood, Christopher and Hugo Frey, 'Defending the empire in retrospect: the discourse of the extreme right' in T. Chafer and A. Sackur (eds), *Promoting the Colonial Idea* (Houndmills: Palgrave, 2002), pp. 195–210.

Fourest, Caroline, *Frère Tariq* (Paris: Grasset & Fasquelle, 2004).

Frégosi, Franck, *Penser l'Islam dans la laïcité; les musulmans de France et la République* (Paris: Fayard, 2008).

Galembert, Claire de and Mustafa Belbah, 'Le Conseil Français du Culte Musulman à l'épreuve des territoires', *French Politics, Culture and Society* 23:1 (2005), 76–86.

Gallo, Max, 'La supériorité de la laïcité', in Yves Charles Zarka (ed.), *L'Islam en France* (Paris: PUF, 2004), pp. 201–4.

Gantin, Karine, 'Who are the French "Indigenous Feminists"? – About an interesting debate that occurred during the Anticolonial Week in Paris, February 2007', *http://www.resistingwomen.net/spip.php?article116*, posted 19 November 2007, accessed 22 June 2008.

Gaspard, Françoise and Farhad Khosrokhavar, *Le Foulard et la République* (Paris: La Découverte, 1995).

Geisser, Vincent and El Yamine Soum, *Discriminer pour mieux régner: enquête sur la diversité dans les partis politiques* (Ivry-sur-Seine: Les Editions de l'Atelier/Editions ouvrières, 2008).

Gemie, Sharif, *French Revolutions, 1815–1914* (Edinburgh: Edinburgh University Press, 1999).

—— 'Stasi's Republic: the school and the "veil", December 2003–March 2004', *Modern and Contemporary France* 12:3 (2004), 387–97.

—— 'An extremism of the center: Jean-Pierre Chevènement, French presidential candidate, 2002', *French Politics, Culture and Society* 22:1 (2004), 76–97.

—— 'The trial of Fatima: anarchists, Muslims and the *Monde Libertaire*, 2003–5', *Anarchist Studies* 14:1 (2006), 9–19.

—— *Brittany, 1750–1950: the Invisible Nation* (Cardiff: University of Wales Press, 2007).

Gill, Hélène, 'Hegemony and ambiguity: discourses, counter-discourses and hidden meanings in French depictions of the conquest and settlement of Algeria', *Modern and Contemporary France* 14:2 (2006), 157–72.

Godechot, Jacques (ed.) *Les Constitutions de la France depuis 1789* (Paris: Flammarion, 1979).

Gordon, Philip H. and Sophie Meunier, 'Globalization and French cultural identity', *French Politics, Culture and Society* 19:1 (2001), 22–42.

Gresh, Alain, 'Les Faux-semblants de la Commission Stasi', *http://www.islam-laicite.org/article187/html*, posted 23 January 2004, accessed 5 March 2004.

Gross, Joan, David McMurray and Ted Swedenburg, 'Arab noise and Ramadan nights: Rai, rap and Franco-Maghrebi identities' in Smadar Lavie and Ted Swedenburg (eds), *Displacement, Diaspora and Geographies of Identity* (Durham and London: Duke University Press, 1996), pp. 119–56.

Guène, Faïza, *Kiffe Kiffe Demain* (Paris: Hachette, 2004).

Guénif-Souilamas, Nacira, 'The other French exception: virtuous racism and the war of the sexes in postcolonial France', *French Politics, Culture and Society* 24:3 (2006), 23–41.

Hajji, Sadek and Stéphanie Marteau, *Voyage dans la France musulmane* (Paris: Plon, 2005).

Hamel, Christelle and Christine Delphy, 'On vous a tant aimé.e.s! Entretien avec Houria Boutelja', *Nouvelles Questions Féministes* 25:1 (2006), 122–35.

Hamel, Ian, 'Quand pourra-t-on critiquer honnêtement Tariq Ramadan?', *http://oumma.com/article.php3?id_article=1333*, posted 5 Jan 2005, accessed 14 March 2005.

Hargreaves, Alec G., 'Algerians in contemporary France: incorporation or exclusion?', *Journal of Algerian Studies* 3 (1998), 31–47.

—— *Multi-Ethnic France: Immigration, Politics, Culture and Society* (2nd edn) (New York & London: Routledge, 2007).

Harries, Richard, *Should A Christian Support Guerillas?* (Guildford: Lutterworth Press, 1982).

Henissart, Paul, *Wolves in the City: The Death of French Algeria* (London: Rupert Hart-Davis, 1970).

Hirsi Ali, Ayaan, *The Caged Virgin: A Muslim Woman's Cry for Reason* (London: Simon & Schuster, 2006).

House, Jim and Neil MacMaster, *Paris 1961: Algerians, State Terror and Memory* (Oxford: Oxford University Press, 2006).

Huard, Raymond, *La Naissance du parti politique en France* (Paris: Sciences-Po, 1996).

Huntington, Samuel P., *The Clash of Civilizations and the Remaking of the World Order* (London: Simon & Schuster, 1997).

International Crisis Group (ICG), *Understanding Islamism* (Middle East/North Africa Report 37, March 2005).

—— *La France face à ses musulmans: émeutes, jihadisme et dépolitisation* (Rapport Europe 172, 2006).

'Interview with photographer Shadafarin Ghadirian', *http://www3.estart.com/iran/women/shadafarin*, accessed 20 April 2005.

Jacquard, Albert and Fadela Amara, *Jamais soumis, jamais soumise* (Paris: Stock, 2007).

Keaton, Trica Danielle, *Muslim Girls and the Other France: Race, Identity Politics and Social Exclusion* (Bloomington: Indiana University Press, 2006).

Khiari, Sadri, 'La pensée politique de Tariq Ramadan', *http://lmsi.net/ spip.php?article256*, posted 29 May 2004, accessed 29 June 2004.

—— 'Construire une organisation politique autonome anticolonialiste', *http://www.indigenes-republique.org/spip.php?page=imprimer&id_article-1162*, posted 13 February 2008, accessed 26 August 2008.

Khiari, Sadri, Laurent Lévy and Alix Héricord, 'Indigènes de la République, réponses à quelques objections ...', *http://oumma.com/ Indigenes-de-la-Republique*, posted 25 February 2005, accessed 10 March 2007.

Khosrokhavar, Farhad, *Quand al-Qaïda parle: témoignages derrière les barreaux* (Paris: Grasset & Fasquelle, 2006).

Kian-Thiébaut, Azadeh, 'L'islam, les femmes et la citoyenneté', *Pouvoirs* 104 (2003), 71–84.

Killian, Caitlin, 'The other side of the veil: North African women in France respond to the headscarf affair', *Gender and Society* 17:4 (2003), 567–90.

Kiwan, Nadia, 'Managing marginalization: young French North-Africans and local associations', *Modern and Contemporary France* 13:4 (2005), 465–81.

Kramer, Jane, 'Taking the veil', *New Yorker* 22 November 2004, pp. 58–71.

Lamont, Michèle, Ann Morning and Margarita Mooney, 'Particular universalisms: North African immigrants respond to French racism', *Ethnic and Racial Studies* 25:3 (2002), 390–414.

Landfried, Julien, 'Réflexions sur le Conseil Français du Culte Musulman' [Interview with Hakim El Ghissassi], *http://www.communautarisme.net/ Reflexions-sur-le-Conseil-Francais-du-Culte-Musulman_a255.html*, posted 9 July 2004, accessed 19 July 2004.

Lapidus, Ira M., 'State and religion in Islamic societies', *Past and Present* 151 (1996), 3–27.

Laurence, Jonathan and Justin Vaisse, *Integrating Islam: Political and Religious Challenges in Contemporary France* (Washington: Brookings Institution Press, 2006).

Lazreg, Marnia, 'Gender and politics in Algeria: unravelling the religious paradigm', *Signs* 15 (1990), 755–80.

Lecorre, Erwann, 'La Marche de TOUTES les femmes? – A propos de la manifestation féministe du 6 mars 2004', *www.lmsi.net/article.php3?id_ article=227*, posted 8 March 2004, accessed 12 March 2004.

Levy, Carl, 'The European Union after 9/11: the demise of a liberal democratic asylum regime?', *Government and Opposition* 40:4 (2005), 26–59.

Lévy, Laurent, *Le Spectre du communautarisme* (Paris: Éditions Amsterdam, 2005).

Lewis, Reina, 'Veils and sales: Muslims and the spaces of postcolonial fashion retail', *Fashion Theory* 11:4 (2007), 423–42.

Lorcin, Patricia M. E., *Imperial Identities: Stereotyping, Prejudice and Race in Colonial Algeria* (London: Tauris, 1999).

MacMaster, Neil, *Colonial Migrants and Racism: Algerians in France, 1900– 1962* (Houndmills: Basingstoke, 1997).

—— 'Imperial facades: Muslim institutions and propaganda in inter-war Paris' in T. Chafer and A. Sackur (eds), *Promoting the Colonial Ideal* (Houndmills: Palgrave, 2002), pp. 71–81.

Majumdar, Margaret A., 'Extra-European national minorities in France and the concept of European identity', *History of European Ideas* 19:4–6 (1994), 647–53.

Malik, Serge, *Histoire secrète de SOS-Racisme* (Paris: Albin Michel, 1990).

Marcos, Subcomandante Insurgente, *Our Word is Our Weapon: Selected Writings* (London: Serpent's Tail, 2001).

Masclet, Olivier, 'Des quartiers sans voix: sur le divorce entre la Gauche et les enfants d'immigrés', *French Politics, Culture and Society* 24:3 (2006), 5–22.

Maspero, François, *Les Passagers du Roissy-Express* (Paris: Seuil, 1990).

Meddeb, Abdelwahab, *Face à l'Islam* (Paris: Textuel, 2004).

Mellah, Salima, 'Le mouvement islamiste algérien entre autonomie et manipulation', *Comité Justice pour l'Algérie* 19 (2004), 21–3; http://www.algerie-tpp.org/tpp/presentation/dossiers_presentes.htm.

Messica, Fabienne and Serge Quadruppani, 'A propos de l'Appel "Nous sommes les indigènes de la République"', http://quadru.free.fr/article. php3?id_article=31, posted 16 March 2005, accessed 5 December 2006.

Milani, Farzaneh, 'On women's captivity in the Islamic world', *Merip* 246 (2008), http://www.merip.org/mer/mer246, accessed 4 June 2008.

Mir-Hosseini, Ziba, 'Is time on Iranian women protestors' side?', *Merip* (June 2006), www.merip.org/mero/mero061606.html.

Mitchell, W. J. T., 'Translator translated (interview with cultural theorist Homi Bhabha)', http://www.prelectur.stanford.edu/lecturers.bhabha/interview.html, originally published in 1995, accessed 18 June 2007.

Mohanty, Chandra Talpade, '"Under Western Eyes" revisited: feminist solidarity through anticapitalist struggles', *Signs*, 28:2 (2002), 499–535.

Morris, Benny, 'On ethnic cleansing', *New Left Review* 26 (2004), 37–51.

Murray, Graham, 'France: the riots and the Republic', *Race and Class* 47:4 (2006), 26–45.

Nair, Parvati, 'Moor – veiled – matters: the *hijab* as troubling interrogative of the relation between the West and Islam', *New Formations* 51 (2004), 39–49.

Nicholet, Claude, *L'Idée républicaine en France (1789–1924)* (Paris: Gallimard, 1994)

Notes from Nowhere, *We are Everywhere: The Irresistible Rise of Global Anticapitalism* (London: Verse, 2003).

Ouassak, Fatima, 'La stigmatisation du garçon arabe: Ni Putes ni Soumises', http://www.indigenes-republique.org/spip.php?article524, posted 1 November 2006, accessed 25 November 2006.

Pattieu, Sylvain, *Les Camarades des frères: trotskistes et libertaires dans la guerre d'Algérie* (Paris: Syllepsie, 2002).

Perucca, Brigitte, 'Une loi contre les dérives', *Le Monde de l'éducation* 321 (January 2004), 3.

Peter, Frank, 'Leading the community of the middle way: a study of the Muslim field in France', *Muslim World* 96 (2006), 707–36.

Pingualt, Jean-Baptiste, 'Jeunes issus de l'immigration portugaise: affirmations identitaires dans les espaces politiques nationaux', *Mouvement social* 209 (2004), 71–89.

Rabineau, Isabelle, 'Dévoilez Chahdortt', *Topo* 11 (November 2004), 19–29.

Rahal-Sidhoum, Dada, 'Féministe et de culture musulmane dans la société française: une identité sans contrôle', *http://www.indigens-republique.org/spip.php?page=imprimer&id_article=680*, posted 5 February 2007, accessed 7 February 2007.

Ramadan, Tariq, *Être Musulman européen: Etude des sources islamiques à la lumière du contexte européen* (translated from the English by Claude Dabbak) (Lyon: Tawhid, 1999).

—— *Aux sources du renouveau musulman: d'al-Afghānī à al-Bannā; un siècle de réformisme islamique* (Lyon: Tawhid, 2002)

—— 'Les musulmans et la mondialisation', *Pouvoirs* 104 (2003), 97–109.

—— 'Critique des (nouveaux) intellectuels communautaires', *http://oumma.com/article.php3?id_article=719*, posted 3 October 2003, accessed 6 June 2007.

—— *La Foi, la voie et la résistance* (2nd edn) (Lyon: Tawhid, 2004).

—— *Peut-on vivre avec l'islam?* (Lausanne: Favre, 2004).

—— 'The Call to Jihad', *http://www.tariqramadan.com/spip.php?article65*, posted 28 September 2004, accessed 27 August 2007.

—— 'C'est l'ensemble de la classe politique française qui se trompe...' *www.saphirnews.com/C-est-l-ensemble* , posted 9 November 2005, accessed 14 Nov 2005.

—— 'Dr Jeckyll et M. Hyde? – A Propos d'un pitoyable portrait dans *Le Monde*', *http://oumma.com/Dr-Jeckyll-et-M-Hyde*, posted 27 February 2006, accessed 2 March 2006.

—— 'Il y a un vrai problème de liberté d'expression en France', *www.saphirnet.info/Tariq-Ramadan-il-y-a* , posted 17 October 2006, accessed 20 October 2006.

Rapport d'activité 2006, PDF file at *http://www.niputesnisoumises.com/mouvement.php?section=historique_2006*; accessed 7 August 2008.

Read, Jen'nan Ghazal and John P. Bartkowski, 'To veil or not to veil? – A case study on identity negotiation among Muslim women in Austin, Texas', *Gender and Society* 14:3 (2000), 395–417.

Rechter, David, 'The Jews: a European minority' in S. Berger (ed.), *A Companion to Nineteenth-Century Europe* (Oxford: Blackwell, 2006), pp. 274–87.

'Riverbend', *Baghdad Burning: Girl Blog from Iraq* (London: Marion Boyars, 2006).

Rivière, Georges, 'The Libertarian Insurrection of the "Arrooch" Assembly Movement in Kabylia (Algeria), 2000–2' translated by Sharif Gemie, *Anarchist Studies* 11:2 (2003), 102–10.

Robine, Jérémy, 'Les «indigènes de la République»: nation et question postcoloniale', *Hérodote* 120 (2006), *http://www.herodote.org/article.php?3id_article=211*.

Roy, Olivier, *L'Islam mondialisé* (Paris: Seuil, 2002).

—— *La Laïcité face à l'Islam* (Paris: Stock, 2005)

Rutherford, Jonathan, 'The third space: interview with Homi Bhabha' in his *Identity: Community, Culture, Difference* (London: Lawrence and Wishart, 1990), pp. 207–21.

Saktander, Ayşe, *Living Islam: Women, Religion and the Politicization of Culture in Turkey* (London: Tauris, 2002),

'Sappho', 'Among the believers', *http://www.sappho.dk/Den%20loebende/bourgetengelsk.html, posted 1 June 2007, accessed 16 July 2008.*

Saunders, Robert A., 'The ummah as Nation: a reappraisal in the wake of the "Cartoons Affair"', *Nations and Nationalism* 14:2 (2008), 303–21.

Sayad, Abdelmalek, *L'Immigration ou les paradoxes et l'altérité, I: L'illusion du provisoire* (Paris: Raisons d'Agir, 2006).

Sellam, Sadek, *La France et ses musulmans: un siècle de politique musulmans, 1895–2005* (Paris: Fayard, 2006).

Sennett, Richard, *The Fall of Public Man* (London: Faber & Faber, 1986 [1977]).

Sieffert, Denis, 'L'affaire Tariq Ramadan: l'ère du soupçon', *http://www.politis.fr/article716.html,* posted 16 October 2003, accessed 29 June 2004.

Silverstein, Paul A., *Algeria in France: Transpolitics, Race and Nation* (Bloomington: Indiana University Press, 2004).

Silverstein Paul, and Chantal Tetreaut, 'Urban violence in France', *Merip* (November 2005), *http://www.merip.org/mero/interventions/silverstein_tetre ault_interv.htm.*

Simon, Patrick, 'The choice of ignorance: the debate on ethnic and racial statistics in France', *French Politics, Culture & Society* 26:1 (2008), 7–31.

Simon-Nahun, Perrine, 'French Judaism', translated by A. Goldhammer in A. Prost and G. Vincent (eds), *A History of Private Life, Vol. V* (Cambridge, Mass.: Harvard University Press, 1991), pp. 347–78.

Smith, Zadie, *White Teeth* (Harmondsworth: Penguin, 2000).

Sopo, Dominique, *SOS Antiracisme* (np: Denoël, 2005).

Stasi, Bernard, *Rapport au président de la République* (np: no publisher, 2003)

—— 'Laïcité: soignons notre copie' in Yves Charles Zarka (ed.), *L'Islam en France* (Paris: PUF, 2004), pp. 177–9.

Stasi, Bernard, with Olivier Picard, *Tous français: Immigration, la chance de la France* (Paris: Hugo, 2007).

Stille, Alexander, *Benevolence and Betrayal; Five Jewish Italian Families under Fascism* (Harmondsworth: Penguin, 1991).

Stora, Benjamin, *La Guerre des mémoires; la France face à son passé colonial, entretiens avec Thierry Leclère* (np: L'Aube, 2007).

Terray, Emmanuel, 'Headscarf hysteria', *New Left Review* 26 (2004), 118–27.

Teulières, Laure, 'Le "pèlerinage des émigrés": itinéraires de dévotion et missions catholiques italiennes dans la France du Sud-Ouest', *Mouvement social* 209 (2004), 53–70.

Tévanian, Pierre, *Le Voile médiatique – un faux débat: L'affaire du foulard islamique* (Paris: Raisons d'Agir, 2005).

Tolan, John V., *Saracens: Islam in the Medieval European Imagination* (New York: Columbia University Press, 2002)

Touati, Aïcha, 'Féministes d'hier et d'aujourd'hui, ou le féminisme à l'épreuve de l'universel', *Nouvelles Questions Féministes* 25:1 (2006), 108–20.

Tyre, Stephen, 'From *Algérie française* to *France musulmane:* Jacques Soustelle and the myth and realities of "integration", 1955–62', *French History* 20:3 (2006), 275–96.

UFAL, 'Pour un 6 mars féministe et laïque sans femmes voilées dans nos cortèges', *http://www.ufal.org/spip/article.php3?id_article=56*, posted 20 February 2004, accessed 9 March 2004.

Valensi, Lucette, 'Confrontations/contradictions' in Gabriel Martinez-Gros and Lucette Valensi, *L'Islam en dissidence: Genèse d'un affrontement* (Paris: Seuil, 2004), pp. 140–302.

Vernet, Juan, *Lo que Europa debe al Islam de España* (Barcelona: El Acantilado, 1999).

Vianès, Michèle, *Un voile sur la République* (Paris: Stock, 2004)

Villiers, Philippe de, *Les Mosquées de Roissy* (Paris: Albin Michel, 2006),

Volovitch-Tavares, Marie Christine, 'L'église de France et l'acceuil des immigrés portugais (1960–1975)', *Mouvement social* 188 (1999), 89–102.

Weil, Patrick, *Le Statut des musulmans en Algérie coloniale: une nationalité française dénaturée* (San Domenico: European University Institute, 2003)

——, 'Lifting the veil', *French Politics, Culture and Society* 22:3 (2004), 142–9.

Weill, Nicolas, 'What's in a scarf? – The debate on *laïcité* in France', *French Politics, Culture and Society* 24:1 (2006), 59–73.

White, Jenny B., 'The paradox of the new Islamic woman in Turkey' in Inger Marie Okkenhaug and Ingvild Flaskerud (eds), *Gender, Religion and Change in the Middle East* (Oxford: Berg, 2005), pp. 123–35.

Whitney, Sarah, 'Gender, class and generation in interwar French Catholicism: the case of the Jeunesse Ouvrière Chrétienne Féminine', *Journal of Family History* 36:4 (2001), 480–507.

Woloch, Isser, 'Left, right and centre: the MRP and the post-war moment', *French History* 21:1 (2007), 85–106.

Zemouri, Aziz, *Faut-il faire taire Tariq Ramadan? suivie d'un entretien avec Tariq Ramadan* (Paris: l'Archipel, 2005).

Zouhar, Halima, 'Le foulard islamique: choix ou soumission', *http://www.oumma.com/Le-foulard-islamique-ou*, posted 17 March 2007, accessed 23 March 2007.

Newspapers consulted
(articles of particular interest have been cited in endnotes)

La Croix
Globe and Mail
Guardian
Le Figaro
L'Humanité
Libération
Le Monde
El País

Television programmes

'Comment peut-on être français?', *Culture et Dépendances*, FR2, 27 January 2006.

The Headmaster and the Headscarves, BBC2, 29 March 2005.

'Itinéraire d'une révoltée', *Envoyé Spécial*, FR2, 17 January 2008.

Les Femmes d'Islam, Yamina Benguigi, FR2, 1994.

'Les religions sont-elles les ennemis des femmes?', *Culture et Dépendances*, FR2, 19 May 2005.

'Y a-t-il un racisme anti-blanc?', *Culture et Dépendances*, FR2, 4 May 2006.

Index